ORDINARY MEN

Also by Christopher R. Browning

FATEFUL MONTHS:
ESSAYS ON THE EMERGENCE OF THE FINAL SOLUTION

THE FINAL SOLUTION AND THE GERMAN FOREIGN OFFICE

ORDINARY
MEN

RESERVE POLICE BATTALION 101
AND THE FINAL SOLUTION IN POLAND

Christopher R. Browning

HARPER PERENNIAL

NEW YORK • LONDON • TORONTO • SYDNEY • NEW DELHI • AUCKLAND

HarperCollins Publishers

"One Day in Józefów: Initiation to Mass Murder," a paper based on a portion of this work, has appeared in Peter Hayes, ed., *Lessons and Legacies: The Meaning of the Holocaust in a Changing World* (Chicago: Northwestern University Press, 1991).

A hardcover edition of this book was published in 1992 by HarperCollins Publishers.

HarperCollins books may be purchased for educational, business, or sales promotional use. For information, please e-mail the Special Markets Department at SPsales@harpercollins.com.

FIRST HARPER PERENNIAL EDITION PUBLISHED 1993, REISSUED 1998. REVISED EDITION PUBLISHED 2017.

Library of Congress has catalogued the previous edition as follows.

Browning, Christopher R.
    Ordinary Men : Reserve Police Battalion 101 and the final solution in Poland / Christopher R. Browning.
        p.   cm
    Includes bibliography references (p.) and index
    ISBN 978-0-06-216790-3
    1. Holocaust, Jewish (1939-1945). 2. World War, 1939–1945—Personal narratives, German. 3. World War, 1939–1945—Atrocities. I. Title.
D804.3.B77   1992
940.53'18—dc20   91-50471

ISBN 978-0-06-230302-8 (revised edition)

23 24 25 26 27 LBC 26 25 24 23 22

for
Raul Hilberg

CONTENTS

ILLUSTRATIONS

SWEDEN

Baltic Sea

•Riga

LATVIA

•Memel   LITHUANIA

REICHSKOMMISSARIAT
OSTLAND

•Königsberg

Gdańsk (Danzig)

Suwałki

EAST PRUSSIA

GERMANY

Bydgoszcz•
(Bromberg)

•Białystok

Wisła River

•Poznań (Posen)

Treblinka✕

Bug River

Chełmno✕
(Kulmhof)

Warsaw•
WARSAW DISTRICT

Łuków•

•Łódź

P O L A N D

Kalisz•

Sobibór✕

REICHSKOMMISSARIAT
UKRAINE

Oder River

Leipzig•

Radom•

GENERAL
GOVERNMENT

•Lublin

Majdanek
✕

SILESIA Opole
(Oppeln)•

RADOM
DISTRICT

LUBLIN
DISTRICT

Katowice•

Bełżec✕

Oświęcim✕
(Auschwitz)

•Kraków

KRAKÓW
DISTRICT

•Lwów
(Lemberg)

SOVIET
UNION

GALICIA

CZECHOSLOVAKIA

RUMANIA

Vienna
AUST.

•Budapest

Danube River

HUNGARY

POLAND IN 1942-1943

▬▬▬ Boundary of Poland before September 1, 1939

████ Incorporated Territories (Annexed by Germany)

▓▓▓▓ Under German civil administration

✕ Extermination camps

0 ▬▬▬▬▬▬ 200 miles

THE LUBLIN DISTRICT

0 ———————— 20 miles

Treblinka

Bug River

P O L A N D

Siedlce

Biała
Podlaska

Międzyrzec   Piszczac

Łukow   Łomazy   Tuczna

                    Komarówka

                    Radzyń   Wisznice

            Czemierniki

Serokomla   Parczew

            Kock

                        Parczew
                        Forest   Sobibór

        Końskowola

        Puławy   Wieprz River

                    Lublin

                        Zakrzów

                        Majdanek   Chełm

                        Piaski   Trawniki

Niezdów   Poniatowa

                    Wisła River

        Krasnik   Wysokie   Izbica

                    Turobin

                                        Zamość

                    Frampol

            Biłgoraj

    Ulanów   Aleksandrów   Józefów

            Tarnogród

PREFACE

In mid-March 1942 some 75 to 80 percent of all victims of the Holocaust were still alive, while 20 to 25 percent had perished. A mere eleven months later, in mid-February 1943, the percentages were exactly the reverse. At the core of the Holocaust was a short, intense wave of mass murder. The center of gravity of this mass murder was Poland, where in March 1942, despite two and a half years of terrible hardship, deprivation, and persecution, every major Jewish community was still intact, and where eleven months later only the remnants of Polish Jewry survived in a few rump ghettos and labor camps. In short, the German attack on the Jews of Poland was not a gradual or incremental program stretched over a long period of time, but a veritable blitzkrieg, a massive offensive requiring the mobilization of large numbers of shock troops. This offensive, moreover, came just when the German war effort in Russia hung in the balance—a time period that opened with the renewed German thrust toward the Crimea and the Caucasus and closed with the disastrous defeat at Stalingrad.

If the German military offensive of 1942 was ultimately a failure, the blitzkrieg against the Jews, especially in Poland, was not. We have long known how the Jews in the major ghettos, especially Warsaw and Lódź, were murdered. But most Polish Jews lived in smaller cities and towns whose populations were often more than 30 percent Jewish, and in some cases even 80 or 90 percent. How had the Germans organized and carried out the destruction of this widespread Jewish population? And where had they found the manpower during this pivotal year of the war for such an astounding logistical achievement in mass murder? The personnel of the death camps was quite minimal. But the manpower needed to clear the smaller ghettos—to round up and either deport or shoot the bulk of Polish Jewry—was not.[1]

My search for the answers to these questions led me to the town of Ludwigsburg near Stuttgart. Here is located the Central Agency for the State Administrations of Justice (Zentrale Stelle der Landesjustizverwaltungen), the Federal Republic of Germany's office for coordinating the investigation of Nazi crimes. I was working through their extensive collection of indictments and judgments for virtually every German trial of Nazi crimes committed against the Jews of Poland when I first encountered the indictment concerning Reserve Police Battalion 101, a unit of the German Order Police.

Though I had been studying archival documents and court records of the Holocaust for nearly twenty years, the impact this indictment had upon me was singularly powerful and disturbing. Never before had I encountered the issue of choice so dramatically framed by the course of events and so openly discussed by at least some of the perpetrators. Never before had I seen the monstrous deeds of the Holocaust so starkly juxtaposed with the human faces of the killers.

It was immediately clear from the indictment, which contained quite extensive verbatim quotations from pretrial interrogations of battalion members, that the case was based upon an unusually rich collection of testimonies. Moreover, many of these testimonies had a "feel" of candor and frankness conspicuously absent from the exculpatory, alibi-laden, and mendacious testimony so often encountered in such court records. The investigation and legal prosecution of Reserve Police Battalion 101 had been a decade-long process (1962 to 1972) conducted by the Office of the State Prosecutor (Staatsanwaltschaft) in Hamburg. This office—surely one of the most diligent and committed prosecutors of Nazi crimes in all of the Federal Republic—still had custody of the court records relating to the case, and I successfully applied for permission to see them.

Unlike so many of the Nazi killing units, whose membership can only be partially reconstructed, Reserve Police Battalion 101's roster was available to the investigators. As most of the men came from Hamburg and many still lived there at the time of the investigation, I was able to study the interrogations of 210 men from a unit consisting of slightly less than 500 when it was sent at full strength to Poland in June 1942. This collection of interrogations provided a representative sample for statistical answers to questions about age, Party and SS membership, and social background. Moreover, about 125 of the testimonies were sufficiently substantive to permit both detailed narrative reconstruction and analysis of the internal dynamics of this killing unit.

Ultimately, the Holocaust took place because at the most basic level individual human beings killed other human beings in large numbers over an extended period of time. The grass-roots perpetrators became "professional killers." The historian encounters numerous difficulties in trying to write about a unit of such men, among them the problem of sources. In the case of Reserve Police Battalion 101, in contrast to many of the killing units operating in the Soviet Union, there are few contemporary documents and none that deal explicitly with its killing activities.[2] The accounts of a handful of Jewish survivors can establish the dates and magnitude of various actions in some of the towns where the battalion operated. But unlike survivor testimony about prominent perpetrators in the ghettos and camps, where prolonged contact was possible, survivor testimony can tell us little about an itinerant unit like Reserve Police Battalion 101. Unknown men arrived, carried out their murderous task, and left. Seldom, in fact, can the survivors even remember the peculiar green uniforms of the Order Police to identify what kind of unit was involved.

In writing about Reserve Police Battalion 101, therefore, I have depended heavily upon the judicial interrogations of some 125 men conducted in the 1960s. To read about the same events experienced by a single unit as filtered through the memories of 125 different men more than twenty years after the fact is disconcerting to a historian looking for certainties. Each of these men played a different role. He saw and did different things. Each subsequently repressed or forgot certain aspects of the battalion's experiences, or reshaped his memory of them in a different way. Thus the interrogations inevitably present a confusing array of perspectives and memories. Paradoxically, I would have had the illusion of being more certain about what happened to the battalion with one detailed recollection instead of 125.

Beyond the differing perspectives and memories, there is also the interference caused by the circumstances in which the testimony was given. Quite simply, some men deliberately lied, for they feared the judicial consequences of telling the truth as they remembered it. Not only repression and distortion but conscious mendacity shaped the accounts of the witnesses. Furthermore, the interrogators asked questions pertinent to their task of collecting evidence for specific, indictable crimes committed by particular people, but did not systematically investigate the broader, often more impressionistic and subjective facets of the policemen's experience that are important to the historian, if not to the lawyer.

As with any use of multiple sources, the many accounts and perspectives had to be sifted and weighed. The reliability of each witness had to be assessed. Much of the testimony had to be partially or totally dismissed in favor of conflicting testimony that was accepted. Many of these judgments were both straightforward and obvious, but others were quite difficult. And as self-conscious as I have tried to be, at times I undoubtedly made purely instinctive judgments without even being aware of it. Other historians looking at the same materials would retell these events in somewhat different ways.

In recent decades the historical profession in general has been increasingly concerned with writing history "from the bottom up," with reconstructing the experiences of the bulk of the population ignored in the history of high politics and high culture hitherto so dominant. In Germany in particular, this trend has culminated in the practice of *Alltagsgeschichte*—"the history of everyday life"—achieved through a "thick description" of the common experiences of ordinary people. When such an approach has been applied to the era of the Third Reich, however, some have criticized it as an evasion—a way to shift attention from the unparalleled horrors of the Nazi regime's genocidal policies to those mundane aspects of life that continued relatively undisturbed. Thus, the very attempt to write a case study or microhistory of a single battalion might seem undesirable to some.

As a methodology, however, "the history of everyday life" is neutral. It becomes an evasion, an attempt to "normalize" the Third Reich, only if it fails to confront the degree to which the criminal policies of the regime inescapably permeated everyday existence under the Nazis. Particularly for the German occupiers stationed in the conquered lands of eastern Europe—literally tens of thousands of men from all walks of life—the mass-murder policies of the regime were not aberrational or exceptional events that scarcely ruffled the surface of everyday life. As the story of Reserve Police Battalion 101 demonstrates, mass murder and routine had become one. Normality itself had become exceedingly abnormal.

Another possible objection to this kind of study concerns the degree of empathy for the perpetrators that is inherent in trying to understand them. Clearly the writing of such a history requires the rejection of demonization. The policemen in the battalion who carried out the massacres and deportations, like the much smaller number who refused or evaded, were human beings. I must recognize that in the same situation, I could have been either a killer or an evader—both were human—if I want to understand and explain the behavior of both as best I can. This recognition does indeed mean an attempt to empathize. What I do not accept, however, are the old clichés that to explain is to excuse, to understand is to forgive. Explaining is not excusing; understanding is not forgiving. Not trying to understand the perpetrators in human terms would make impossible not only this study but any history of Holocaust perpetrators that sought to go beyond one-dimensional caricature. Shortly before his death at the hands of the Nazis, the French Jewish historian Marc Bloch wrote, "When all is said and done, a single word, 'understanding,' is the beacon light of our studies."[3] It is in that spirit that I have tried to write this book.

One condition placed upon my access to the judicial interrogations must be made clear. Regulations and laws for the protection of privacy have become increasingly restrictive in Germany, especially in the past decade. The state of Hamburg and its court records are no exception to this trend. Before receiving permission to see the court records of Reserve Police Battalion 101, therefore, I had to promise not to use the men's real names. The names of the battalion commander, Major Wilhelm Trapp, and the three company commanders, Captain Wolfgang Hoffmann, Captain Julius Wohlauf, and Lieutenant Hartwig Gnade, appear in other documentation in archives outside Germany. I have used their real names, for in their cases there is no confidentiality to breach. However, I have used pseudonyms (designated at first occurrence by an asterisk) for all other battalion members who appear in the text of this book. The notes refer to those giving testimony simply by first name and last initial. While this promise of confidentiality and use of pseudonyms is, in my opinion, an unfortunate limitation on strict historical accuracy, I do not believe it undermines the integrity or primary usefulness of this study.

A number of people and institutions provided indispensable support during the research and writing of this study. Oberstaatsanwalt (Senior Prosecutor) Alfred Streim made available to me the incomparable collection of German judicial records in Ludwigsburg. Oberstaatsanwältin Helge Grabitz encouraged me to work with the court records in Hamburg, supported my application for access, and generously helped in every way during my stay there. Pacific Lutheran University provided me with financial awards for the two trips to German archives that initiated and concluded my research on this project. The Alexander von Humboldt Foundation likewise aided one research visit in Germany. The bulk of the research and writing was completed during sabbatical leave from Pacific Lutheran University, and with the support of a Fulbright Research Grant to Israel. Daniel Krauskopf, executive secretary of the United States–Israel Educational Foundation, deserves special thanks for facilitating my research in both Israel and Germany.

Peter Hayes of Northwestern University and Saul Friedlander of UCLA offered opportunities to present initial research findings at conferences they organized at their respective institutions. Many friends and colleagues listened patiently, offered suggestions, and provided encouragement along the way. Philip Nordquist, Dennis Martin, Audrey Euyler, Robert Hoyer, Ian Kershaw, Robert Gellately, Yehuda Bauer, Dinah Porat, Michael Marrus, Bettina Birn, George Mosse, Elisabeth Domansky, Gitta Sereny, Carlo Ginzburg, and the late Uwe Adam deserve special mention. To Raul Hilberg I owe a special debt. In 1982 he called attention to the indispensability of the Order Police to the Final Solution, continuing as so often in the past to set the agenda for further Holocaust research.[4] He then personally interested himself in the publication of this study. For such help, both now and on earlier occasions in my career, the dedication of this book is an inadequate expression of my esteem and gratitude. For the continued support and understanding of my family, who have patiently endured the gestation period of another book, I am particularly grateful.

Tacoma, November 1991

ORDINARY MEN

1

One Morning in Józefów

IN THE VERY EARLY HOURS OF JULY 13, 1942, THE MEN OF Reserve Police Battalion 101 were roused from their bunks in the large brick school building that served as their barracks in the Polish town of Biłgoraj. They were middle-aged family men of working- and lower-middle-class background from the city of Hamburg. Considered too old to be of use to the German army, they had been drafted instead into the Order Police. Most were raw recruits with no previous experience in German occupied territory. They had arrived in Poland less than three weeks earlier.

It was still quite dark as the men climbed into the waiting trucks. Each policeman had been given extra ammunition, and additional boxes had been loaded onto the trucks as well.[1] They

1

were headed for their first major action, though the men had not yet been told what to expect.

The convoy of battalion trucks moved out of Biłgoraj in the dark, heading eastward on a jarring washboard gravel road. The pace was slow, and it took an hour and a half to two hours to arrive at the destination—the village of Józefów—a mere thirty kilometers away. Just as the sky was beginning to lighten, the convoy halted outside Józefów. It was a typical Polish village of modest white houses with thatched straw roofs. Among its inhabitants were 1,800 Jews.

The village was totally quiet.[2] The men of Reserve Police Battalion 101 climbed down from their trucks and assembled in a half-circle around their commander, Major Wilhelm Trapp, a fifty-three-year-old career policeman affectionately known by his men as "Papa Trapp." The time had come for Trapp to address the men and inform them of the assignment the battalion had received.

Pale and nervous, with choking voice and tears in his eyes, Trapp visibly fought to control himself as he spoke. The battalion, he said plaintively, had to perform a frightfully unpleasant task. This assignment was not to his liking, indeed it was highly regrettable, but the orders came from the highest authorities. If it would make their task any easier, the men should remember that in Germany the bombs were falling on women and children.

He then turned to the matter at hand. The Jews had instigated the American boycott that had damaged Germany, one policeman remembered Trapp saying. There were Jews in the village of Józefów who were involved with the partisans, he explained according to two others. The battalion had now been ordered to round up these Jews. The male Jews of working age were to be separated and taken to a work camp. The remaining Jews—the women, children, and elderly—were to be shot on the spot by the battalion. Having explained what awaited his men, Trapp then made an extraordinary offer: if any of the older men among them did not feel up to the task that lay before him, he could step out.[3]

The Order Police

How did a battalion of middle-aged reserve policemen find themselves facing the task of shooting some 1,500 Jews in the Polish village of Józefów in the summer of 1942? Some background is needed, both on the institution of the Order Police (Ordnungspolizei, or Orpo) and on its role in the Nazi policy of murdering the Jews of Europe.

The Order Police resulted from the third attempt in interwar Germany to create large police formations with military training and equipment.[1] In the wake of the German defeat in World War I, revolution broke out in Germany. As the army dissolved, military officers and government officials fearful of being swept away by revolutionary forces organized counterrevolutionary paramilitary units known as the Freikorps. When the domestic situation stabilized in 1919, many of the Freikorps men were merged with regular police into large formations stationed in barracks and on hand to combat any further resurgence of the revolutionary threat. The Allies, however, demanded the dissolution of these police formations in 1920 as a potential violation of the clause of the Versailles Treaty limiting Germany's standing army to 100,000 men.

After the Nazi regime was established in 1933, a "police army" (Armee der Landespolizei) of 56,000 men was created. These units were stationed in barracks and given full military training as part of Germany's covert rearmament. When Hitler openly defied the disarmament provisions of the Versailles Treaty and reintroduced military conscription in 1935, the "police army" was merged into the rapidly enlarging regular army to provide cadres of commissioned and noncommissioned officers. The "police army" played no small role as a training ground for future army officers. As of 1942, no fewer than ninety-seven generals in the German army had previously served in the "police army" of 1933–35.[2]

The preservation of large military formations within the police had to await the appointment of Heinrich Himmler, already head of the SS, as chief of German police in 1936, with jurisdiction over all police units in the Third Reich. Himmler divided the various German police into two branches, each under a main office in Berlin. Under the Security Police (Sicherheitspolizei) Main Office of Reinhard Heydrich were the notorious Secret State Police (Geheime Staatspolizei, or Gestapo), to combat the regime's political enemies, and the Criminal Police (Kriminalpolizei, or Kripo), which was basically a detective force for nonpolitical crimes. The second branch of the police was the Order Police Main Office under Kurt Daluege. Daluege had charge of the city or municipal police (Schutzpolizei, or Schupo), the rural police, equivalent perhaps to county troopers (Gendarmerie), and the small-town or community police (Gemeindepolizei).

By 1938 Daluege had over 62,000 policemen under his

jurisdiction. Nearly 9,000 of them were organized into police companies called *Polizei-Hundertschaften* of 108 men each. In each of ten cities in Germany, three police companies were brought together into yet larger "police training units" (*Polizei-Ausbildungsabteilungen*).

In 1938 and 1939, the Order Police expanded rapidly as the increasing threat of war gave prospective recruits a further inducement. If they enlisted in the Order Police, the new young policemen were exempted from conscription into the army. Moreover, because the police battalions—like U.S. National Guard units—were organized regionally, they seemed to offer the guarantee of completing one's alternative to regular military service not only more safely but closer to home.

With the outbreak of war in September 1939, the Order Police had reached a strength of 131,000 men. The big threat to its large military formations was, of course, absorption into the German army, a move avoided through a compromise for which the Order Police paid a heavy price. Many of its best units were formed into a police division of nearly 16,000 men that was put at the disposal of the army. (It subsequently fought in the Ardennes in 1940 and took part in the attack on Leningrad in 1941, before Himmler got it back in 1942 as the Fourth SS-Polizei Grenadier Division.) Two police regiments raised in newly seized Danzig were also transferred to the army in October 1939. Finally, the Order Police provided over 8,000 men for the army's military police, or Feldgendarmerie. In return the other draft-age men of the Order Police remained exempt from military conscription.

To replenish its ranks, the Order Police was allowed to recruit 26,000 young German men—9,000 volunteers born between 1918 and 1920, and 17,000 volunteers born between 1909 and 1912—as well as 6,000 so-called "ethnic Germans," or *Volksdeutsche*, who had lived outside Germany prior to 1939. In addition, the Order Police received authorization to conscript 91,500 reservists born between 1901 and 1909—an age group not as yet subject to the military draft. Order Police conscription was gradually extended to still older men, and by mid-1940, the size of the Order Police had grown to 244,500.[3]

The Order Police had scarcely been taken into account in prewar mobilization plans, and little thought had been given to its possible wartime use, but Germany's military success and rapid expansion quickly created the need for more occupation forces behind the lines. With the outbreak of war, twenty-one police battalions of approximately 500 men each were formed from the various police companies and training units in Germany; thirteen of them were attached to the armies invading Poland. They were subsequently involved in rounding up Polish soldiers cut off behind the advancing lines, collecting weapons and military equipment abandoned by the retreating Poles, and providing other services to secure the rear areas.

The number of police battalions rapidly expanded to 101 by mid-1940, as the 26,000 new young recruits and many of the older drafted reservists were formed into battalion units as well. Thirteen battalions were stationed in German-occupied central Poland, known as the General Government, and seven were stationed in the western Polish territories annexed to the Third Reich, the "incorporated territories." Ten were stationed in the occupied Czech lands of Bohemia and Moravia, known as the Protectorate. In addition, six battalions were stationed in Norway, and four in the Netherlands.[4] The Order Police were quickly becoming an essential source of manpower for holding down German-occupied Europe.

The new battalions were created in two ways. First, to provide the necessary cadres of noncommissioned officers, career policemen and prewar volunteers from the initial battalions that went into Poland in 1939 were promoted and distributed to the newly formed units, whose ranks were filled with older drafted reservists. These battalions were designated "reserve police battalions." Second, particular units (given numbers from 251 to 256 and 301 to 325) were formed from among the 26,000 young volunteers allocated to the Order Police in the fall of 1939. They would become, in effect, the new elite formations of the Order Police.[5]

The presence of the Order Police in the General Government was felt in two ways. First, in each of the four districts into which the General Government had been divided—Kraków, Lublin, Radom, and Warsaw (a fifth, Galicia, was added in 1941)—a permanent regimental commander (Kommandeur der Ordnungspolizei, or KdO) and staff were established. Each district regiment was composed of three battalions that were constantly changing as they were rotated out from Germany on tours of duty. Second, there was a thin network of smaller units of Order Police throughout the General Government. In each of the major Polish cities, a Schutzpolizei station was established. Its primary task was to supervise the Polish municipal police. In addition, there were thirty to forty small Gendarmerie posts in the medium-sized towns of each district. Both the Schutzpolizei and the Gendarmerie units, like the three battalion commanders, reported to the district commander of the Order Police, the KdO. By the end of 1942, the total strength of the Order Police in the General Government had reached 15,186 men. The Polish police under Order Police supervision numbered 14,297.[6]

One chain of command led upward from the Order Police battalions, as well as from the network of smaller units, through the district KdO to the overall commander of the Order Police in the General Government (Befehlshaber der Ordnungspolizei, or BdO) in the capital city of Kraków, and finally to Daluege's main office in Berlin. This was the normal chain of command for matters solely concerning the local Order Police units. However, there was a second chain of command for all policies and operations that involved the joint action of the Order Police with the Security Police and other SS units. In the General Government, Heinrich Himmler had appointed a Higher SS and Police Leader (HSSPF), Friedrich-Wilhelm Krüger, as his personal representative, with special responsibility to coordinate any actions involving more than one agency of Himmler's sprawling

SS and police empire. In each district in the General Government, there was an SS and Police Leader (SSPF) who had the same responsibilities and powers on the district level that Krüger exercised for the General Government. For the district of Lublin, where Reserve Police Battalion 101 was stationed in 1942–43, the SSPF was the brutal and unsavory Odilo Globocnik, a crony of Himmler's, who had been removed from his position as party chief in Austria for corruption. Thus Order Police units in the Lublin district could receive orders either from Daluege and the Berlin main office through the BdO in Kraków and the district KdO, or from Himmler through the HSSPF, Krüger, and the district SSPF, Globocnik. As the murder of Polish Jewry was a program involving every branch of the SS and the police, it was the latter chain of command that would be crucial for Order Police participation in the Final Solution.

3

The Order Police and the Final Solution: Russia 1941

THE INITIAL PARTICIPATION OF THE ORDER POLICE IN THE Final Solution—the Nazi mass murder of European Jewry—occurred not in Poland but in Russia in the summer and fall of 1941. In preparation for the invasion of Russia and the "war of destruction" Hitler intended to wage there, four special mobile units of the SS known as Einsatzgruppen were formed and trained in the late spring of 1941. The core of these units came from Heydrich's Security Police (Gestapo and Kripo) as well as his intelligence apparatus (Security Service, or SD). They were supplemented by small units of Waffen-SS (the military branch of Himmler's SS). In addition, however, the three companies of Order Police Battalion 9 were distributed to three of the four Einsatzgruppen.[1] Order Police members thus constituted about

500 of the total of 3,000 men assigned to the four Einsatzgruppen.

The Einsatzgruppen were only the thin cutting edge of German units that became involved in political and racial mass murder in Russia. In early July a fifth ad hoc Einsatzgruppe made up of personnel from the Security Police in the General Government was sent into Russia. Most of these men became the permanent Security Police force in the areas of the 1939–41 Soviet occupation zone in former eastern Poland, while the original four Einsatzgruppen pressed deep into Russia behind the advancing German armies.

For the occupation of Russia, Himmler had appointed three Higher SS and Police Leaders for the northern, central, and southern regions respectively. These men were in charge of coordinating all SS operations in occupied Russia. In the euphoric days of mid-July 1941, when ultimate victory seemed in sight after Germany's stupendous initial military successes, Hitler ordered the intensification of the pacification program behind the advancing German lines. On July 16 he announced that Germany would never withdraw from its newly won territories in the east; instead he would create there "a Garden of Eden," taking all necessary measures to accomplish this. It was fortunate that Stalin had given the order for partisan warfare, Hitler said, because "it gives us the opportunity to exterminate anyone who is hostile to us. Naturally the vast area must be pacified as quickly as possible; this will happen best through shooting anyone who even looks askance at us."[2]

Himmler was not slow to respond to such exhortations from his master. Within a week, he had reinforced HSSPF Central Erich von dem Bach-Zelewski and HSSPF South Friedrich Jeckeln with an additional SS brigade each, thus adding more than 11,000 men to the SS murder campaign.[3] Moreover, at least eleven police battalions—nine of them 300-level and thus composed of recent young volunteers—were distributed among the three HSSPFs in Russia, adding another 5,500 Order Police to the 500 already assigned to the Einsatzgruppen.[4] Between late July and mid-August, Himmler toured the eastern front, personally urging his men to carry out the mass murder of Russian Jewry.

But the Order Police actually inaugurated their murderous career in Russia before this massive buildup in the later part of July. The site was the nearly half-Jewish city of Białystok. On the eve of the German invasion of Russia—dubbed Operation Barbarossa—Major Weis of Police Battalion 309 met with his company commanders. As in every other unit of the German army and police moving into Russia, he disclosed several orders that were to be passed on to the men verbally. The first was the notorious *Kommissarbefehl*, or "commissar order," according to which so-called political commissars—all Communist functionaries in the army as well as those in the civil administration suspected of being in any way anti-German—were to be denied prisoner of war status and executed.[5] The second order was the "Barbarossa decree," which removed the actions of German soldiers toward Russian civilians from the jurisdiction of military courts and explicitly approved collective reprisal against entire villages.[6] It was, in fact, a "shooting license" against Russian civilians. Major Weis then went further. The war, he said, was a war against Jews and Bolsheviks, and he wanted it understood that the battalion should proceed ruthlessly against Jews. In his view, the meaning of the Führer's orders was that the Jews, regardless of age or sex, were to be destroyed.[7]

After entering the city of Białystok, Major Weis on June 27 ordered his battalion to comb the Jewish quarter and seize male Jews, but he did not specify what was to be done with them. That was apparently left to the initiative of the company captains, who had been oriented to his way of thinking in the preinvasion meeting. The action began as a pogrom: beating, humiliation, beard burning, and shooting at will as the policemen drove Jews to the marketplace or synagogue. When several Jewish leaders appeared at the headquarters of the 221st Security Division of

General Pflugbeil and knelt at his feet, begging for army protection, one member of Police Battalion 309 unzipped his fly and urinated on them while the general turned his back.

What started as a pogrom quickly escalated into more systematic mass murder. Jews collected at the marketplace were taken to a park, lined up against a wall, and shot. The killing lasted until dark. At the synagogue, where at least 700 Jews had been collected, gasoline was poured at the entryways. A grenade was tossed into the building, igniting a fire. Police shot anyone trying to escape. The fire spread to nearby houses in which Jews were hiding, and they too were burned alive. The next day, thirty wagonloads of corpses were taken to a mass grave. An estimated 2,000 to 2,200 Jews had been killed. When General Pflugbeil sent a messenger to Major Weis to inquire about the fire, the major was found drunk. He claimed to know nothing about what was happening. Weis and his officers subsequently submitted a false report of the events to Pflugbeil.[8]

If the first Order Police massacre of Jews in Białystok, on June 27, was the work of an individual commander who correctly intuited and anticipated the wishes of his Führer, the second, in mid-July, involved clear and systematic instigation from the very highest echelons of the SS—namely Erich von dem Bach-Zelewski, Kurt Daluege, and Heinrich Himmler. Police Battalion 309 moved eastward, and Police Battalions 316 and 322 entered Białystok in its wake. The official daily record, or war diary (*Kriegstagebuch*), and various reports and orders of Police Battalion 322 are among the rare surviving Order Police documents that have reached the West from Soviet archives. They allow us to trace subsequent events in Białystok.

The preinvasion orientation of Police Battalion 322 was apparently not as vicious as that of Police Battalion 309, but it was certainly not free of ideological exhortation. Major General Retzlaff delivered a farewell address to the battalion in Warsaw on June 10. Every member had to be careful, he advised, "to appear before the Slavic peoples as a master and show them that he was a German."[9] Before leaving for Russia on July 2, the men were informed that any "political commissar was to be shot" and that they had to be "tough, determined, and ruthless."[10]

The battalion arrived in Białystok on July 5, and two days later was ordered to carry out a "thorough search of the city . . . for Bolshevik commissars and Communists." The war diary entry of the following day makes clear what this meant: "a search of the Jewish quarter," allegedly for plunder seized by Jews before the German arrival. The German police in fact carried off twenty wagonloads of booty during the search. By July 8 the battalion had shot twenty-two people. "It was a matter . . . almost exclusively of Jews."[11]

On this same afternoon of the July 8 search, the battalion received a surprise visit from the Reichsführer SS and chief of German police, Heinrich Himmler, and the commander of the Order Police, Kurt Daluege. The battalion commander, Major Nagel, was invited to the dinner given that evening by HSSPF Central, Bach-Zelewski, in Himmler's honor. The following morning Daluege held a review of the police battalions in Białystok in Himmler's presence. In his speech Daluege emphasized that the Order Police "could be proud to be participating in the defeat of the world enemy, Bolshevism. No other campaign had the significance of the present one. Now Bolshevism will finally be destroyed for the benefit of Germany, Europe, yes, the entire world."[12]

Two days later, on July 11, Colonel Montua of the Police Regiment Center (which included Police Battalions 316 and 322) issued the following order:

Confidential!

1. By order of the Higher SS and Police Leader . . . all male Jews between the ages of 17 and 45 convicted as plunderers are to be shot according to martial law. The shootings are to take place away from cities, villages, and thoroughfares.
The graves are to be leveled in such a way that no pilgrimage site can arise. I forbid photographing and the permitting of

spectators at the executions. Executions and grave sites are not to be made known.

2. The battalion and company commanders are especially to provide for the spiritual care of the men who participate in this action. The impressions of the day are to be blotted out through the holding of social events in the evenings.

Furthermore the men are to be instructed continuously about the political necessity of the measures.[13]

The war diary falls strangely silent about what happened in Białystok following Montua's ordering of executions, but subsequent judicial proceedings in Germany unveiled the course of events.[14] There was, of course, no investigation, trial, and conviction of so-called plunderers to be shot according to martial law. Male Jews who appeared to be between the ages of seventeen and forty-five were simply rounded up and brought to the stadium in Białystok on July 12. When the stadium was nearly filled, Bach-Zelewski visited the site, and valuables were collected from the Jews. It was a very hot day, during which the Jews neither received water nor were allowed to go to the toilet.

Beginning either the same day or the following morning, trucks from the motor pools of both police battalions began shuttling the Jews from the stadium to antitank ditches in a forested area outside the city. Most of Battalion 316 and one company of Battalion 322 guarded the shooting site and were formed into firing squads. Bach-Zelewski again appeared on the scene and gave a justifying speech. The shooting lasted until nightfall, and then the policemen attempted to carry on the executions under the headlights of their trucks. When this proved unsatisfactory, the action was broken off and completed the following day. The German courts concluded that at least 3,000 Jews had been shot (though it must be kept in mind that for judicial convenience such figures always represent an uncontested minimal estimate of victims, and not the most probable number, so as to remove that issue from judicial dispute).

The murder campaign against Russian Jewry accelerated in the late summer and fall of 1941, and the war diary of Police Battalion 322 reveals its continuing involvement. On July 23 the battalion's formal subordination to the rear area army commander was severed. "For the imminent tasks of the battalion, it is placed directly under the HSSPF Gruppenführer von dem Bach."[15] As the three companies of Police Battalion 322 moved from Białystok to Minsk during the month of August, Lieutenant Riebel's Third Company particularly distinguished itself by ongoing executions of Jews in its path. Following sweeps by the Third Company through the forest regions around Białowieża on August 2, the war diary noted, "Before departure 3d Company must carry out the liquidation of Jews."[16] Riebel subsequently reported, "In the early morning hours of August 10, the liquidation of the Jews lodged in the Białowieża prisoner collection camp was carried out by 3d Company. Seventy-seven male Jews between 16 and 45 were shot. The action was performed without incident. There was not a single case of resistance."[17] This was not an isolated action, for five days later Riebel reported, "The Jewish action in Narevka-Mala was carried out by 3d Company on August 15, 1941. In it 259 women and 162 children were moved to Kobrin. All male persons between 16 and 65 years of age were shot. On August 15, 1941, a total of one Pole for plundering and 232 Jews were shot. The Jewish execution was performed smoothly and without incident."[18]

By late August the battalion was in Minsk, where Bach-Zelewski and Daluege met on August 29.[19] As in Białystok earlier, their meeting was the prelude to Order Police participation in another major mass shooting of Jews. On August 30 the battalion commander, Major Nagel, was summoned to discuss "a basic Jewish action" scheduled to take place on August 31 and September 1. The battalion was to provide two companies.[20]

On August 31 the First and Third Companies of Police Battalion 322 (now designated the Seventh and Ninth Companies of Police Regiment Center) moved into the Minsk ghetto, where they seized some 700 Jews, including 74 women. The following day Riebel's Ninth Company took part in the execution of more than 900 Jews, including all of those seized the day before. For this first shooting of large numbers of Jewish women, the author of the war diary felt the need to provide a justification. They were shot, he explained, "because they had been encountered without the Jewish star during the roundup. . . . Also in Minsk it has been discovered that especially Jewesses removed the marking from their clothing."[21] Ever anxious to get credit for his company's body count, Riebel dutifully reported, "In the Jewish action of September 1, the Jews seized on August 31 were shot. Shot by 9th Company were 290 men and 40 women. The executions proceeded smoothly. No one resisted."[22]

In a subsequent action in Mogilev in early October, the need to explain the shooting of Jewish women was no longer felt. For October 2, the war diary recorded, "9th Company. From 3:30 p.m. the entire company. Jewish action in the ghetto of Mogilev together with the staff of the Higher SS and Police Leader Russia Central and Ukrainian auxiliary police: 2,208 Jews of both sexes seized, 65 shot on the spot attempting to escape." On the following day: "7th and 9th Companies together with the staff of the Higher SS and Police Leader Russia Central—execution of a total of 2,208 Jews and Jewesses outside Mogilev not far from the forest camp (7th Company 378, 9th Company 545 shootings)."[23]

The involvement of the police battalions in the central region of Russia was not unique. The scant surviving documentation indicates similar involvement in both the south and the north. HSSPF Russia South, Friedrich Jeckeln, who commanded a total of five police battalions (304 and 320 in addition to Police Regiment South, consisting of 45, 303, and 314—thus, all but one of them composed of recent young volunteers), was careful in his cryptic daily reports to give credit where credit was due. The following emerges from an incomplete collection of these reports.[24]

AUGUST 19:	Battalion 314 shot 25 Jews. Battalion 45 at Slavuta shot 522 Jews.
AUGUST 22:	Battalion 45 shot 66 and 471 Jews in two actions.
AUGUST 23:	Battalion 314 shot 367 Jews in a "cleansing action."
AUGUST 24:	Battalion 314 shot 294 Jews, Battalion 45 shot 61 Jews, and the "police squadron" (horse-mounted police) 113 Jews.
AUGUST 25:	Police Regiment South shot 1,324 Jews.
AUGUST 27:	According to the first of two reports, Police Regiment South shot 549 Jews and Battalion 314 shot 69 Jews. The second credited Police Regiment South with shooting 914 Jews.
AUGUST 28:	Police Regiment South shot 369 Jews.
AUGUST 29:	Battalion 320 provided the "cordon" while the staff company of the HSSPF shot 15,000 Jews at Kamenets Podolsky on August 26–27 and another 7,000 on August 28.
AUGUST 31:	Battalion 320 shot 2,200 Jews in Minkovtsy.
SEPTEMBER 1:	Police Regiment South shot 88 Jews; Battalion 320 shot 380.
SEPTEMBER 2:	Police Regiment South shot 45 Jews.
SEPTEMBER 4:	Police Regiment South shot 4,144 Jews.
SEPTEMBER 6:	Police Regiment South shot 144 Jews.
SEPTEMBER 11:	Police Regiment South shot 1,548 Jews.
SEPTEMBER 12:	Police Regiment South shot 1,255 Jews.
OCTOBER 5:	Police Battalion 304 shot 305 Jews.

Postwar judicial interrogations in the Federal Republic of Germany, stemming from this scant documentation, uncovered further information about the murderous swath Police Battalions 45 and 314 cut across the Soviet Union in the fall of 1941. Police Battalion 45 had reached the Ukrainian town of Shepetovka on July 24, when its commander, Major Besser, was summoned by the head of Police Regiment South, Colonel Franz. Franz told Besser that by order of Himmler the Jews in Russia were to be destroyed and his Police Battalion 45 was to take part in this task. Within days the battalion had massacred the several hundred remaining Jews of Shepetovka, including women and children. Three-figure massacres in various Ukrainian towns followed in August. In September the battalion provided cordon, escort, and shooters for the execution of thousands of Jews in Berdichev and Vinnitsa. The battalion's brutal activities climaxed in Kiev on September 29 and 30, when the policemen again provided cordon, escort, and shooters for the murder of over 33,000 Jews in the ravine of Babi Yar. The battalion continued to carry out smaller executions (Khorol, Krementshug, Poltava) until the end of the year.[25] Police Battalion 314 also began with relatively small three-figure massacres, starting on July 22. It then joined Police Battalion 45 in the execution of several thousand Jews in Vinnitsa in September 1941, and shot 7,000 to 8,000 Jews in Dnepropetrovsk on October 10–14. The last shooting uncovered in the investigation dated to late January 1942 in Kharkov.[26]

The documentation from southern Russia provides a sketchy overview of the broad and continuous participation of Order Police units in the mass shootings of Jews, but it lacks detail; the documentation for northern Russia is just the opposite. Here we have no overview, but we do have one extraordinarily vivid description of an operation by Police Battalion 11, which had been stationed in the Kovno region since early July 1941, its Third Company charged with guarding the Kovno ghetto.[27] In mid-October the battalion commander was sent to Minsk with two companies of Battalion 11 and two companies of Lithuanian auxiliary police. The operations officer of the 707th Security

Division gave the policemen their first task (which they later claimed to be the first of only two such actions): the execution of all Jews in the village of Smolevichi, east of Minsk, as an alleged deterrent and warning to the civilian population not to help the partisans. The battalion commander claimed that he protested but was merely told by the operations officer and division commander that the German police could provide the cordon and leave the shooting to the Lithuanians. The massacre of the Smolevichi Jews was carried out as ordered.

In late October the two companies of Order Police and their Lithuanian auxiliaries were ordered by the army to liquidate all the Jews in Slutsk, south of Minsk, a town of some 12,000 inhabitants, one-third Jewish. Again the measure was justified as a deterrent for the protection of German troops. What happened in Slutsk on October 27 was the subject of a report from the head of the German civil administration there to his boss, Wilhelm Kube, in Minsk.

Slutsk, 30 October 1941

Regional Commissioner Slutsk
To: General Commissioner in Minsk
Concerning: Jewish action

In reference to my telephone report of October 27, 1941, I submit the following to you in writing:
On the morning of October 27 about 8 o'clock, a first lieutenant of Police Battalion 11 from Kovno (Lithuania) appeared. He introduced himself as the adjutant of the battalion commander of the Security [sic] Police. The first lieutenant declared that the police battalion had been assigned the task of carrying out the liquidation of all Jews in the city of Slutsk within two days. The battalion commander was approaching with a force of four companies, two of them Lithuanian auxiliaries, and the action had to begin immediately. I thereupon answered the first lieutenant that in any case I first of all had to discuss the action with the commander. About one-half hour later the police battalion arrived in

Slutsk. As requested, the discussion with the battalion commander then took place immediately after his arrival. I explained first of all to the commander that it would scarcely be possible to carry out the action without prior preparation, because all [the Jews] had been sent to work and there would be frightful confusion. At the very least, he was obligated to give one day's notice. I then asked him to postpone the action for one day. He nonetheless rejected this, noting that he had to carry out actions in the cities all around and only two days were available for Slutsk. At the end of these two days Slutsk had to be absolutely free of Jews. I immediately lodged the sharpest protest against this, in which I emphasized that a liquidation of the Jews could not take place arbitrarily. The larger portion of Jews still present in the city consisted of craftsmen and their families. One simply could not do without the Jewish craftsmen, because they were indispensable for the maintenance of the economy. Furthermore I referred to the fact that White Russian craftsmen were, so to say, utterly unavailable, that therefore all vital enterprises would be paralyzed with a single blow if all Jews were liquidated. At the conclusion of our discussion I mentioned that the craftsmen and specialists, insofar as they were indispensable, had identification on hand, and that these Jews were not to be taken out of the workshops. It was further agreed that all Jews still in the city, especially the craftsmen's families, whom I also did not want to have liquidated, should first of all be brought to the ghetto for the purpose of sorting. Two of my officials were to be authorized to carry out the sorting. The commander in no way opposed my position, so in good faith I believed that the action would therefore be carried out accordingly.

Several hours after the action began, the greatest difficulties were already becoming apparent. I discovered that the commander was not at all abiding by our arrangement. Contrary to the agreement, all Jews without exception were being taken from the factories and workshops and sent off. A portion of the Jews were in any case taken through the ghetto, where many were grabbed and selected out by me, but most were loaded directly on trucks and without further ado liquidated outside the city. Shortly after noon, complaints were already coming from all sides that the workshops could no longer operate because all Jewish craftsmen had been removed. Because the commander had driven on to Baranovichi, I contacted the deputy commander, a captain, after a long search and demanded that the action be immediately stopped, because it was not taking place according to my instructions and the economic damage already inflicted could not be made good. The captain was very astonished by my viewpoint and explained that he had received instructions from the commander to make the city free of Jews without exception, as they had also done in other cities. The cleansing had to take place on political grounds, and nowhere had economic factors so far played a role. Upon my energetic interventions he then nonetheless stopped the action toward evening.

What else concerns this action, I must to my greatest regret emphasize, is last of all that it bordered on sadism. During the action the city itself offered a horrible picture. With indescribable brutality, by the German policemen as well but especially by the Lithuanians, the Jews and also White Russians were taken out of their lodgings and driven together. There was shooting everywhere in the city, and in the individual streets bodies of Jews who had been shot piled up. The White Russians had the greatest difficulty in extricating themselves from the roundup. Aside from the fact that the Jews, among them also craftsmen, were brutally mistreated in a frightfully barbarous way before the eyes of the White Russians, the latter were likewise beaten with truncheons and clubs. One can no longer speak of a Jewish action, it appeared much more like a revolution. I and all my officials were in the midst of this all day without a break, in order to save what could still be saved. Repeatedly I literally had to drive German police officials as well as Lithuanians out of the workshops with drawn revolver. My own gendarmes were given the same task but because of the wild shooting often had to get off the streets in order not to be shot themselves. The entire scene was altogether more than ghastly. In the afternoon a large number of horse-drawn carts without drivers stood around in the streets, so that I had to assign the city administration immediately to take care of them. Afterward it turned out that they were Jewish wagons that had been assigned by the army to transport ammunition. The Jews had simply been taken down from the wagons and marched off, without anyone caring for the wagons.

I was not present at the shootings outside the city. Thus I can say nothing about the brutality. But it suffices when I emphasize that long after being thrown in the grave, some of those shot worked their way out again. Concerning the economic damage I note that the tannery was most frightfully affected. Twenty-six experts worked there. In one blow fifteen of the best specialists among them were shot. Another four jumped from the wagons while underway and escaped, while seven avoided being seized through flight. Five men worked in the wheelwright shop, four of whom were shot, and the shop must now be kept going with only one wheelwright. Still other craftsmen are missing, such as cabinetmakers, smiths, etc. So far it has not been possible for me to get a precise overview. As I already mentioned at the beginning, the families of the craftsmen were also supposed to have been spared. Today it appears, however, that in almost every family some people are missing. Reports come in from everywhere, from which it can be concluded that in some such families the craftsman himself, in others the wife, and in yet others the children are missing. Thus almost all families have been torn apart. In these circumstances it must be very doubtful if the remaining craftsmen are enthusiastic about their work and produce accordingly, the more so in that at the moment they are still walking around with faces beaten bloody on account of the brutality. The White Russians, whose full trust had been won, stood there aghast. Although they are intimidated and do not dare to express their opinions freely, one nonetheless hears it said that this day represented no page of glory for Germany and that it will never be forgotten. I am of the opinion that through this action much has been destroyed that we had achieved over the last months, and that it will be a long time before we can again win the trust of the population.

In conclusion I find myself compelled to point out that during the action the police battalion plundered in an outrageous way, and indeed not only in Jewish houses, but just as much in the houses of the White Russians. They took with them anything useful, such as boots, leather, textiles, gold, and other valuables. According to the accounts of members of the army, watches were torn from the arms of Jews publicly in the streets, rings were pulled off fingers in the most brutal way. One senior paymaster reported that a Jewish girl was ordered by the police immediately to fetch 5,000 rubles, then her father would be released. This girl is said to have run around everywhere trying to get the money. Also within the ghetto the individual barracks that were nailed shut by the civil administration and provided with a Jewish inventory were broken into and robbed by the police. Even in the barracks in which the unit was lodged, window frames and doors were torn out for the camp fire. Even though I had a talk with the commander's adjutant on Tuesday morning concerning the plundering and he promised me in the course of the conversation that no police would henceforth enter the city, several hours later I was forced once again to arrest two fully armed Lithuanians, because they were caught looting. On the night of Tuesday to Wednesday, the battalion left the city in the direction of Baranovichi. The population was manifestly happy as the news spread through the city.

So much for the report. I will come to Minsk in the near future in order once again to discuss the matter orally. At the moment I am not able to continue the Jewish action. First peace must return. I hope to be able to restore peace as quickly as possible and despite the difficulties to revive the economy. I now ask only that one request be granted me: "In the future spare me without fail from this police battalion." Carl[28]

Though the documentation of police battalion participation in the mass murder of Russian Jewry is not extensive, it does suffice to disprove beyond any reasonable doubt the chief postwar alibi of the Order Police leadership—namely, that Daluege had reached an agreement with Himmler whereby the Order Police would assist the Security Police, providing guard duty and any services short of shooting, but were forbidden to be the executioners themselves. This alibi, akin to the postwar claim of the Waffen-SS that they were soldiers like any others and did not participate in the ideologically grounded programs of the rest of the SS, was successfully pleaded before at least one German court in the trial of Police Battalion 11. The defendants persuaded the court that after only two executions—upon army orders in the Minsk region—they were able to invoke Daluege's arrangement to secure their recall to Kovno.[29]

As the documentation shows, the direct participation of the Order Police in the mass executions of Russian Jews in the summer and fall of 1941 was pervasive, occurring within the jurisdictions of the northern, central, and southern HSSPFs as well as in Białystok. Moreover, the mid-July massacre in Białystok took place directly after Daluege and Himmler met there with Bach-Zelewski, and the September 1 massacre in Minsk occurred immediately after Daluege's visit with Bach-Zelewski in that city. Clearly, Daluege was not forbidding but rather inciting Order Police participation in the mass murder.

Order Police involvement in mass shootings in Russia after the fall of 1941 is not well documented and in all probability was much less frequent. The major exception was extensive Order Police participation in the shooting of Jews in the Pinsk region in the fall of 1942.[30] In the military crisis of the 1941–42 winter, many police battalions were pressed into frontline duty. Others had to contend with growing partisan resistance. Moreover, the number of men recruited from native populations into auxiliary units under the Order Police increased nearly tenfold in 1942, from 33,000 to 300,000.[31] There was a constant tendency to assign the actual shooting duties to these units, in order to shift the psychological burden from the German police to their collaborators. This psychological burden was serious and extended even to Bach-Zelewski himself. Himmler's SS doctor, reporting to the Reichsführer on Bach-Zelewski's incapacitating illness in the spring of 1942, noted that the SS leader was suffering "especially from visions in connection with the shootings of Jews that he himself had led, and from other difficult experiences in the east."[32]

4

The Order Police and the Final Solution: Deportation

JUST AS THE ROLE OF THE ORDER POLICE IN THE MASSACRE OF Russian Jewry was beginning to wind down in the fall of 1941, Daluege took on a new and vital assignment contributing to the Final Solution: guarding the deportation trains "to the east." In late September 1941 Hitler approved the commencement of Jewish deportations from the Third Reich, to be organized by Reinhard Heydrich through his Jewish expert in Berlin, Adolf Eichmann, and the regional Security Police offices throughout Germany.[1] The only exceptions on the local level were in Vienna and Prague, where the deportations were to be handled by the Central Agencies for Jewish Emigration, created by Eichmann before the war and staffed by his handpicked men. Almost immediately, Heydrich reached agreement with Daluege on a division of labor. Daluege's Order Police would guard the transports that Heydrich's Security Police organized. Before each deportation wave, the local Order Police were instructed to accommodate Security Police requests for the agreed-upon transport guards. Ordinarily, the Order Police supplied one officer and fifteen men to each transport.[2]

What was the scale of these operations? Between the fall of 1941 and the spring of 1945, over 260 deportation trains took German, Austrian, and Czech Jews directly to the ghettos and death camps "in the east" (i.e., Poland and Russia) or to the transit ghetto of Theresienstadt north of Prague and from there "to the east."[3] A minimum of 147 trains from Hungary, 87 from Holland, 76 from France, 63 from Slovakia, 27 from Belgium, 23 from Greece, 11 from Italy, 7 from Bulgaria, and 6 from Croatia—that is, close to 450 additional trains from western and southern Europe—were taken over by German guards at some point in their journey.[4] No estimate has even been made of the number of Jewish deportation trains that traveled from Polish cities to the nearby death camps, but it was clearly in the many hundreds. Virtually all of these trains were guarded by Order Police.

What did this mean in terms of what the Order Police experienced? One graphic report by Lieutenant Paul Salitter on guarding a deportation train from Düsseldorf to Riga on December 11, 1941, has already been published in both English and German.[5] Two other reports—on deportation trains from Vienna to Sobibór and from Kołomyja in Galicia to Bełżec—are noteworthy for an understanding of what numerous Order Police units did more than one thousand times during the war. First, the Vienna transport.

152d Police Precinct   Vienna, June 20, 1942
Report of Experiences
Subject: Transport commando for the Jewish Transport
Vienna-Aspangbahnhof to Sobibór, June 14, 1942

The transport commando consisted of Reserve Lieutenant Fischmann as leader, two sergeants, and 13 reserve policemen of the 1st Reserve Police Company East. The duty of the transport commando began at 11 a.m. on June 14, 1942, at the Aspangbahnhof, in accordance with the prior telephone request of SS-Hauptsturmführer Brunner.

1. The loading of the Jews:
Under the direction and supervision of SS-Hauptsturmführer Brunner and SS-Hauptscharführer Girzik of the Central Agency for Jewish Emigration, the loading of the Jews into the special train waiting in the Aspangbahnhof began at noon and went smoothly. The guard duty of the transport commando commenced at this time. A total of 1,000 Jews were deported. The transfer of the Jews as listed occurred at 4 p.m. Because of a shortage of cars, the transport commando had to make do with a third- instead of a second-class car.

2. Trip from Vienna to Sobibór:
The train Da 38 was dispatched from Vienna at 7:08 p.m. on June 14, 1942, and traveled to Sobibór, not as scheduled to Izbica, via Lundenburg [Břeclar], Brünn [Brno], Neisse [Nysa], Oppeln [Opole], Częstochowa, Kielce, Radom, Dęblin, Lublin, and Chelm. Arrival in Sobibór on June 17, 1942, at 8:05 a.m. On arrival in Lublin at 9 p.m. on June 16, SS-Obersturmführer Pohl was waiting for the train at the station and had 51 Jews capable of work between the ages of 15 and 50 removed from the train and taken to a work camp. At the same time he gave the order to take the remaining 949 Jews to the work camp in Sobibór. Both lists of names, three wagons of baggage (with food supplies) as well as 100,000 zlotys were turned over to SS-Obersturmführer Pohl in Lublin. At 11 p.m. the train departed from Lublin for Sobibór. At the Jewish camp in Trawniki some 30 kilometers beyond Lublin the three baggage wagons and food supplies were surrendered to SS-Scharführer Mayerhofer.

3. Delivery of the Jews in Sobibór:
At 8:15 a.m. on June 17 the train drove into the work camp next to the Sobibór train station, where the camp commandant, First Lieutenant Stangl, took delivery of the 949 Jews. The unloading of the train cars began immediately and was completed by 9:15 a.m.

4. Trip from Sobibór to Vienna:
The return trip in the special train began about 10 a.m., immediately after the completion of the unloading of the Jews, from Sobibór to Lublin, where we arrived at 2:30 a.m. on June 18. No travel expenses were paid for this train. The trip continued from Lublin at 8:13 a.m. on June 18 by regularly scheduled express train to Kraków, where we arrived at 5:30 p.m. on the same day. In Kraków we billeted with the Third Company of Reserve Police Battalion 74. On June 19 this company handed out one day's rations to each of the 16 men. From Kraków the return trip was again continued on a regularly scheduled express train at 8:08 p.m. on June 19. Arrival in Vienna east train station at 6:30 a.m. on June 20.

5. The transport commando stopover in Kraków:
The stopover of the transport commando in Kraków lasted 26½ hours.

6. Crossing the border:
The special train crossed the border between the Reich and the General Government on the outward journey on June 15 at 1:45 p.m., the regularly scheduled express train on the return trip at 12:15 a.m. on June 20.

7. Provisions:
The men of the transport commando were provided with cold rations for four days. This consisted of sausage, bread, marmalade, and butter, but was nonetheless not sufficient. In Kraków the daily ration of the Third Company of Reserve Battalion 74 was good and sufficient.

8. Suggestions:

In future it will be necessary to provide the men of the transport commando with marching rations, because the cold rations do not keep in the summer months. The sausage—it was a soft sausage—was already opened and cut up when handed out on June 15, and had to be consumed no later than the third day because of the danger of spoiling. On the fourth day the men had to be satisfied with marmalade, because the butter was also already rancid due to the tremendous heat in the train car. The size of the ration was also rather meager.

9. Incidents:

No incidents occurred either on the outward journey, the stopovers in the train stations, or the return trip.

(signed) Fischmann
Precinct Lieutenant of the Schutzpolizei[6]

The deportation of largely unsuspecting Viennese Jews, most of them elderly and/or female, passed with so little incident that Lieutenant Fischmann could concentrate on the hardships of a third- rather than second-class car, insufficient rations, and the summer heat that spoiled his butter. No mention, of course, was made of what the incarcerated Jews, without food or water, must have been suffering in the closed cattle cars during the sixty-one-hour journey. But Fischmann was quite conscious, as he delivered 949 Jews to the alleged work camp in Sobibór, that the Jews selected for work, the luggage, and the food supplies did not accompany them there. At Sobibór the gas chambers were deep in the forest and not visible from the unloading ramp. But contrary to most Order Police denials, Fischmann and his commando apparently entered the camp and watched the unloading.

The Order Police who guarded the deportation train from Kołomyja in Galicia found the experience considerably more trying than the incident-free transport from Vienna. Indeed, in

Galicia, where the Jews had been subjected to open-air massacres in the summer and fall of 1941 and to a first wave of deportations in the spring of 1942, the resumption of deportations in August 1942 clearly no longer entailed an unknown fate for many of the victims. In mid-September 1942 an Order Police captain of Reserve Police Battalion 133 in Police Regiment 24 reported on the experiences of one week of deportation operations.

7./Pol. 24.   Lemberg [Lwów], September 14, 1942
To: Commander of the Order Police in the district of
   Galicia, Lemberg
Subject: Jewish Resettlement

After carrying out Jewish resettlement actions on the 3d and 5th of September in Skole, Stryj, and Khodorov, for which Captain of the Schutzpolizei Kröpelin was in charge of the Order Police involved and which has already been reported in detail, the 7th Company of the 24th Police Regiment arrived as ordered in Kołomyja on the evening of September 6. I immediately contacted Kriminal Kommissar and SS-Obersturmführer Leitmaritz, head of the branch office of the Security Police in Kołomyja, and First Lieutenant Hertel of the Schutzpolizei station in Kołomyja.

Contrary to the experience in Stryj, the action planned for September 7 in Kołomyja was well prepared and made easy for all units involved. The Jews had been informed by the above-mentioned agencies and the Labor Office to gather at the collection point of the Labor Office for registration on September 7 at 5:30 a.m. Some 5,300 Jews were actually assembled there at the appointed time. With all the manpower of my company, I sealed the Jewish quarter and searched thoroughly, whereby some 600 additional Jews were hunted down.

The loading of the transport train was completed about 7 p.m. After the Security Police released some 1,000 from the total rounded up, 4,769 Jews were resettled. Each car of the transport was loaded with 100 Jews. The great heat prevailing that day made the entire action very difficult and greatly impeded the transport. After the regular nailing up and sealing of all cars, the transport train got underway to Bełżec about 9 p.m. with a guard of one officer and nine men. With the coming of deep darkness in the night, many Jews escaped by squeezing through the air holes after removing the barbed wire. While the guard was able to shoot many of them immediately, most of the escaping Jews were eliminated that night or the next day by the railroad guard or other police units. This transport was delivered in Bełżec without noteworthy incident, although given the length of the train and the deep darkness, the guard had proved to be too weak, as the commander of the transport guard from 6th Company of Police Regiment 24, who returned directly to Stanislawów, was able to report to me in person on September 11.

On September 8, some 300 Jews—old and weak, ill, frail, and no longer transportable—were executed. According to the order of September 4, of which I was first informed on September 6, concerning use of ammunition, 90% of all those executed were shot with carbines and rifles. Only in exceptional cases were pistols used.

On September 8 and 10, actions in Kuty, Kosov, Horodenka, Zaplatov, and Śniatyn were carried out. Some 1,500 Jews had to be driven on foot marches 50 kilometers from Kuty or 35 kilometers from Kosov to Kołomyja, where they were kept overnight in the courtyard of the Security Police prison with the other Jews brought together from the region. Other than the Jews rounded up in Horodenka and Śniatyn, who had already been loaded onto ten cars at each location by the Security Police, another 30 cars were loaded in Kołomyja. The total number sent to Bełżec on the resettlement train of September 10 amounted to 8,205.

In the actions in the area around Kołomyja on September 8 and 10, some 400 Jews had to be eliminated by shooting for the well-known reasons. In the great roundup of Jews to be resettled by September 10 in Kołomyja, the Security Police loaded all Jews into the 30 available train cars despite the objections I expressed. Given the great heat prevailing on those days and the strain on the Jews from the long foot marches or from waiting for days without being given any provisions worth noting, the excessively great overloading of most of the cars with 180 to 200 Jews was catastrophic in a way that had tremendously adverse effects on the transport.

How densely the ten cars each in Horodenka and Śniatyn were loaded with Jews by the Security Police is beyond my knowledge. In any case, both transports arrived in Kołomyja with completely inadequate guard, so that the barbed wire closing the air holes was almost entirely removed. As quickly as possible I had this train moved out of the train station in Kołomyja and coupled with the 30 cars standing on a side track far from the station. The Jewish police (Ordnungsdienst) and members of the train station construction crew from Kołomyja were employed until the onset of darkness to close up all the insufficiently sealed cars in the usual regulation manner. A commando of one officer and fifteen men under the leadership of Captain Zitzmann was assigned to guard the parked resettlement train of 50 cars until departure and to prevent any escape attempt. Given the already described strains on the Jews, the negative effect of the heat, and the great overloading of most of the cars, the Jews attempted time and again to break out of the parked train cars, as darkness had already set in toward 7:30 p.m. At 7:50 p.m. the guard commando of the resettlement train, with nine men under Corporal Jäcklein, arrived at the side track. Breakout attempts from the parked train could not be prevented in the darkness, nor could the escaping Jews be shot in flight. In all train cars the Jews had completely undressed because of the heat.

As the train left Kołomyja on schedule at 8:50 p.m., the guard took up their stations. The guard commando, as initially stipulated by me, was divided into five men in a passenger car at the front and five men in a passenger car at the end of the train. On account of the length of the train and its total load of 8,205 Jews, this distribution proved to be unsuitable. Next time Corporal J. will arrange a distribution of the guards along the entire train. Throughout the entire trip the policemen had to remain in the cabooses, in order to be able to counter the escape attempts of the Jews. Shortly into the journey the Jews attempted to break through the sides and even through the ceilings of certain train cars. They were partially successful in perpetrating this scheme, so that already five stations before Stanislawów, Corporal J. had to ask the stationmaster in Stanislawów by telephone to lay out nails and boards in order to seal the damaged cars as required by orders and to request the station guard to watch the train. As the train entered Stanislawów, the train station workers and the station guards were present to carry out the necessary repairs and in addition take over guarding the train.

The work took one and one-half hours. When the train subsequently resumed its journey, it was discovered at the next stop some stations later that once again large holes had been broken by the Jews in some of the train cars and that for the most part the barbed wire fastened on the outside of the ventilation windows had been torn off. In one train car the Jews had even been working with hammer and saw. Upon interrogation they explained that the Security Police had left these tools with them, because they could make good use of them at their next work place. Corporal J. made the Jews hand over the tools. During the further journey, at every station stop, help was needed to nail up the train, because otherwise the rest of the trip would not have been at all possible. At 11:15 a.m. the train reached Lemberg. Because no relief for the escort commando arrived, the escort commando J. had to continue guarding the train until Bełżec. After a brief halt at the Lemberg train station, the train continued to the suburban station of Klaporov, where nine train cars marked with the letter "L" and destined for the labor camp were turned over to SS-Obersturmführer Schulze and unloaded. SS-Obersturmführer Schulze then had some additional 1,000 Jews loaded. About 1:30 p.m. the transport departed for Bełżec.

With the change of engine in Lemberg, such an old engine was hooked up that further travel was possible only with continuous interruptions. The slow journey was time and again used by the strongest Jews to press themselves through the holes they had forced open and to seek their safety in flight, because in jumping from the slow-moving train they were scarcely injured. Despite the repeated requests to the engineer to go faster, this was not possible, so that the frequent stops on open stretches became increasingly unpleasant.

Shortly beyond Lemberg the commando had already shot off the ammunition they had with them and also used up a further 200 rounds that they had received from army soldiers, so that for the rest of the journey they had to resort to stones while the train was moving and to fixed bayonets when the train was stopped.

The ever greater panic spreading among the Jews due to the great heat, overloading of the train cars, and stink of dead bodies—when unloading the train cars some 2,000 Jews were found dead in the train—made the transport almost unworkable. At 6:45 p.m. the transport arrived in Bełżec, and around 7:30 p.m. was turned over by Corporal J. to the SS-Obersturmführer and head of the camp there. Until the unloading of the transport around 10 p.m., J. had to remain in the camp, while the escort commando was used to guard the train cars parked outside the camp. Because of the special circumstances described, the number of Jews who escaped from this transport cannot be specified. Nonetheless, it can be assumed that at least two-thirds of the escaping Jews were shot or rendered harmless in some other way.

In the actions themselves for the period of September 7–10, 1942, no special incidents occurred. The cooperation between

the Security Police and the Order Police units involved was
good and without friction.

(signed) Westermann
Reserve Lieutenant of the Schutzpolizei
and Company Commander[7]

This document demonstrates many things: the desperate
attempts of the deported Jews to escape the death train; the
scanty manpower employed by the Germans (a mere 10 men to
guard over 8,000 Jews); the unimaginably terrible conditions—
forced marches over many miles, terrible heat, days without food
and water, the packing of 200 Jews into each train car, etc.—that
led to fully 25 percent of the deported Jews dying on the train
from suffocation, heat prostration, and exhaustion (to say nothing
of those killed in the shooting, which was so constant that the
guards expended their entire ammunition supply as well as
replenishment); the casual mention that even before the deportations hundreds of Jews judged too old, frail, or sick to get to the
train were routinely shot in each action. Moreover, the document makes clear that this action was only one among many in
which members of Reserve Police Battalion 133 participated
alongside the Security Police in Galicia during the late summer
of 1942.

Such documents, however, do not tell us much that we would
like to know about the "grass-roots" perpetrators of the Final
Solution. These men were not desk murderers who could take
refuge in distance, routine, and bureaucratic euphemisms that
veiled the reality of mass murder. These men saw their victims
face to face. Their comrades had already shot all the Jews deemed
too weak to be deported, and they subsequently worked viciously
for hours to prevent their victims from escaping the train and
hence the gas chambers awaiting them in Bełżec. No one participating in the events described in this report could have had the
slightest doubt about what he was involved in, namely a mass
murder program to exterminate the Jews of Galicia.

But how did these men first become mass murderers? What happened in the unit when they first killed? What choices, if any, did they have, and how did they respond? What happened to the men as the killing stretched on week after week, month after month? Documents like the one on the Kołomyja transport give us a vivid snapshot of a single incident, but they do not reveal the personal dynamics of how a group of normal middle-aged German men became mass murderers. For that we must return to the story of Reserve Police Battalion 101.

5

Reserve Police Battalion 101

WHEN GERMANY INVADED POLAND IN SEPTEMBER 1939, POLICE Battalion 101, based in Hamburg, was one of the initial battalions attached to a German army group and sent to Poland. Crossing the border from Oppeln in Silesia, the battalion passed through Częstochowa to the Polish city of Kielce. There it was involved in rounding up Polish soldiers and military equipment behind German lines and guarding a prisoner of war camp. On December 17, 1939, the battalion returned to Hamburg, where about a hundred of its career policemen were transferred to form additional units. They were replaced by middle-aged reservists drafted in the fall of 1939.[1]

In May 1940, after a period of training, the battalion was

dispatched from Hamburg to the Warthegau, one of the four regions in western Poland annexed to the Third Reich as the incorporated territories. Stationed first in Poznań (Posen) until late June, and then in Łódź (renamed Litzmannstadt by the victorious Germans), it carried out "resettlement actions" for a period of five months. As part of a demographic scheme of Hitler and Himmler's to "germanize" these newly annexed regions, that is, to populate them with "racially pure" Germans, all Poles and other so-called undesirables—Jews and Gypsies—were to be expelled from the incorporated territories into central Poland. In accordance with provisions of an agreement between Germany and the Soviet Union, ethnic Germans living in Soviet territory were to be repatriated and resettled in the recently evacuated farms and apartments of the expelled Poles. The "racial purification" of the incorporated territories desired by Hitler and Himmler was never achieved, but hundreds of thousands of people were shoved around like so many pieces on a chessboard in pursuit of their vision of a racially reorganized eastern Europe.

The battalion's summary report boasted of its zealous participation in the "resettlement":

> In actions night and day without pause, 100% of the battalion's strength was employed in all of the districts of the Warthegau. On the average some 350 Polish peasant families were evacuated daily. . . . During the peak of the evacuation period they [the men of the battalion] could not return to quarters for eight days and nights. The men had the opportunity to sleep only while traveling at night by truck. . . . In the biggest action, the battalion evacuated about 900 families . . . on one day with only its own forces and 10 translators.

In all the battalion evacuated 36,972 people out of a targeted 58,628. About 22,000 people escaped the evacuations by fleeing.[2]

One drafted reservist, Bruno Probst,* recalled the battalion's role in these actions.

> In the resettlement of the native population, primarily in the small villages, I experienced the first excesses and killings. It was always thus, that with our arrival in the villages, the resettlement commission was already there. . . . This so-called resettlement commission consisted of members of the black [-uniformed] SS and SD as well as civilians. From them we received cards with numbers. The houses of the village were also designated with the same numbers. The cards handed to us designated the houses that we were to evacuate. During the early period we endeavored to fetch all people out of the houses, without regard for whether they were old, sick, or small children. The commission quickly found fault with our procedures. They objected that we struggled under the burden of the old and sick. To be precise, they did not initially give us the order to shoot them on the spot, rather they contented themselves with making it clear to us that nothing could be done with such people. In two cases I remember that such people were shot at the collection point. In the first case it was an old man and in the second case an old woman. . . . both persons were shot not by the men but by noncommissioned officers.[3]

Others in the battalion also remembered the resettlement actions, but no one else remembered or admitted to such violence.[4] One policeman did recall that the battalion had provided the Security Police with firing squads for the execution of 100 to 120 Poles during its stay in Poznań.[5]

Following its five-month resettlement campaign, the battalion carried out "pacification actions." Combing villages and woods, they caught 750 Poles who had evaded the earlier evacuations.

* Pseudonyms are designated throughout by an asterisk at first occurrence.

Their task was made more difficult because even the newly arrived ethnic Germans did not always report the unauthorized presence of the Poles they had displaced, wishing to avail themselves of cheap labor.[6]

On November 28, 1940, the battalion took up guard duty around the Łódź ghetto, which had been sealed seven months earlier, at the end of April 1940, when the 160,000 Jews of Łódź were cut off from the rest of the city by a barbed wire fence. Guarding the ghetto now became the major duty of Police Battalion 101, which had a standing order to shoot "without further ado" any Jew who ignored the posted warnings and came too close to the fence. This order was obeyed.[7]

None of Battalion 101's men, however, remembered excesses such as occurred while the First Company of Police Battalion 61 was guarding the Warsaw ghetto. There the company captain openly encouraged shooting at the ghetto wall. The most notorious shooters were not rotated to other duties but were kept permanently on ghetto guard duty. The company recreation room was decorated with racist slogans, and a Star of David hung above the bar. A mark was made on the bar door for each Jew shot, and "victory celebrations" were reportedly held on days when high scores were recorded.[8]

Stationed outside the ghetto wire, the battalion members had more contact with the non-Jewish population than with the incarcerated Jews. Bruno Probst recalled that the guards on the thoroughfare that cut between the two halves of the Łódź ghetto occasionally amused themselves by setting their watches ahead as a pretext for seizing and beating Poles who were allegedly violating the curfew. He also recalled that drunken guards, intending to kill a Pole on New Year's eve, shot an ethnic German by mistake and covered it up by switching the victim's identity card.[9]

In May 1941 the battalion returned to Hamburg and was "practically dissolved." All remaining prewar recruits beneath the rank of noncommissioned officer were distributed to other units, and the ranks were filled with drafted reservists. The battalion had become, in the words of one policeman, a "pure reserve battalion."[10]

During the next year, from May 1941 to June 1942, the battalion was reformed and underwent extensive training. Only a few incidents from this period remained in the memories of the men. One was the bombing of Lübeck in March 1942, for units of the battalion were sent to the damaged city immediately afterward.[11] Another involved the deportation of Hamburg Jews.

From mid-October 1941 to late February 1942, 59 transports carried more than 53,000 Jews and 5,000 Gypsies from the Third Reich "to the east," in this case Łódź, Riga, Kovno (Kaunas), and Minsk. The five transports to Kovno and the first transport to Riga were massacred upon arrival.[12] The remaining transports were not "liquidated" immediately. Rather the deportees were initially incarcerated in the ghettos of Łódź (where the 5,000 Austrian Gypsies were sent), Minsk, and Riga.

Four such transports that were spared immediate death came from Hamburg. The first, with 1,034 Jews, departed on October 25, 1941, for Łódź. The second, with 990 Jews, left for Minsk on November 8. The third, with 408 Jews from Hamburg and 500 from Bremen, left for Minsk on November 18. The fourth left Hamburg for Riga with 808 Jews on December 4.[13]

Men from Reserve Police Battalion 101 were involved in various phases of the Hamburg deportations. The collection point for the deportations was the Freemason lodge house on the Moorweide, which had been confiscated by the Security Police. Flanked by the university library and an apartment block, within several hundred yards of the heavily used Dammtor train station, the collection point was scarcely an inconspicuous location out of the sight of Hamburg citizens. Some Order Police of Battalion 101 provided guard duty at the Freemason lodge house, where the Jews were collected, registered, and loaded on trucks to the Sternschanze train station.[14] Other men of Battalion 101 guarded the station, where the Jews were loaded onto the trains.[15] And finally, Battalion 101 provided the escort for at least three of the four transports—the first, on October 25, to Łódź; the second, on November 8, to Minsk; and the last, on December 4, to Riga.[16] According to Hans Keller,* escort duty on the Jewish transports was "highly coveted" because of the chance to travel, and was assigned only to a "favored" few.[17]

Bruno Probst, who accompanied the November 8 transport to Minsk, recalled:

> In Hamburg the Jews were told at the time that they would be allocated a whole new settlement territory in the east. The Jews were loaded into normal passenger cars . . . accompanied by two cars of tools, shovels, axes, etc., as well as large kitchen equipment. For the escort commando a second-class carriage was attached. There were no guards in the cars of the Jews themselves. The train had to be guarded on both sides only at stops. After about four days' journey we reached Minsk in the late afternoon. We learned of this destination for the first time only during the journey, after we had already passed Warsaw. In Minsk an SS commando was waiting for our transport. Again without guard, the Jews were then loaded onto the waiting trucks. Only their baggage, which they had been allowed to bring from Hamburg, had to be left behind in the train. They were told it would follow. Then our commando was finally driven to a Russian barracks, in which an active [i.e., not reserve] German police battalion was lodged. There was a Jewish camp nearby. . . . From conversations with members of the above-mentioned police battalion we learned that some weeks ago this unit had already shot Jews in Minsk. We concluded from this fact that our Hamburg Jews were to be shot there also.

Not wanting to be involved, the escort's commander, Lieutenant Hartwig Gnade, did not remain at the barracks. Instead he and his men returned to the station and took a late-night train out of Minsk.[18]

We have no description of the escort duty to Riga from Hamburg, but the Salitter report on the Order Police escort of the December 11 Jewish transport from Düsseldorf to Riga provides graphic evidence that policemen there learned as much as the Hamburg policemen did in Minsk. As Salitter noted:

> Riga consisted of some 360,000 inhabitants, including some 35,000 Jews. The Jews were everywhere dominant in the business world. Their businesses were nonetheless immediately closed and confiscated after the entry of German troops. The Jews themselves were lodged in a ghetto on the Düna [Dvina] that was sealed by barbed wire. At the moment only 2,500 male Jews who are used for labor are said to be in the ghetto. The other Jews have either been sent to similar employment elsewhere or shot by the Latvians. . . . They [the Latvians] hate the Jews in particular. From the time of liberation to the present, they have participated very amply in the extermination of these parasites. It is, however, incomprehensible to them, as I was especially able to discover from Latvian railway personnel, why the Germans bring their Jews to Latvia instead of exterminating them in their own country.[19]

In June 1942, Reserve Police Battalion 101 was assigned another tour of duty in Poland. By then, only a few noncommissioned officers who had been on the first Polish action remained, and less than 20 percent of the men had been on the second in the Warthegau. A few of these had witnessed what they called "excesses" in Poznań and Łódź. A few more had accompanied one of the Hamburg Jewish transports to Łódź, Minsk, or Riga. At the latter two destinations, as we have seen, it was difficult not to learn something about the mass murder of Jews in Russia. But for the most part, Reserve Police Battalion 101 was now composed of men without any experience of German occupation methods in eastern Europe, or for that matter—with the exception of the very oldest who were World War I veterans—any kind of military service.

The battalion consisted of 11 officers, 5 administrative officials (in charge of financial matters relating to pay, provisioning, lodging, etc.), and 486 noncommissioned officers and men.[20] To reach full strength, some non-Hamburg contingents were added at the last minute from nearby Wilhelmshaven and Rendsburg (in Schleswig-Holstein), and from distant Luxembourg. Still, the vast majority of the rank and file had been born and reared in Hamburg and its environs. The Hamburg element was so dominant and the ethos of the battalion so provincial that not just the Luxembourgers but also the contingents from Wilhelmshaven and Rendsburg felt themselves to be outsiders.[21]

The battalion was divided into three companies, each of approximately 140 men when at full strength. Two companies were commanded by police captains, the third by the senior reserve lieutenant in the battalion. Each company was divided into three platoons, two of them commanded by reserve lieutenants and the third by the platoon's senior sergeant. Each platoon was divided into four squads, commanded by a sergeant or corporal. The men were equipped with carbines, the noncommissioned officers with submachine guns. Each company also had a heavy machine-gun detachment. Apart from the three companies, there was the personnel of the battalion staff, which included, in addition to the five administrative officials, a doctor and his aide as well as various drivers, clerks, and communications specialists.

The battalion was commanded by fifty-three-year-old Major Wilhelm Trapp, a World War I veteran and recipient of the Iron Cross First Class. After the war he became a career policeman and rose through the ranks. He had recently been promoted from captain of Second Company, and this was his first battalion command. Though Trapp had joined the Nazi Party in December 1932 and thus technically qualified as an "old Party fighter," or *Alter Kämpfer*, he had never been taken into the SS or even given an equivalent SS rank, in spite of the fact that Himmler and Heydrich consciously tried to merge and intertwine the state and Party components of their SS and police empire. Trapp was clearly not considered SS material. He was soon to come into conflict with his two captains, both young SS men, who even in their testimony more than twenty years later made no attempt to conceal their contempt for their commander as weak, unmilitary, and unduly interfering in the duties of his officers.[22]

The two police captains, who also held the equivalent SS rank of Hauptsturmführer, were young men in their late twenties. Wolfgang Hoffmann, born in 1914, had joined the National Socialist Student Union (NS-Schülerbund) in 1930 as a sixteen-year-old, the Hitler Youth in 1932 at eighteen, and the SS one year later, all before he had graduated from *Gymnasium* (a college-preparatory high school) in 1934. He joined the police force in Breslau in 1936 and entered the Nazi Party in 1937, the same year he completed officer training and was commissioned as a lieutenant of the Schutzpolizei. He joined Reserve Police Battalion 101 in the spring of 1942. The following June, at the age of twenty-eight, he was promoted to the rank of captain.[23] He commanded Third Company.

Julius Wohlauf, born in 1913, graduated from *Gymnasium* in 1932. In April 1933 he joined the Nazi Party and SA. In 1936 he joined the SS, and the same year he began his training to become a police officer. He was commissioned a lieutenant of the Schutzpolizei in 1938. He too was assigned to Reserve Police Battalion 101 in early 1942 and was promoted to captain in June 1942, just before the departure for Poland.[24] He commanded First Company and served as Trapp's deputy battalion commander. In contrast to the elderly Trapp, Hoffmann and Wohlauf represented precisely the combination of well-educated professional police officer, early enthusiast for National Socialism, and young SS member that was the Himmler-Heydrich ideal for the SS and police.

Trapp's adjutant was First Lieutenant Hagen,* about whom little is known except that he was killed in the spring of 1943. In addition the battalion had seven reserve lieutenants, that is, men who were not career policemen like Hoffmann and Wohlauf but were selected to receive officer training after they were drafted into the Order Police, because of their middle-class status, education, and success in civilian life. From oldest to youngest, they were:

> Hartwig Gnade, born 1894, a forwarding agent and Nazi Party member since 1937, commander of Second Company;
> Paul Brand,* born 1902;
> Heinz Buchmann,* born 1904, owner of a family lumber business, Party member since 1937;
> Oscar Peters,* born 1905;
> Walter Hoppner,* born 1908, tea importer, Party member briefly in 1930, rejoined in the spring of 1933;
> Hans Scheer,* born 1908, and a Party member since May 1933;
> Kurt Drucker,* born 1909, a salesman and party member since 1939.[25]

Thus, their ages ranged from thirty-three to forty-eight. Five were Party members, but none belonged to the SS.

Of the thirty-two noncommissioned officers on whom we have information, twenty-two were party members and seven were in the SS. They ranged in age from twenty-seven to forty years old; their average age was thirty-three and a half. They were not reservists but rather prewar recruits to the police.

Of the rank and file, the vast majority were from the Hamburg area. About 63 percent were of working-class background, but few were skilled laborers. The majority of them held typical Hamburg working-class jobs: dock workers and truck drivers were most numerous, but there were also many warehouse and construction workers, machine operators, seamen, and waiters. About 35 percent were lower-middle-class, virtually all of them white-collar workers. Three-quarters were in sales of some sort; the other one-quarter performed various office jobs, in both the government and private sector. The number of independent artisans and small businessmen was very small. Only a handful (2 percent) were middle-class professionals, and very modest ones at that, such as druggists and teachers. The average age of the men was thirty-nine; over half were between thirty-seven and forty-two, a group considered too old for the army but most heavily conscripted for reserve police duty after September 1939.[26]

Among the rank and file policemen, about 25 percent (43 from a sample of 174) were Party members in 1942. Six were *Alte Kämpfer* who had joined the Party before Hitler came to power; another six joined in 1933. Despite the domestic ban on new Party members from 1933 to 1937, another six men who worked aboard ships were admitted by the Party section for members living overseas. Sixteen joined in 1937, when the ban on new membership was lifted. The remaining nine joined in 1939 or later. The men of lower-middle-class background held Party membership in an only slightly higher proportion (30 percent) than those from the working class (25 percent).[27]

The men of Reserve Police Battalion 101 were from the lower orders of German society. They had experienced neither social nor geographic mobility. Very few were economically independent. Except for apprenticeship or vocational training, virtually none had any education after leaving *Volksschule* (terminal secondary school) at age fourteen or fifteen. By 1942, a surprisingly high percentage had become Party members. However, because the interrogating officials did not record such information, we do not know how many had been Communists, socialists, and/or labor union members before 1933. Presumably a not insignificant number must have been, given their social origins. By virtue of their age, of course, all went through their formative period in the pre-Nazi era. These were men who had known political standards and moral norms other than those of the Nazis. Most came from Hamburg, by reputation one of the least nazified cities in Germany, and the majority came from a social class that had been anti-Nazi in its political culture. These men would not seem to have been a very promising group from which to recruit mass murderers on behalf of the Nazi vision of a racial utopia free of Jews.

6

Arrival in Poland

SOMETIME IN THE SUMMER OF 1941, AFTER THE ONSLAUGHT against Russian Jewry was under way, Himmler confided to the SS and Police Leader in Lublin, Odilo Globocnik, Hitler's intention to murder the Jews of Europe as well. Moreover, Himmler put Globocnik in charge of the single most important element of this "Final Solution to the Jewish Question in Europe"—the destruction of the Jews of the General Government, who constituted the bulk of Polish Jewry. A method different from the firing squad operations used against Russian Jewry was deemed essential for the murder of European Jews, however—one that was more efficient, less public, and less burdensome psychologically for the killers.

The organizational and technological answer to these needs

was the extermination camp. The victims would be deported to special camps where—by virtue of assembly-line procedures requiring very limited manpower, most of it prisoner labor— they would be gassed in relative secrecy. Preparations for gassing began at three locations in the fall of 1941: Auschwitz/ Birkenau near Katowice in Silesia and Chełmno near Łódź in the Warthegau, both in the incorporated territories, and Bełżec in Globocnik's Lublin district. Large-scale gassing began at Chełmno in early December 1941 and at Birkenau in mid-February 1942.[1] Gassing at Globocnik's camp at Bełżec did not begin until mid-March 1942.

The task Globocnik faced was enormous, but he was given virtually no manpower to accomplish it. For expertise and assistance in building and operating the extermination center at Bełżec, Globocnik was able to draw on personnel from the "euthanasia program" in Germany, but this was a handful of men that at its maximum never exceeded one hundred. This number by itself was insufficient to staff a single extermination camp, and two more were yet to be built by Globocnik at Sobibór and Treblinka. But the extermination camps were not Globocnik's biggest problem. Far more pressing was the manpower required to clear the ghettos—to round up the victims and force them onto the death trains. In the Lublin district alone there were nearly 300,000 Jews; in all of the General Government, about 2,000,000!

While Germany's military fate hung in the balance in the crucial year of 1942, where were the men for such a staggering logistical task? In fact, aside from the assignment itself, Himmler gave Globocnik virtually nothing, and he had to improvise. He had to create "private" armies out of his own resources and ingenuity to accomplish the task with which Himmler had entrusted him.

For the coordination of the mass murder campaign against Polish Jewry—dubbed Operation Reinhard after Reinhard Heydrich was slain in Czechoslovakia in June 1942—Globocnik formed a special staff under his deputy and fellow Austrian

Hermann Höfle. The key people on this staff included Christian Wirth and his adjutant, Josef Oberhauser, in charge of the extermination centers; Helmuth Pohl, another Austrian, in charge of incoming transports; Georg Michalsen, Kurt Claasen, and yet another Austrian, Ernst Lerch, to oversee and often personally conduct operations in the field; and Georg Wippern, in charge of collecting, sorting, and utilizing the Jewish property collected at the extermination camps and in the vacated ghettos.

As the SS and Police Leader in the Lublin district, Globocnik was responsible for coordinating all regional operations that involved the joint action of mixed SS units. Thus the entire SS and police network in the Lublin district, though already stretched thin, was at his disposal. Most important, this meant the two branches of the Security Police (Gestapo and Kripo) on the one hand and various units of the Order Police on the other. In addition to its main headquarters in the city of Lublin, the Security Police had four branch offices in the district. Each contained a Gestapo section for "Jewish affairs."

The presence of the Order Police was felt in three ways. First, each of the major towns in the Lublin district had a Schutzpolizei agency. Included in its responsibilities was the supervision of the Polish municipal police. Second, scattered throughout the towns in the countryside were small detachments of Gendarmerie. Finally, three battalions of Order Police were stationed in the Lublin district. The Security Police branches along with the Schutzpolizei and Gendarmerie units provided small numbers of policemen who knew the local conditions. But the three Order Police battalions, totaling 1,500 men, represented the single largest police manpower pool Globocnik could draw on. Clearly they were indispensable, but still not sufficient to meet his needs.

Globocnik also utilized two other sources of manpower. The first was the Sonderdienst (Special Service), composed of small units of ethnic Germans who had been mobilized and trained after the German conquest and assigned to the head of the civil administration in each county of the district in the summer of

1940.[2] Second, and far more important, were the so-called Trawnikis. Unable to satisfy his manpower needs out of local resources, Globocnik prevailed upon Himmler to recruit non-Polish auxiliaries from the Soviet border regions. The key person on Globocnik's Operation Reinhard staff for this task was Karl Streibel. He and his men visited the POW camps and recruited Ukrainian, Latvian, and Lithuanian "volunteers" (Hilfswillige, or Hiwis) who were screened on the basis of their anti-Communist (and hence almost invariably anti-Semitic) sentiments, offered an escape from probable starvation, and promised that they would not be used in combat against the Soviet army. These "volunteers" were taken to the SS camp at Trawniki for training. Under German SS officers and ethnic German noncommissioned officers, they were formed into units on the basis of nationality. Alongside the Order Police, they constituted the second major manpower pool from which Globocnik would form his private armies for the ghetto-clearing campaign.

The first murderous onslaught against Lublin Jewry began in mid-March 1942 and continued until mid-April. About 90 percent of the 40,000 inhabitants of the Lublin ghetto were killed either through deportation to the extermination camp at Bełżec or execution on the spot, and 11,000 to 12,000 more Jews were sent to Bełżec from the nearby towns Izbica, Piaski, Lubartów, Zamość, and Krasnik. During the same period some 36,000 Jews from the neighboring district of Galicia to the east of Lublin were also deported to Bełżec.

From mid-April to late May the killing operations at Bełżec were temporarily halted as the small wooden building with three gas chambers was torn down and a large stone building with six larger gas chambers was erected. When killing operations resumed at Bełżec in late May, the camp primarily received Jews deported from the neighboring district of Kraków to the west, not from the Lublin district itself.

However, Sobibór, Globocnik's second extermination camp in the Lublin district, had begun operating in early May. For the next six weeks it received deportations from the Lublin counties of Zamość, Puławy, Krasnystaw, and Chełm. By June 18, scarcely three months after the first deportations from the Lublin ghetto, about 100,000 Jews from the Lublin district had been killed, along with 65,000 from Kraków and Galicia, the vast majority by gassing at Bełżec and Sobibór.[3]

The deportations to the death camps were only part of a vast relocation of central European Jewry. At the same time that Polish Jews were being deported from their homes to the extermination camps, trainloads of Jews from Germany, Austria, the Protectorate, and the puppet state of Slovakia were being dumped into the Lublin district. Some of these transports, such as the June 14 train from Vienna guarded by Lieutenant Fischmann, were also sent directly to Sobibór. Others, however, were unloaded in various ghettos, with the foreign Jews temporarily taking the places of those who had recently been killed.

This vast shuffling of Jews as well as the mass murder in Bełżec and Sobibór stopped temporarily on June 19, when a shortage of rolling stock brought to a halt all Jewish transports in the General Government for a period of twenty days.[4] Two death trains per week from the Kraków district to Bełżec resumed on July 9, and the steady flow of transports from Warsaw to the newly opened extermination center at Treblinka began on July 22. However, the main rail line to Sobibór was under repair, rendering that camp virtually inaccessible until the fall. In the Lublin district itself, therefore, deportations to the extermination camps did not resume in early July.

It was during this enforced lull in the Final Solution in the General Government that Reserve Police Battalion 101 arrived in the Lublin district. On June 20, 1942, the battalion received orders for a "special action" in Poland.[5] The nature of this "special action" was not specified in the written orders, but the men were led to believe that they would be performing guard duty. There is no indication whatsoever that even the officers suspected the true nature of the duties that awaited them.

The battalion entrained at the Sternschanze station,[6] the same point from which some of its men had deported Hamburg Jews to the east the previous fall. It arrived in the Polish town of Zamość in the southern part of the Lublin district on June 25. Five days later the battalion headquarters was shifted to Biłgoraj, and various units of the battalion were quickly stationed in the nearby towns of Frampol, Tarnogród, Ulanów, Turobin, and Wysokie, as well as the more distant Zakrzów.[7]

Despite the temporary lull in the killing, SS and Police Leader Odilo Globocnik and his Operation Reinhard staff were not about to allow the newly arrived police battalion to remain entirely inactive in regard to the Lublin Jews. If the killing could not be resumed, the process of consolidating the victims in transit ghettos and camps could be. For most of the policemen of Reserve Police Battalion 101, the searing memory of the subsequent action in Józefów blotted out lesser events that had occurred during their four-week stay south of Lublin. However, a few did remember taking part in this consolidation process—collecting Jews in smaller settlements and moving them to larger ghettos and camps. In some cases only so-called work Jews were seized, put on trucks, and sent to camps around Lublin. In other cases, the entire Jewish population was rounded up and put on trucks or sent off on foot. Sometimes the Jews from the smaller surrounding villages were then collected and resettled in their place. None of these actions involved mass executions, though Jews who were too old, frail, or sick to be transported were shot in at least some instances. The men were uniformly uncertain about the towns from which they had deported Jews and the places to which the Jews had been relocated. No one recalled the names Izbica and Piaski, though these were the two major "transit" ghettos south of Lublin that were used for collecting Jews.[8]

Apparently, Globocnik lost patience with this consolidation process and decided to experiment with renewed killing. As deportation to the extermination camps was not possible at the time, mass execution through firing squad was the available alternative. Reserve Police Battalion 101 was the unit to be tested.

7

Initiation to Mass Murder: The Józefów Massacre

IT WAS PROBABLY ON JULY 11 THAT GLOBOCNIK OR SOMEONE ON his staff contacted Major Trapp and informed him that Reserve Police Battalion 101 had the task of rounding up the 1,800 Jews in Józefów, a village about thirty kilometers slightly south and east of Biłgoraj. This time, however, most of the Jews were not to be relocated. Only the male Jews of working age were to be sent to one of Globocnik's camps in Lublin. The women, children, and elderly were simply to be shot on the spot.

Trapp recalled the units that were stationed in nearby towns. The battalion reassembled in Biłgoraj on July 12, with two exceptions: the Third Platoon of Third Company, including Captain Hoffmann, stationed in Zakrzów, as well as a few men of First Company already stationed in Józefów. Trapp met with

First and Second Company commanders, Captain Wohlauf and Lieutenant Gnade, and informed them of the next day's task.[1] Trapp's adjutant, First Lieutenant Hagen, must have informed other officers of the battalion, for Lieutenant Heinz Buchmann learned from him the precise details of the pending action that evening.

Buchmann, then thirty-eight years old, was the head of a family lumber business in Hamburg. He had joined the Nazi Party in May 1937. Drafted into the Order Police in 1939, he had served as a driver in Poland. In the summer of 1940 he applied for a discharge. Instead he was sent to officer training and commissioned as a reserve lieutenant in November 1941. He was given command of the First Platoon of First Company in 1942.

Upon learning of the imminent massacre, Buchmann made clear to Hagen that as a Hamburg businessman and reserve lieutenant, he "would in no case participate in such an action, in which defenseless women and children are shot." He asked for another assignment. Hagen arranged for Buchmann to be in charge of the escort for the male "work Jews" who were to be selected out and taken to Lublin.[2] His company captain, Wohlauf, was informed of Buchmann's assignment but not the reason for it.[3]

The men were not officially informed, other than that they would be awakened early in the morning for a major action involving the entire battalion. But some had at least a hint of what was to come. Captain Wohlauf told a group of his men that an "extremely interesting task" awaited them the next day.[4] Another man, who complained that he was being left behind to guard the barracks, was told by his company adjutant, "Be happy that you don't have to come. You'll see what happens."[5] Sergeant Heinrich Steinmetz* warned his men of Third Platoon, Second Company, that "he didn't want to see any cowards."[6] Additional ammunition was given out.[7] One policeman reported that his unit was given whips, which led to rumors of a *Judenaktion*.[8] No one else, however, remembered whips.

Departing from Biłgoraj around 2:00 a.m., the truck convoy

arrived in Józefów just as the sky was beginning to lighten. Trapp assembled the men in a half-circle and addressed them. After explaining the battalion's murderous assignment, he made his extraordinary offer: any of the older men who did not feel up to the task that lay before them could step out. Trapp paused, and after some moments one man from Third Company, Otto-Julius Schimke,* stepped forward. Captain Hoffmann, who had arrived in Józefów directly from Zakrzów with the Third Platoon of Third Company and had not been part of the officers' meetings in Biłgoraj the day before, was furious that one of his men had been the first to break ranks. Hoffmann began to berate Schimke, but Trapp cut him off. After he had taken Schimke under his protection, some ten or twelve other men stepped forward as well. They turned in their rifles and were told to await a further assignment from the major.[9]

Trapp then summoned the company commanders and gave them their respective assignments. The orders were relayed by the first sergeant, Kammer,* to First Company, and by Gnade and Hoffmann to Second and Third Companies. Two platoons of Third Company were to surround the village.[10] The men were explicitly ordered to shoot anyone trying to escape. The remaining men were to round up the Jews and take them to the marketplace. Those too sick or frail to walk to the marketplace, as well as infants and anyone offering resistance or attempting to hide, were to be shot on the spot. Thereafter, a few men of First Company were to escort the "work Jews" who had been selected at the marketplace, while the rest of First Company was to proceed to the forest to form the firing squads. The Jews were to be loaded onto the battalion trucks by Second Company and Third Platoon of Third Company and shuttled from the marketplace to the forest.[11]

After making the assignments, Trapp spent most of the day in town, either in a schoolroom converted into his headquarters, at the homes of the Polish mayor and the local priest, at the marketplace, or on the road to the forest.[12] But he did not go to the forest itself or witness the executions; his absence there was conspicuous. As one policeman bitterly commented, "Major Trapp was never there. Instead he remained in Józefów because he allegedly could not bear the sight. We men were upset about that and said we couldn't bear it either."[13]

Indeed, Trapp's distress was a secret to no one. At the marketplace one policeman remembered hearing Trapp say, "Oh, God, why did I have to be given these orders," as he put his hand on his heart.[14] Another policeman witnessed him at the schoolhouse. "Today I can still see exactly before my eyes Major Trapp there in the room pacing back and forth with his hands behind his back. He made a downcast impression and spoke to me. He said something like, 'Man, . . . such jobs don't suit me. But orders are orders.' "[15] Another man remembered vividly "how Trapp, finally alone in our room, sat on a stool and wept bitterly. The tears really flowed."[16] Another also witnessed Trapp at his headquarters. "Major Trapp ran around excitedly and then suddenly stopped dead in front of me, stared, and asked if I agreed with this. I looked him straight in the eye and said, 'No, Herr Major!' He then began to run around again and wept like a child."[17] The doctor's aide encountered Trapp weeping on the path from the marketplace to the forest and asked if he could help. "He answered me only to the effect that everything was very terrible."[18] Concerning Józefów, Trapp later confided to his driver, "If this Jewish business is ever avenged on earth, then have mercy on us Germans."[19]

While Trapp complained of his orders and wept, his men proceeded to carry out the battalion's task. The noncommissioned officers divided some of their men into search teams of two, three, or four, and sent them into the Jewish section of Józefów. Other men were assigned as guards along the streets leading to the marketplace or at the marketplace itself. As the Jews were driven out of their houses and the immobile were shot, the air was filled with screams and gunfire. As one policeman noted, it was a small town and they could hear everything.[20] Many policemen admitted seeing the corpses of those who had been shot during the search, but only two admitted having shot.[21] Again, several policemen admitted having heard that all the patients in the Jewish "hospital" or "old people's home" had been shot on the spot, though no one admitted having actually seen the shooting or taken part.[22]

The witnesses were least agreed on the question of how the men initially reacted to the problem of shooting infants. Some claimed that along with the elderly and sick, infants were among those shot and left lying in the houses, doorways, and streets of the town.[23] Others, however, stressed quite specifically that in this initial action the men still shied from shooting infants during the search and clearing operation. One policeman was emphatic "that among the Jews shot in our section of town there were no infants or small children. I would like to say that almost tacitly everyone refrained from shooting infants and small children." In Józefów as later, he observed, "Even in the face of death the Jewish mothers did not separate from their children. Thus we tolerated the mothers taking their small children to the market-place in Józefów."[24] Another policeman likewise noted "that tacitly the shooting of infants and small children was avoided by almost all the men involved. During the entire morning I was able to observe that when being taken away many women carried infants in their arms and led small children by the hand."[25] According to both witnesses, none of the officers intervened when infants were brought to the marketplace. Another policeman, however, recalled that after the clearing operation his unit (Third Platoon, Third Company) was reproached by Captain Hoffmann. "We had not proceeded energetically enough."[26]

As the roundup neared completion, the men of First Company were withdrawn from the search and given a quick lesson in the gruesome task that awaited them. They were instructed by the battalion doctor and the company's first sergeant. One musically inclined policeman who frequently played the violin on social evenings along with the doctor, who played a "wonderful accordion," recalled:

> I believe that at this point all officers of the battalion were present, especially our battalion physician, Dr. Schoenfelder.* He now had to explain to us precisely how we had to shoot in order to induce the immediate death of the victim. I remember exactly that for this demonstration he drew or outlined the contour of a human body, at least from the shoulders upward, and then indicated precisely the point on which the fixed bayonet was to be placed as an aiming guide.[27]

After First Company had received instructions and departed for the woods, Trapp's adjutant, Hagen, presided over the selection of the "work Jews." The head of a nearby sawmill had already approached Trapp with a list of twenty-five Jews who worked for him, and Trapp had permitted their release.[28] Through an interpreter Hagen now called for craftsmen and able-bodied male workers. There was unrest as some 300 workers were separated from their families.[29] Before they had been marched out of Józefów on foot, the first shots from the woods were heard. "After the first salvos a grave unrest grew among these craftsmen, and some of the men threw themselves upon the ground weeping. . . . It had to have become clear to them at this point that the families they had left behind were being shot."[30]

Lieutenant Buchmann and the Luxembourgers in First Company marched the workers a few kilometers to a country loading station on the rail line. Several train cars, including a passenger car, were waiting. The work Jews and their guards were then taken by train to Lublin, where Buchmann delivered them to a camp. According to Buchmann, he did not put them in the notorious concentration camp at Majdanek but in another camp instead. The Jews were not expected, he said, but the camp administration was glad to take them. Buchmann and his men returned to Biłgoraj the same day.[31]

Meanwhile, First Sergeant Kammer had taken the initial contingent of shooters in First Company to a forest several kilometers from Józefów. The trucks halted on a dirt road that ran along the edge, at a point where a pathway led into the woods. The men climbed down from their trucks and waited.

When the first truckload of thirty-five to forty Jews arrived, an equal number of policemen came forward and, *face to face*, were paired off with their victims. Led by Kammer, the policemen and Jews marched down the forest path. They turned off into the woods at a point indicated by Captain Wohlauf, who busied himself throughout the day selecting the execution sites. Kammer then ordered the Jews to lie down in a row. The policemen stepped up behind them, placed their bayonets on the backbone above the shoulder blades as earlier instructed, and on Kammer's orders fired in unison.

In the meantime more policemen of First Company had arrived at the edge of the forest to fill out a second firing squad. As the first firing squad marched out of the woods to the unloading point, the second group took their victims along the same path into the woods. Wohlauf chose a site a few yards farther on so that the next batch of victims would not see the corpses from the earlier execution. These Jews were again forced to lie face down in a row, and the shooting procedure was repeated.

Thereafter, the "pendulum traffic" of the two firing squads in and out of the woods continued throughout the day. Except for a midday break, the shooting proceeded without interruption until nightfall. At some point in the afternoon, someone "organized" a supply of alcohol for the shooters. By the end of a day of nearly continuous shooting, the men had completely lost track of how many Jews they had each killed. In the words of one policeman, it was in any case "a great number."[32]

When Trapp first made his offer early in the morning, the real nature of the action had just been announced and time to think and react had been very short. Only a dozen men had instinctively seized the moment to step out, turn in their rifles, and thus excuse themselves from the subsequent killing. For many the reality of what they were about to do, and particularly that they themselves might be chosen for the firing squad, had probably not sunk in. But when the men of First Company were summoned to the marketplace, instructed in giving a "neck shot," and sent to the woods to kill Jews, some of them tried to make up for the opportunity they had missed earlier. One policeman approached First Sergeant Kammer, whom he knew well. He confessed that the task was "repugnant" to him and asked for a different assignment. Kammer obliged, assigning him to guard duty on the edge of the forest, where he remained throughout the day.[33] Several other policemen who knew Kammer well were given guard duty along the truck route.[34] After shooting for some time, another group of policemen approached Kammer and said they could not continue. He released them from the firing squad and reassigned them to accompany the trucks.[35] Two policemen made the mistake of approaching Captain (and SS-Hauptsturmführer) Wohlauf instead of Kammer. They pleaded that they too were fathers with children and could not continue. Wohlauf curtly refused them, indicating that they could lie down alongside the victims. At the midday pause, however, Kammer relieved not only these two men but a number of other older men as well. They were sent back to the marketplace, accompanied by a noncommissioned officer who reported to Trapp. Trapp dismissed them from further duty and permitted them to return early to the barracks in Biłgoraj.[36]

Some policemen who did not request to be released from the firing squads sought other ways to evade. Noncommissioned officers armed with submachine guns had to be assigned to give so-called mercy shots "because both from excitement *as well as intentionally* [italics mine]" individual policemen "shot past" their victims.[37] Others had taken evasive action earlier. During the clearing operation some men of First Company hid in the Catholic priest's garden until they grew afraid that their absence would be noticed. Returning to the marketplace, they jumped aboard a truck that was going to pick up Jews from a nearby village, in order to have an excuse for their absence.[38] Others hung around the marketplace because they did not want to round up Jews during the search.[39] Still others spent as much time as possible searching the houses so as not to be present at the marketplace, where they feared being assigned to a firing squad.[40] A driver assigned to take Jews to the forest made only one trip before he asked to be relieved. "Presumably his nerves were not strong enough to drive more Jews to the shooting site," commented the man who took over his truck and his duties of chauffeuring Jews to their death.[41]

After the men of First Company departed for the woods, Second Company was left to complete the roundup and load Jews onto the trucks. When the first salvo was heard from the woods, a terrible cry swept the marketplace as the collected Jews realized their fate.[42] Thereafter, however, a quiet composure— indeed, in the words of German witnesses, an "unbelievable" and "astonishing" composure—settled over the Jews.[43]

If the victims were composed, the German officers grew increasingly agitated as it became clear that the pace of the executions was much too slow if they were to finish the job in one day. "Comments were repeatedly made, such as, 'It's not getting anywhere!' and 'It's not going fast enough!' "[44] Trapp reached a decision and gave new orders. Third Company was called in from its outposts around the village to take over close guard of the marketplace. The men of Lieutenant Gnade's Second Company were informed that they too must now go to the woods to join the shooters. Sergeant Steinmetz of Third Platoon once again gave his men the opportunity to report if they did not feel up to it. No one took up his offer.[45]

Lieutenant Gnade divided his company into two groups assigned to different sections of the woods. He then visited Wohlauf's First Company to witness a demonstration of the executions.[46] Meanwhile, Lieutenant Scheer and Sergeant Hergert* took the First Platoon of Second Company, along with some men of Third Platoon, to a certain point in the woods. Scheer divided his men into four groups, assigned them each a shooting area, and sent them back to fetch the Jews they were to kill. Lieutenant Gnade arrived and heatedly argued with Scheer that the men were not being sent deep enough into the woods.[47]

By the time each group had made two or three round trips to the collection point and carried out their executions, it was clear to Scheer that the process was too slow. He asked Hergert for advice. "I then made the proposal," Hergert recalled, "that it would suffice if the Jews were brought from the collection point to the place of execution by only two men of each group, while the other shooters of the execution commando would already have moved to the next shooting site. Furthermore, this shooting site was moved somewhat forward from execution to execution and thus always got closer to the collection point on the forest path. We then proceeded accordingly."[48] Hergert's suggestion speeded the killing process considerably.

In contrast to First Company, the men of Second Company received no instruction on how to carry out the shooting. Initially bayonets were not fixed as an aiming guide, and as Hergert noted, there was a "considerable number of missed shots" that "led to the unnecessary wounding of the victims." One of the policemen in Hergert's unit likewise noted the difficulty the men had in aiming properly. "At first we shot freehand. When one aimed too high, the entire skull exploded. As a consequence, brains and bones flew everywhere. Thus, we were instructed to place the bayonet point on the neck."[49] According to Hergert, however, using fixed bayonets as an aiming guide was no solution. "Through the point-blank shot that was thus required, the bullet struck the head of the victim at such a trajectory that often the entire skull or at least the entire rear skullcap was torn off, and blood, bone splinters, and brains sprayed everywhere and besmirched the shooters."[50]

Hergert was emphatic that no one in First Platoon was given the option of withdrawing beforehand. But once the executions began and men approached either him or Scheer because they could not shoot women and children, they were given other duties.[51] This was confirmed by one of his men. "During the execution word spread that anyone who could not take it any longer could report." He went on to note, "I myself took part in some ten shootings, in which I had to shoot men and women. I simply could not shoot at people anymore, which became apparent to my sergeant, Hergert, because at the end I repeatedly shot past. For this reason he relieved me. Other comrades were also relieved sooner or later, because they simply could no longer continue."[52]

Lieutenant Drucker's Second Platoon and the bulk of Sergeant Steinmetz's Third Platoon were assigned to yet another part of the forest. Like Scheer's men, they were divided into small groups of five to eight each rather than large groups of thirty-five to forty as in Wohlauf's First Company. The men were told to place the end of their carbines on the cervical vertebrae at the base of the neck, but here too the shooting was done initially without fixed bayonets as a guide.[53] The results were horrifying. "The shooters were gruesomely besmirched with blood, brains, and bone splinters. It hung on their clothing."[54]

When dividing his men into small groups of shooters, Drucker had kept about a third of them in reserve. Ultimately, everyone was to shoot, but the idea was to allow frequent relief and "cigarette breaks."[55] With the constant coming and going from the trucks, the wild terrain, and the frequent rotation, the men did not remain in fixed groups.[56] The confusion created the opportunity for work slowdown and evasion. Some men who hurried at their task shot far more Jews than others who delayed as much as they could.[57] After two rounds one policeman simply "slipped off" and stayed among the trucks on the edge of the forest.[58] Another managed to avoid taking his turn with the shooters altogether.

It was in no way the case that those who did not want to or could not carry out the shooting of human beings with their own hands could not keep themselves out of this task. No strict control was being carried out here. I therefore remained by the arriving trucks and kept myself busy at the arrival point. In any case I gave my activity such an appearance. It could not be avoided that one or another of my comrades noticed that I was not going to the executions to fire away at the victims. They showered me with remarks such as "shit-head" and "weakling" to express their disgust. But I suffered no consequences for my actions. I must mention here that I was not the only one who kept himself out of participating in the executions.[59]

By far the largest number of shooters at Józefów who were interrogated after the war came from the Third Platoon of Second Company. It is from them that we can perhaps get the best impression of the effect of the executions on the men and the dropout rate among them during the course of the action.

Hans Dettelmann,* a forty-year-old barber, was assigned by Drucker to a firing squad. "It was still not possible for me to shoot the first victim at the first execution, and I wandered off and asked . . . Lieutenant Drucker to be relieved." Dettelmann told his lieutenant that he had a "very weak nature," and Drucker let him go.[60]

Walter Niehaus,* a former Reemtsma cigarette sales repre-sentative, was paired with an elderly woman for the first round. "After I had shot the elderly woman, I went to Toni [Anton] Bentheim* [his sergeant] and told him that I was not able to carry out further executions. I did not have to participate in the shooting anymore. . . . my nerves were totally finished from this one shooting."[61]

For his first victim August Zorn* was given a very old man. Zorn recalled that his elderly victim

could not or would not keep up with his countrymen, because he repeatedly fell and then simply lay there. I regularly had to lift him up and drag him forward. Thus, I only reached the execution site when my comrades had already shot their Jews. At the sight of his countrymen who had been shot, my Jew threw himself on the ground and remained lying there. I then cocked my carbine and shot him through the back of the head. Because I was already very upset from the cruel treatment of the Jews during the clearing of the town and was completely in turmoil, I shot too high. The entire back of the skull of my Jew was torn off and the brain exposed. Parts of the skull flew into Sergeant Steinmetz's face. This was grounds for me, after returning to the truck, to go to the first sergeant and ask for my release. I had become so sick that I simply couldn't anymore. I was then relieved by the first sergeant.[62]

Georg Kageler,* a thirty-seven-year-old tailor, made it through the first round before encountering difficulty. "After I had carried out the first shooting and at the unloading point was allotted a mother with daughter as victims for the next shooting, I began a conversation with them and learned that they were Germans from Kassel, and I took the decision not to participate further in the executions. The entire business was now so repugnant to me that I returned to my platoon leader and told him that I was still sick and asked for my release." Kageler was sent to guard the marketplace.[63] Neither his pre-execution conversation with his victim nor his discovery that there were German Jews in Józefów was unique. Schimke, the man who had first stepped out, encountered a Jew from Hamburg in the marketplace, as did a second policeman.[64] Yet another policeman remembered that the first Jew he shot was a decorated World War I veteran from Bremen who begged in vain for mercy.[65]

Franz Kastenbaum,* who during his official interrogation had denied remembering anything about the killing of Jews in Poland, suddenly appeared uninvited at the office of the Hamburg state prosecutor investigating Reserve Police Battalion 101. He told how he had been a member of a firing squad of seven or eight men that had taken its victims into the woods and shot them in the neck at point-blank range. This procedure had been repeated until the fourth victim.

The shooting of the men was so repugnant to me that I missed the fourth man. It was simply no longer possible for me to aim accurately. I suddenly felt nauseous and ran away from the shooting site. I have expressed myself incorrectly just now. It was not that I could no longer aim accurately, rather that the fourth time I intentionally missed. I then ran into the woods, vomited, and sat down against a tree. To make sure that no one was nearby, I called loudly into the woods, because I wanted to be alone. Today I can say that my nerves were totally finished. I think that I remained alone in the woods for some two to three hours.

Kastenbaum then returned to the edge of the woods and rode an empty truck back to the marketplace. He suffered no consequences; his absence had gone unnoticed because the firing squads had been all mixed up and randomly assigned. He had come to make this statement, he explained to the investigating attorney, because he had had no peace since attempting to conceal the shooting action.[66]

Most of those who found the shooting impossible to bear quit very early.[67] But not always. The men in one squad had already shot ten to twenty Jews each when they finally asked to be relieved. As one of them explained, "I especially asked to be relieved because the man next to me shot so impossibly. Apparently he always aimed his gun too high, producing terrible wounds in his victims. In many cases the entire backs of victims' heads were torn off, so that the brains sprayed all over. I simply couldn't watch it any longer."[68] At the unloading point, Sergeant Bentheim watched men emerge from the woods covered with blood and brains, morale shaken and nerves finished. Those who asked to be relieved he advised to "slink away" to the marketplace.[69] As a result, the number of policemen gathered on the marketplace grew constantly.[70]

As with First Company, alcohol was made available to the policemen under Drucker and Steinmetz who stayed in the forest and continued shooting.[71] As darkness approached at the end of a long summer day and the murderous task was still not finished, the shooting became even less organized and more hectic.[72] The forest was so full of dead bodies that it was difficult to find places to make the Jews lie down.[73] When darkness finally fell about 9:00 p.m.—some seventeen hours after Reserve Police Battalion 101 had first arrived on the outskirts of Józefów—and the last Jews had been killed, the men returned to the marketplace and prepared to depart for Biłgoraj.[74] No plans had been made for the burial of the bodies, and the dead Jews were simply left lying in the woods. Neither clothing nor valuables had been officially collected, though at least some of the policemen had enriched themselves with watches, jewelry, and money taken from the victims.[75] The pile of luggage the Jews had been forced to leave at the marketplace was simply burned.[76] Before the policemen climbed into their trucks and left Józefów, a ten-year-old girl appeared, bleeding from the head. She was brought to Trapp, who took her in his arms and said, "You shall remain alive."[77]

When the men arrived at the barracks in Biłgoraj, they were depressed, angered, embittered, and shaken.[78] They ate little but drank heavily. Generous quantities of alcohol were provided, and many of the policemen got quite drunk. Major Trapp made the rounds, trying to console and reassure them, and again placing the responsibility on higher authorities.[79] But neither the drink nor Trapp's consolation could wash away the sense of shame and horror that pervaded the barracks. Trapp asked the men not to talk about it,[80] but they needed no encouragement in that direction. Those who had not been in the forest did not want to learn more.[81] Those who had been there likewise had no desire to speak, either then or later. By silent consensus within Reserve Police Battalion 101, the Józefów massacre was simply not discussed. "The entire matter was a taboo."[82] But repression during waking hours could not stop the nightmares. During the first night back from Józefów, one policeman awoke firing his gun into the ceiling of the barracks.[83]

Several days after Józefów the battalion, it would seem, narrowly missed participation in yet another massacre. Units of First and Second Company, under Trapp and Wohlauf, entered Alekzandrów—a so-called street village composed of houses strung out along the road twelve kilometers west of Józefów. A small number of Jews was rounded up, and both the policemen and the Jews feared that another massacre was imminent. After some hesitation, however, the action was broken off, and Trapp permitted the Jews to return to their houses. One policeman remembered vividly "how individual Jews fell on their knees before Trapp and tried to kiss his hands and feet. Trapp, however, did not permit this and turned away." The policemen returned to Biłgoraj with no explanation for the strange turn of events.[84] Then, on July 20, precisely one month after its departure from Hamburg and one week after the Józefów massacre, Reserve Police Battalion 101 left Biłgoraj for redeployment in the northern sector of the Lublin district.

8

Reflections
on a Massacre

At Józefów a mere dozen men out of nearly 500 had responded instinctively to Major Trapp's offer to step forward and excuse themselves from the impending mass murder. Why was the number of men who from the beginning declared themselves unwilling to shoot so small? In part, it was a matter of the suddenness. There was no forewarning or time to think, as the men were totally "surprised" by the Józefów action.[1] Unless they were able to react to Trapp's offer on the spur of the moment, this first opportunity was lost.[2]

As important as the lack of time for reflection was the pressure for conformity—the basic identification of men in uniform with their comrades and the strong urge not to separate themselves from the group by stepping out. The battalion had only recently been brought up to full strength, and many of the men did not yet know each other well; the bonds of military comradeship were not yet fully developed. Nonetheless, the act of stepping out that morning in Józefów meant leaving one's comrades and admitting that one was "too weak" or "cowardly." Who would have "dared," one policeman declared emphatically, to "lose face" before the assembled troops.[3] "If the question is posed to me why I shot with the others in the first place," said another who subsequently asked to be excused after several rounds of killing, "I must answer that no one wants to be thought a coward." It was one thing to refuse at the beginning, he added, and quite another to try to shoot but not be able to continue.[4] Another policeman—more aware of what truly required courage—said quite simply, "I was cowardly."[5]

Most of the interrogated policemen denied that they had any choice. Faced with the testimony of others, many did not contest that Trapp had made the offer but claimed that they had not heard that part of the speech or could not remember it. A few policemen made the attempt to confront the question of choice but failed to find the words. It was a different time and place, as if they had been on another political planet, and the political values and vocabulary of the 1960s were useless in explaining the situation in which they had found themselves in 1942. Quite atypical in describing his state of mind that morning of July 13 was a policeman who admitted to killing as many as twenty Jews before quitting. "I thought that I could master the situation and that without me the Jews were not going to escape their fate anyway. . . . Truthfully I must say that at the time we didn't reflect about it at all. Only years later did any of us become truly conscious of what had happened then. . . . Only later did it first occur to me that had not been right."[6]

In addition to the easy rationalization that not taking part in the shooting was not going to alter the fate of the Jews in any case, the policemen developed other justifications for their behavior. Perhaps the most astonishing rationalization of all was that of a thirty-five-year-old metalworker from Bremerhaven:

I made the effort, and it was possible for me, to shoot only children. It so happened that the mothers led the children by the hand. My neighbor then shot the mother and I shot the child that belonged to her, because I reasoned with myself that after all without its mother the child could not live any longer. It was supposed to be, so to speak, soothing to my conscience to release children unable to live without their mothers.[7]

The full weight of this statement, and the significance of the word choice of the former policeman, cannot be fully appreciated unless one knows that the German word for "release" (*erlösen*) also means to "redeem" or "save" when used in a religious sense. The one who "releases" is the *Erlöser*—the Savior or Redeemer!

In terms of motivation and consciousness, the most glaring omission in the interrogations is any discussion of anti-Semitism. For the most part the interrogators did not pursue this issue. Nor were the men, for understandable reasons as potential defendants, eager to volunteer any illuminating comments. With few exceptions the whole question of anti-Semitism is marked by silence. What is clear is that the men's concern for their standing in the eyes of their comrades was not matched by any sense of human ties with their victims. The Jews stood outside their circle of human obligation and responsibility. Such a polarization between "us" and "them," between one's comrades and the enemy, is of course standard in war.

It would seem that even if the men of Reserve Police Battalion 101 had not consciously adopted the anti-Semitic doctrines of the regime, they had at least accepted the assimilation of the Jews into the image of the enemy. Major Trapp appealed to this generalized notion of the Jews as part of the enemy in his early-morning speech. The men should remember, when shooting Jewish women and children, that the enemy was killing German women and children by bombing Germany.

If only a dozen policemen stepped out at the beginning to extricate themselves from the impending mass murder, a much larger number either sought to evade the shooting by less conspicuous methods or asked to be released from the firing squads once the shooting had begun. How many policemen belonged to these categories cannot be ascertained with any certainty, but an estimate in the range of 10 to 20 percent of those actually assigned to the firing squads does not seem unreasonable. Sergeant Hergert, for instance, admitted excusing as many as five from his squad of forty or fifty men. In the Drucker-Steinmetz group, from which the greatest number of shooters was interrogated, we can identify six policemen who quit within four rounds and an entire squad of five to eight who were released considerably later. While the number of those who evaded or dropped out was thus not insignificant, it must not obscure the corollary that at least 80 percent of those called upon to shoot continued to do so until 1,500 Jews from Józefów had been killed.

Even twenty or twenty-five years later those who did quit shooting along the way overwhelmingly cited sheer physical revulsion against what they were doing as the prime motive but did not express any ethical or political principles behind this revulsion. Given the educational level of these reserve police-men, one should not expect a sophisticated articulation of abstract principles. The absence of such does not mean that their revulsion did not have its origins in the humane instincts that Nazism radically opposed and sought to overcome. But the men themselves did not seem to be conscious of the contradiction between their feelings and the essence of the regime they served. Being too weak to continue shooting, of course, posed problems for the "productivity" and morale of the battalion, but it did not challenge basic police discipline or the authority of the regime in general. Indeed, Heinrich Himmler himself sanctioned the toleration of this kind of weakness in his notorious Posen speech of October 4, 1943, to the SS leadership. While exalting obedience as one of the key virtues of all SS men, he explicitly noted an exception, namely, "one whose nerves are finished, one who is weak. Then one can say: Good, go take your pension."[8]

Politically and ethically motivated opposition, explicitly identified by the policemen as such, was relatively rare. One man said he decisively rejected the Jewish measures of the Nazis because he was an active Communist Party member and thus rejected National Socialism in its entirety.[9] Another said he opposed the shooting of Jews because he had been a Social Democrat for many years.[10] A third said he was known to the Nazis as "politically unreliable" and a "grumbler" but gave no further political identity.[11] Several others grounded their attitude on opposition to the regime's anti-Semitism in particular. "This attitude I already had earlier in Hamburg," said one landscape gardener, "because due to the Jewish measures already carried out in Hamburg I had lost the greater part of my business customers."[12] Another policeman merely identified himself as "a great friend of the Jews" without explaining further.[13]

The two men who explained their refusal to take part in the greatest detail both emphasized the fact that they were freer to act as they did because they had no careerist ambitions. One policeman accepted the possible disadvantages of his course of action "because I was not a career policeman and also did not want to become one, but rather an independent skilled craftsman, and I had my business back home. . . . thus it was of no consequence that my police career would not prosper."[14]

Lieutenant Buchmann had cited an ethical stance for his refusal; as a reserve officer and Hamburg businessman, he could not shoot defenseless women and children. But he too stressed the importance of economic independence when explaining why his situation was not analogous to that of his fellow officers. "I was somewhat older then and moreover a reserve officer, so it was not particularly important to me to be promoted or otherwise to advance, because I had my prosperous business back home. The company chiefs . . . on the other hand were young men and career policemen who wanted to become something." But

Buchmann also admitted to what the Nazis would undoubtedly have condemned as a "cosmopolitan" and pro-Jewish outlook. "Through my business experience, especially because it extended abroad, I had gained a better overview of things. Moreover, through my earlier business activities I already knew many Jews."[15]

The resentment and bitterness in the battalion over what they had been asked to do in Józefów was shared by virtually everyone, even those who had shot the entire day. The exclamation of one policeman to First Sergeant Kammer of First Company that "I'd go crazy if I had to do that again" expressed the sentiments of many.[16] But only a few went beyond complaining to extricate themselves from such a possibility. Several of the older men with very large families took advantage of a regulation that required them to sign a release agreeing to duty in a combat area. One who had not yet signed refused to do so; another rescinded his signature. Both were eventually transferred back to Germany.[17] The most dramatic response was again that of Lieutenant Buchmann, who asked Trapp to have him transferred back to Hamburg and declared that short of a direct personal order from Trapp, he would not take part in Jewish actions. In the end he wrote to Hamburg, explicitly requesting a recall because he was not "suited" to certain tasks "alien to the police" that were being carried out by his unit in Poland.[18] Buchmann had to wait until November, but his efforts to be transferred were ultimately successful.

The problem that faced Trapp and his superiors in Lublin, therefore, was not the ethically and politically grounded opposition of a few but the broad demoralization shared both by those who shot to the end and those who had not been able to continue. It was above all a reaction to the sheer horror of the killing process itself. If Reserve Police Battalion 101 was to continue to provide vital manpower for the implementation of the Final Solution in the Lublin district, the psychological burden on the men had to be taken into account and alleviated.

In subsequent actions two vital changes were introduced and

henceforth—with some notable exceptions—adhered to. First, most of the future operations of Reserve Police Battalion 101 involved ghetto clearing and deportation, not outright massacre on the spot. The policemen were thus relieved of the immediate horror of the killing process, which (for deportees from the northern Lublin district) was carried out in the extermination camp at Treblinka. Second, while deportation was a horrifying procedure characterized by the terrible coercive violence needed to drive people onto the death trains as well as the systematic killing of those who could not be marched to the trains, these actions were generally undertaken jointly by units of Reserve Police Battalion 101 and the Trawnikis, SS-trained auxiliaries from Soviet territories, recruited from the POW camps and usually assigned the very worst parts of the ghetto clearing and deportation.

Concern over the psychological demoralization resulting from Józefów is indeed the most likely explanation of that mysterious incident in Alekzandrów several days later. Probably Trapp had assurance that Trawniki men would carry out the shooting this time, and when they did not show up, he released the Jews his men had rounded up. In short, the psychological alleviation necessary to integrate Reserve Police Battalion 101 into the killing process was to be achieved through a twofold division of labor. The bulk of the killing was to be removed to the extermination camp, and the worst of the on-the-spot "dirty work" was to be assigned to the Trawnikis. This change would prove sufficient to allow the men of Reserve Police Battalion 101 to become accustomed to their participation in the Final Solution. When the time came to kill again, the policemen did not "go crazy." Instead they became increasingly efficient and calloused executioners.

9

Łomazy:
The Descent of Second Company

EVEN BEFORE THE MASSACRE AT JÓZEFÓW ON JULY 13, ORDERS
had already been given for a redeployment of the police
battalions in the Lublin district.[1] The district was divided into
northern, central, and southern "security sectors." Reserve
Police Battalion 101 was assigned to the northern sector, which
encompassed, from west to east, the counties (*Kreise*) of Puławy,
Radzyń, and Biała Podlaska. Lieutenant Gnade's Second Company was assigned Biała Podlaska, and Gnade stationed his
company staff in the county seat of Biała. First Platoon was
divided between Piszczac and Tuczna to the southeast, while
Second Platoon was at Wisznice due south. Third Platoon was
stationed in Parczew to the southwest, actually in the neighboring county of Radzyń.

The Final Solution in the county of Biała Podlaska had commenced on June 10, 1942, when 3,000 Jews were deported from Biała to Sobibór. Hundreds of Jews from smaller communities were concentrated in the village of Łomazy, halfway between Biała and Wisznice.[2] Then the murder campaign came to a halt, until the arrival of Lieutenant Gnade's Second Company. The Jews of Łomazy were to be the target of Reserve Police Battalion 101's first joint killing action with a unit from Trawniki. Second Company was to provide the bulk of the manpower for the roundup. The primary function of the Trawniki unit was to provide the shooters, thus alleviating the chief psychological burden the German policemen had experienced at Józefów.

In early August one squad of Third Platoon, some fifteen to eighteen men, was stationed directly in Łomazy under Sergeant Heinrich Bekemeier.* Gruppe Bekemeier, as it was known, passed several uneventful weeks in a town that was half Polish and half Jewish. Though the Jewish population lived apart from the Poles, the Jewish quarter of town was neither fenced nor guarded.[3] The German policemen were housed in the school in the Jewish quarter.

On August 16, only one day before the impending action, Heinrich Bekemeier in Łomazy received a telephone call from Lieutenant Gnade informing him that there would be a Jewish "resettlement" the next morning and his men were to be ready at 4:00 a.m. It was "clear" to Bekemeier what this meant.[4] The same day Gnade summoned Lieutenants Drucker and Scheer to Biała. Allegedly in the presence of an SD officer, he informed them of the next day's action, which was to be carried out in cooperation with the SS. The entire Jewish population was to be shot.[5] Second Platoon in nearby Wisznice was provided with trucks for a half-hour ride early in the morning.[6] Since no trucks were available for First Platoon, horse-drawn Polish farm wagons were commandeered, and the policemen rode all night to reach Łomazy by early morning.[7]

In Łomazy Gnade held a meeting with his noncommissioned

officers, who received instructions for clearing the Jewish quarter and assembling the Jews in the schoolyard. The NCOs were told that the Hiwis from Trawniki would do the shooting, so the policemen would for the most part be spared. Nonetheless, the roundup was to be conducted "as had been done before," which is to say that infants and the old, sick, and frail who could not be easily taken to the assembly point were to be shot on the spot. According to one squad leader, however, most children were once again brought to the assembly point. As in Józefów, the men encountered not only German Jews but specifically Hamburg Jews during the clearing action. The Jews quickly filled the schoolyard and overflowed into the adjoining sports field. With some shooting, the roundup was finished in a short two hours.[8]

The 1,700 Jews of Łomazy were then forced to sit and wait. A group of sixty to seventy young men was selected out, given shovels and spades, loaded onto trucks, and driven to the woods. Several of the young Jews jumped from the moving trucks and made good their escape. Another attacked a German corporal, the battalion boxing champion, who promptly knocked his desperate assailant senseless. In the woods the Jews were set to work digging a mass grave.[9]

Back in Łomazy, the wait of the doomed Jews and their police guards stretched into hours. Suddenly a contingent of fifty Hiwis from Trawniki marched into town, led by a German SS officer. "I can still remember exactly," one policeman testified, "that immediately after their arrival these Trawnikis took a break. I saw that in addition to food they also took bottles of vodka out of their packs and drank from them." The SS officer and Gnade began drinking heavily as well. Other NCOs also smelled of alcohol but unlike the two commanders were not visibly drunk.[10] Buttered bread was prepared for the policemen.[11]

As the grave digging neared completion and after the Hiwis and policemen finished their meal, the one-kilometer "march to death" in the forest began.[12] Some policemen rode the farmers' wagons to the forest, where they set up a new cordon.[13] Others began to march the Jews in groups of 200 or 300 at a time. Those who collapsed on the way were simply shot.[14] This process proved too slow, and the decision was taken to march all the remaining Jews in a single large group. Pieces of rope were collected from the Polish villagers, tied together, and laid on the ground around the collected Jews. The Jews were then ordered to stand up, lifting the rope that surrounded them, and march toward the forest.

Sergeant Toni Bentheim described what followed:

> The march proceeded extremely sluggishly. Presumably at the front they went too fast and pulled on the rope, so that at the back end they bunched together in a giant cluster, and scarcely a Jew could put one foot in front of another. Inevitably people fell, and the group had not even left or had just left the sports field when the first ones to fall were regularly hanging on the rope and being dragged along. Inside the cluster people were even trampled. The Jews who fell in this way and lay on the ground behind the column were ruthlessly driven forward or shot. But even these first shots did not alter the situation, and the cluster of people bunched together at the end could not untangle themselves and move forward. As at this point we were without assignment, I alone or with several of my comrades followed the Jews, because I had already concluded that one would never make headway in this manner. When no change was apparent after the first shots, I bellowed loudly something like, "What's the point of this nonsense. Away with the rope." Due to my shout the entire formation came to a halt, including the Hiwis, who as I remember turned toward me quite perplexed. I shouted at them once again to the effect—they were all armed—that the business with the rope was nonsense. Away with the rope. . . . After my second call the Jews let the rope drop, and the entire group was able to move forward as a normal column. I myself then returned to the schoolyard. Agitated and vexed, I immediately went into the school and drank a schnapps.[15]

As the columns of marching Jews reached the forest, they were separated by sex and sent to one of three collecting areas.

Here they were ordered to undress. Women were allowed to keep their shifts. In some areas the men were totally naked; elsewhere they were allowed to keep their underpants. Policemen in each area were appointed to collect clothing and valuables. They were warned that they would be searched afterward. The Jews approached with their bundles of clothing, which were laid on a pile and searched. After depositing their valuables in a large container or throwing them onto an open blanket, the Jews were made to lie face down and wait once more, often for hours, while their exposed skin burned under the hot August sun.[16]

The preponderance of testimony indicates that Lieutenant Gnade was "a Nazi by conviction" and an anti-Semite. He was also unpredictable—affable and approachable at times, brutal and vicious at others. His worst traits became more pronounced under the influence of alcohol, and by all accounts that afternoon in Łomazy Gnade was drunk senseless. In Poland he in fact degenerated into a "drunkard."[17] Gnade's increasing dependence on alcohol was not unusual in the battalion. As one nondrinking policeman noted, "Most of the other comrades drank so much solely because of the many shootings of Jews, for such a life was quite intolerable sober."[18]

If Gnade's drinking was commonplace, the streak of sadism he began to display at Łomazy was not. The previous fall Gnade had put his men on the night train from Minsk to avoid becoming involved in the execution of the Jews he had brought there from Hamburg. At Józefów he had not distinguished himself from his fellow officers with any especially sadistic behavior. All this changed in the forest outside Łomazy as Gnade sought to entertain himself while waiting for the Jews to finish digging the grave.

> Even before the shooting began, First Lieutenant Gnade had personally picked out some twenty to twenty-five elderly Jews. They were exclusively men with full beards. Gnade made the old men crawl on the ground in the area before the

grave. Before he gave them the order to crawl, they had to undress. While the totally naked Jews crawled, First Lieutenant Gnade screamed to those around, "Where are my noncommissioned officers? Don't you have any clubs yet?" The noncommissioned officers went to the edge of the forest, fetched themselves clubs, and vigorously beat the Jews with them.[19]

When preparations for the shooting were complete, Gnade began to chase Jews from the undressing areas to the grave.[20]

In small groups the Jews were forced to run between a thin cordon of guards some thirty to fifty meters from the undressing areas to the grave.[21] The grave itself had mounds of dirt piled high on three sides; the fourth side was an incline down which the Jews were driven. In their state of intoxicated excitement, the Hiwis initially began shooting the Jews at the entry to the grave. "As a result, the Jews killed first blocked the slope. Thus some Jews went into the grave and pulled the corpses away from the entry. Immediately large numbers of Jews were driven into the grave, and the Hiwis took their positions on the walls that had been thrown up. From there they shot the victims."[22] As the shooting continued, the grave began to fill. "The Jews who followed had to climb on and later even clamber over those shot earlier, because the grave was filled with corpses almost to the edge."[23]

The Hiwis, often with bottle in hand, as well as Gnade and the SS officer, became increasingly drunk.[24] "While First Lieutenant Gnade shot with his pistol from the dirt wall, whereby he was in constant danger of falling into the grave, the SD [sic] officer climbed into the grave just like the Hiwis and shot from there, because he was so drunk he could no longer stand on the wall." Groundwater mixed with blood began to rise in the grave, so that the Hiwis were soon standing in it over their knees. The number of shooters steadily diminished as one by one the Hiwis fell into a drunken stupor. Gnade and the SS officer then began to scream reproaches at one another loudly enough to be heard by everyone standing within thirty meters of the grave. The SS officer yelled, "Your shit police don't shoot at all." Gnade retorted, "Good, then my men will have to shoot too."[25]

Lieutenants Drucker and Scheer summoned their NCOs and passed on the order to form firing squads and carry out the executions in the same way as the Hiwis. According to Sergeant Hergert, the NCOs rejected the Hiwis' methods "because the groundwater already stood more than half a meter. Moreover, corpses already lay—to be more precise, floated—all over the grave area. I remember as especially horrifying that large numbers of the Jews who were shot had not been fatally hit during the execution and nonetheless were covered by the following victims without being given mercy shots."[26]

The NCOs decided that the execution should continue with two firing squads on opposite sides of the grave. The Jews were forced to lie down in rows along each side of the grave and were shot by the police standing on the opposite wall. Men from all three platoons were formed into squads of eight to ten and were relieved by others in rotation after five or six shots. After about two hours the Hiwis were roused from their stupor and resumed shooting in place of the German policemen. The shooting was finished around 7:00 p.m., and the work Jews who had been kept aside covered the grave. The work Jews were then shot as well.[27] The thin covering of the overfilled grave continued to move.[28]

First and Second Platoons returned to their stations that evening, but Gruppe Bekemeier remained in Łomazy. A few days later it carried out a sweep of the Jewish quarter. Searching the cellars and looking for bunkers dug under the floorboards of the houses, the policemen seized another twenty to thirty Jews. Bekemeier telephoned Gnade, who ordered shooting. Accompanied by three or four Polish policemen, Bekemeier and his men took the Jews to the edge of the forest, forced them to lie down, and shot them in the neck from behind, once again using the bayonet as an aiming guide. Each man shot at least once, some twice. The Polish mayor was ordered to bury the bodies.[29]

The massacre at Łomazy—the second four-figure shooting

carried out by the men of Reserve Police Battalion 101—differed from the massacre at Józefów in significant ways. On the part of the victims, there seem to have been many more escape attempts at Łomazy,[30] presumably because the young, able-bodied work Jews were not spared and the victims were more aware of their impending fate from the beginning. Despite greater efforts by the Jews to hide or escape, in terms of efficiency the killing procedure was a considerable advance over the improvised and amateurish methods employed at Józefów. Roughly one-third as many men killed even more Jews (1,700) in about half the time. Moreover, valuables and clothing were collected, and the bodies disposed of in a mass grave.

Psychologically, the burden on the killers was much reduced. The Hiwis, not just liquored up after the event to help them forget but drunk from the start, did most of the shooting. According to Sergeant Bentheim, his men were "overjoyed" that they were not required to shoot this time.[31] Those spared such direct participation seem to have had little if any sense of participation in the killing. After Józefów, the roundup and guarding of Jews to be killed by someone else seemed relatively innocuous.

Even the policemen who did have to replace the Hiwis and shoot for several hours in the late afternoon did not recall the experience with anything like the horror that predominated in their accounts of Józefów. This time the men did not have to pair off with their victims face to face. The personal tie between victim and killer was severed. In sharp contrast to Józefów, only one policeman recalled the identity of a particular Jew he had shot.[32] In addition to the depersonalization of the killing process, through rapid rotation the men were spared the sense of unremitting, endless killing that had been so salient at Józefów. Their direct participation in the killing was not only less personal but more finite. Habituation played a role as well. Having killed once already, the men did not experience such a traumatic shock the second time. Like much else, killing was something one could get used to.

One other factor sharply distinguished Łomazy from Józefów and may well have been yet another kind of psychological "relief" for the men—namely, this time they did not bear the "burden of choice" that Trapp had offered them so starkly on the occasion of the first massacre. No chance to step out was given to those who did not feel up to shooting; no one systematically excused those who were visibly too shaken to continue. Everyone assigned to the firing squads took his turn as ordered.[33] Therefore, those who shot did not have to live with the clear awareness that what they had done had been avoidable.

This is not to say that the men had no choice, only that it was not offered to them so openly and explicitly as at Józefów. They had to exert themselves to evade killing. Even Sergeant Hergert, who was most emphatic that there was no call for volunteers and that virtually every man in the company had to take a turn at shooting, conceded that some men may have "slipped off" into the woods.[34] Apparently the number of evaders was quite small, however, for in contrast to Józefów, only two men testified to having deliberately avoided shooting in some way. Georg Kageler claimed to have been part of a group that had twice escorted Jews from Łomazy to the forest and then "more or less 'slipped away' to escape a further assignment."[35] Paul Metzger* was assigned to an outer cordon at the edge of the forest to block Jews who bolted from the undressing areas and ran for their lives. At Józefów, Metzger had "slipped off" among the trucks after two rounds of shooting. Now, at Łomazy, when one fleeing Jew suddenly ran toward him, Metzger let him pass. As he recalled, "First Lieutenant Gnade, who was . . . already drunk by then, wanted to know which sentry had allowed the Jew to run away. I did not report myself, and none of my comrades reported. Because of his drunkenness, First Lieutenant Gnade was unable to investigate the matter, and so I was not held to account."[36]

The actions of Kageler and Metzger involved at least some risk, but neither suffered any consequence for his evasion. Most of the policemen, however, seem to have made no effort to avoid shooting. At Łomazy following orders reinforced the natural tendency to conform to the behavior of one's comrades. This was much easier to bear than the situation at Józefów, where the policemen were allowed to make personal decisions concerning their participation but the "cost" of not shooting was to separate themselves from their comrades and to expose themselves as "weak."

Trapp had not only offered a choice but he had set a tone. "We have the task to shoot Jews, but not to beat or torture them," he had declared.[37] His own personal distress had been apparent to all at Józefów. Thereafter, however, most "Jewish actions" were carried out in company and platoon strength, not by the full battalion. The company commanders—like Gnade at Łomazy—and not Trapp were thus in a position to set the tone for the behavior expected and encouraged from the men. Gnade's gratuitous and horrific sadism at the grave's edge was only one instance of how he chose to exercise leadership in this regard, but such examples soon multiplied. When Gnade and the SS commander of the Trawnikis, both still drunk, encountered Toni Bentheim in the Łomazy schoolyard after the massacre, Gnade asked, "Well, how many did you shoot, then?" When the sergeant replied none, Gnade responded contemptuously. "One can't expect otherwise, you're Catholic after all."[38] With such leadership and the help of the Trawnikis at Łomazy, the men of Second Company took a major step toward becoming hardened killers.

10

The August Deportations to Treblinka

F AR FROM ANY RAILWAY STATION, ŁOMAZY WAS A TOWN IN which Jews had been concentrated in June 1942 but from which they could not be easily deported. Hence the massacre of August 17. Most of the Jews in the northern Lublin district, however, resided in the towns of Radzyń, Łuków, Parczew, and Międzyrzec, all proximate to rail connections. Henceforth the major contribution of Reserve Police Battalion 101 to the Final Solution was no longer local massacre but ghetto clearing and deportation to the extermination camp at Treblinka, located some 110 kilometers to the north of the battalion headquarters in Radzyń.

The first deportation train to Treblinka left Warsaw late on July 22, 1942, and reached the extermination camp the following morning. Thereafter Jewish transports from Warsaw and the surrounding district arrived daily. Between August 5 and August 24, some 30,000 Jews of Radom and Kielce were also shipped to Treblinka. Though the camp's killing capacity was stretched to the breaking point, Globocnik impatiently decided to commence deportations from northern Lublin as well. The Jews of Parzcew and Międzyrzec in the county of Radzyń, at the center of Reserve Police Battalion 101's security zone, were the first targets.

Steinmetz's Third Platoon of Second Company, minus Gruppe Bekemeier, which had been detached to Łomazy, was stationed in Parczew. More than 5,000 Jews lived in the city's Jewish quarter, which was not separated from the rest of the town by either wire or wall. But the lack of a sealed ghetto did not mean that the Jewish community there had not suffered all the usual discrimination and humiliation of the German occupation. As Steinmetz recalled, when his policemen arrived, the main street was already paved with Jewish gravestones.[1] In early August some 300 to 500 Jews in Parczew had been loaded onto horse-drawn wagons and driven five or six kilometers into the woods under police guard. There the Jews had been turned over to a unit of SS men. The policemen left before hearing any shots, and the fate of the Jews remained unknown to them.[2]

Rumors of a much larger deportation circulated in Parczew, and many Jews fled to the woods.[3] Most were still in town, however, when policemen of the First and Second Companies of Reserve Police Battalion 101, along with a unit of Hiwis, descended upon Parczew early on August 19—just two days after the Łomazy massacre. Trapp gave another speech, informing the men that the Jews were to be taken to the train station two or three kilometers out of town. He indicated "indirectly" but without ambiguity that once again the old and frail who could not march were to be shot on the spot.[4]

Second Company set up the cordon, and First Company carried out the search action in the Jewish quarter.[5] By afternoon, a long column of Jews stretched from the marketplace to the train station. About 3,000 of Parczew's Jews were deported that day. Several days later, this time without the help of any Hiwis, the entire operation was repeated, and the remaining 2,000 Jews of Parczew were sent to Treblinka as well.[6]

In the policemen's memories, the Parczew deportations were relatively uneventful. Everything went smoothly, there was little shooting, and the participation of the Hiwis in the first deportation does not seem to have been marked by their usual drunkenness and brutality. Presumably because so little "dirty work" needed to be done, the Hiwis were not even deemed necessary for the second deportation. While the policemen did not know precisely where the Jews were being sent or what was to be done with them, "it was clear and well known to us all," as Heinrich Steinmetz admitted, "that for the Jews affected these deportations meant the path to death. We suspected that they would be killed in some sort of camp."[7] Spared direct participation in the killing, the men of Reserve Police Battalion 101 seem scarcely to have been disturbed by this awareness—even though there were more victims in the Parczew deportations than in the Józefów and Łomazy massacres combined. Out of sight was truly out of mind. Indeed, for some men of Steinmetz's platoon, the most vivid memory was that they were assigned guard duty in a swampy meadow north of Parczew, where they had to stand all day with wet feet.[8]

Far more memorable for Reserve Police Battalion 101 was the deportation of 11,000 Jews from Międzyrzec to Treblinka on August 25–26.[9] In August 1942 Międzyrzec was the largest ghetto in the county of Radzyń, with a Jewish population of more than 12,000, in comparison to 10,000 Jews in Łuków and 6,000 in the town of Radzyń. In June 1942 ghetto administration in the Lublin district had been transferred from the civil authorities to the SS, and these three ghettos were henceforth supervised by men dispatched from the Radzyń branch office of the Security Police.[10]

Like Izbica and Piaski in the south of the Lublin district, Międzyrzec was destined to become a "transit ghetto" in which

Jews from the surrounding region were collected and sent to Treblinka. To receive more Jews from elsewhere, the ghetto in Międzyrzec had to be periodically emptied of its inhabitants. The first and largest such clearing took place on August 25–26, in a combined action of First Company, Third Platoon of Second Company, and First Platoon of Third Company from Reserve Police Battalion 101, a unit of Hiwis, and the Radzyń Security Police.[11]

When the battalion headquarters moved from Biłgoraj to Radzyń in late July, the men of First Company were stationed there as well as in Kock, Łuków. and Komarówka. First Platoon of Third Company was also stationed in the county of Radzyń, in the town of Czemierniki, and Third Platoon of Second Company in Parczew. These five platoons were now mobilized for the Międzyrzec action. Some of the policemen arrived in Międzyrzec on the night of August 24, one unit accompanying a convoy of wagons bringing additional Jews.[12] Most of the men, however, assembled in Radzyń in the early hours of August 25 under the supervision of First Sergeant Kammer. The initial absence of Captain Wohlauf was explained when the convoy of trucks stopped in front of his private residence on the way out of town. Wohlauf and his young bride—four months pregnant, with a military coat draped over her shoulders and a peaked military cap on her head—emerged from the house and climbed aboard one of the trucks. "While Captain Wohlauf sat up front next to the driver," one policeman recalled, "I now had to give up my seat to make room for his wife."[13]

Prior to joining Reserve Police Battalion 101, Captain Wohlauf had experienced several career difficulties. He had been sent to Norway with Police Battalion 105 in April 1940, but his commander there eventually demanded his recall. Wohlauf was energetic and bright, he noted, but lacked all discipline and was much too impressed with himself.[14] Sent back to Hamburg, Wohlauf was judged by his next commander as lacking interest in home front service and requiring strict supervision.[15] At this point, in the spring of 1941, Wohlauf was assigned to Police

Battalion 101, which had just returned from Łódź, and his professional fortunes changed. Within months the new battalion commander, Trapp, recommended him for promotion and a company command. Wohlauf was soldierly, energetic, full of life, and possessed leadership qualities, Trapp wrote. Moreover, he sought to act on National Socialist principles and instructed his men accordingly. He was "ready at any time without reservation to go the limit for the National Socialist state."[16] Wohlauf was promoted to the rank of captain, took over First Company, and became Trapp's deputy commander.

To the men, Wohlauf seemed quite pretentious. One policeman remembered that Wohlauf rode standing in his car like a general. Another remarked that he was disparagingly called "the little Rommel."[17] The chief clerk of First Company recalled his energy, his determination to take charge of all aspects of his command, and his ability to get things done.[18] His reluctant platoon commander, Lieutenant Buchmann, judged him a much more "upright and genuine" person than Lieutenant Gnade (admittedly a not very high standard of comparison) and not a prominent anti-Semite. He was an officer who took his responsibilities seriously, but above all he was a young man just married and consumed in romance.[19]

Indeed, the sudden departure of Reserve Police Battalion 101 for Poland had caught Wohlauf by surprise, upsetting plans for a June 22 wedding. No sooner had he arrived in Biłgoraj in late June than he beseeched Trapp to let him return briefly to Hamburg to marry his girlfriend, because she was already pregnant. At first Trapp refused but then granted him a special leave. Wohlauf was married on June 29, and returned to Poland just in time for Józefów. Once his company was stationed in Radzyń, Wohlauf had his new bride visit him there for their honeymoon.[20]

Wohlauf may have brought his bride along to witness the Międzyrzec deportation because he could not stand to be separated from her in the fresh bloom of their honeymoon, as Buchmann suggested. On the other hand, the pretentious and self-important captain may have been trying to impress his new bride by showing her he was master over the life and death of Polish Jewry. The men clearly thought the latter, and their reaction was uniformly one of indignation and outrage that a woman was brought to witness the terrible things they were doing.[21] The men of First Company, if not their captain, could still feel shame.

When the convoy carrying Wohlauf, his bride, and most of First Company arrived in Międzyrzec, less than thirty kilometers to the north of Radzyń, the action was already underway. The men could hear shooting and screaming, as the Hiwis and Security Police had begun the roundup. The men waited while Wohlauf went off to get instructions. Twenty or thirty minutes later he returned and issued the company assignments. Some men were sent to outer guard duty, but most of them were assigned to the clearing action alongside the Hiwis. The usual orders were given to shoot anyone trying to escape, as well as the sick, old, and frail who could not march to the train station just outside town.[22]

While the men waited for Wohlauf's return, they encountered a Security Police officer already quite drunk, despite the early hour.[23] It was soon apparent that the Hiwis were also drunk.[24] They shot so often and so wildly that the policemen frequently had to take cover to avoid being hit.[25] The policemen "saw the corpses of Jews who had been shot everywhere in the streets and houses."[26]

Driven by the Hiwis and policemen, thousands of Jews streamed into the marketplace. Here they had to sit or squat without moving or getting up. As the hours passed on this very hot August day of the late summer heat wave, many Jews fainted and collapsed. Moreover, beating and shooting continued in the marketplace.[27] Having removed her military coat as the temperature rose, Frau Wohlauf was clearly visible in her dress on the marketplace, watching the events at close range.[28]

About 2:00 p.m. the outer guard was called to the marketplace, and one or two hours later the march to the train station began.

The entire force of Hiwis and policemen was employed to drive the thousands of Jews along the route. Once again, shooting was common. The "foot sick" who could go no farther were shot and left lying on the side of the road. Corpses lined the street to the train station.[29]

One final horror was reserved to the end, for the train cars now had to be loaded. While the Hiwis and Security Police packed 120 to 140 Jews into each car, the reserve policemen stood guard and observed. As one remembered:

> When it didn't go well, they made use of riding whips and guns. The loading was simply frightful. There was an unearthly cry from these poor people, because ten or twenty cars were being loaded simultaneously. The entire freight train was dreadfully long. One could not see all of it. It may have been fifty to sixty cars, if not more. After a car was loaded, the doors were closed and nailed shut.[30]

Once all the cars were sealed, the men of Reserve Police Battalion 101 quickly departed without waiting to see the train pull away.

The clearing of the Międzyrzec ghetto was the largest deportation operation the battalion would carry out during its entire participation in the Final Solution. Only 1,000 Jews in Międzyrzec had been given temporary work permits to remain in the ghetto until they could be replaced with Poles.[31] Thus some 11,000 were targeted for deportation. The policemen knew that "many hundreds" of Jews were shot in the course of the operation, but of course they did not know exactly how many.[32] The surviving Jews who collected and buried the bodies did know, however, and their count was 960.[33]

This figure needs to be put into some wider perspective in order to show the ferocity of the Międzyrzec deportation even by the Nazi standards of 1942. About 300,000 Jews were deported from Warsaw between July 22 and September 21, 1942. The total number of Jews killed by gunfire over this two-month period was recorded as 6,687.[34] In Warsaw, therefore, the ratio between those killed on the spot and those deported was approximately 2 percent. The same ratio for Międzyrzec was nearly 9 percent. The Jews of Międzyrzec did not march "like sheep to the slaughter." They were driven with an almost unimaginable ferocity and brutality that left a singular imprint even on the memories of the increasingly numbed and callous participants from Reserve Police Battalion 101. This was no case of "out of sight, out of mind."

Why the contrast between the relatively uneventful and hence unmemorable deportations from Parczew and the horror of Międzyrzec only one week later? On the German side, the key factor was the ratio between perpetrators and victims. For the more than 5,000 Jews of Parczew, the Germans had two companies of Order Police and a unit of Hiwis, or 300 to 350 men. For Międzyrzec, with twice the number of Jews to be deported, the Germans used five platoons of Order Police, the local Security Police, and a unit of Hiwis, or 350 to 400 men. The greater the pressure on the German ghetto clearers in terms of manpower, the greater their ferocity and brutality to get the job done.

Globocnik's impatient attempt to commence deportations to Treblinka from northern Lublin simultaneous with those from the districts of Warsaw and Radom proved too much for the capacity of the extermination camp. In late August the number of Jews waiting to be killed and the number of corpses that could not be disposed of quickly enough piled up. The overburdened killing machinery broke down. The deportations throughout the Warsaw, Radom, and Lublin districts were temporarily halted, including a train scheduled for two trips from Łuków to Treblinka beginning August 28.[35] Globocnik and his extermination camp supervisor, Christian Wirth, rushed to Treblinka to reorganize the camp. Franz Stangl was summoned from Sobibór, which was relatively inactive while rail line repairs made it inaccessible to all but nearby sites, and named commandant. After a week of reorganization, deportations from Warsaw to Treblinka resumed on September 3, followed by deportations from the Radom district in mid-September. Meanwhile, the men of Reserve Police Battalion 101 enjoyed a brief respite, for only in late September did the killing resume in northern Lublin.

Late-September Shootings

Shortly before the deportation program resumed in the northern security zone of the Lublin district, Reserve Police Battalion 101 was involved in several more mass shootings. The first of these occurred in the village of Serokomla, some nine kilometers northwest of Kock. Serokomla had already experienced one massacre in May 1940, at the hands of ethnic Germans organized into vigilante-style units known as the Selbstschutz ("self-defense"). These units had been created in occupied Poland in the fall of 1939 and the spring of 1940 under the leadership of Heinrich Himmler's crony Ludolph von Alvensleben. After conducting a series of massacres, including one at Serokomla, the Selbstschutz was reorganized into "special service" units known as the Sonderdienst and placed under the local county heads of the civil administration.[1]

Serokomla was visited again by the Germans in September 1942. Lieutenant Brand's platoon of First Company was stationed in nearby Kock. Brand ordered Sergeant Hans Keller and ten men of the platoon to round up Jews in the outlying areas around Serokomla and bring them to the village.[2] Then, early on the morning of September 22, Brand's platoon drove out of Kock and waited at a crossroads northwest of town. They were joined by other units of First Company under Captain Wohlauf, arriving from Radzyń twenty kilometers to the northeast, as well as the First Platoon of Third Company under Lieutenant Peters, which was stationed in Czemierniki fifteen kilometers to the east. Under the command of Captain Wohlauf, the reserve policemen drove to Serokomla.

Shortly before reaching the village, Wohlauf halted the convoy and gave orders. Machine guns were set up on two hills just outside the town, vantage points from which the entire area could be seen. Some men from Brand's platoon were assigned to cordon off the Jewish quarter of the village, and the rest of First Company was detailed to collect the Jewish population.[3]

As yet Wohlauf had said nothing about shooting, except that the men were to proceed as usual—an indirect reference understood to mean that those attempting to hide or escape as well as those unable to walk were to be shot on the spot. However, Lieutenant Peters's platoon, which had been held in reserve, was sent to an area of gravel pits and mounds of waste material less than a kilometer outside the village. To Sergeant Keller, who could observe the deployment from his machine-gun nests atop the two nearby hills, it was obvious that the Jews of Serokomla were going to be shot, though Wohlauf had only spoken to the men of "resettlement."

The collection of the Jews of Serokomla—some 200 or 300—was completed by 11:00 a.m. on what was turning out to be a warm, sunny day. Then Wohlauf "suddenly" declared that all the Jews were to be shot.[4] Additional men from First

Company were sent to the gravel pits under the command of Sergeant Jurich* to join the shooters from Lieutenant Peters's platoon. At around noon, the remaining men of First Company began marching the Jews out of town in groups of twenty to thirty.

Lieutenant Peters's platoon had been in the cordon at Józefów and was thus spared duty in the firing squads. They had likewise been absent from Second Company's shooting at Łomazy. At Serokomla, however, their turn had come.

Without the experienced help of the Hiwis, as at Łomazy, Wohlauf organized the executions along the lines of the Józefów shooting. The groups of twenty to thirty Jews, which had been marched out of town in succession to the gravel pits, were turned over to an equal number of Peters's and Jurich's commandos. Thus each policeman once again faced the individual Jew he was going to shoot. The Jews were not forced to undress, nor was there a collection of valuables. There was also no selection for labor. All the Jews, regardless of age and sex, were to be shot.

The policemen in the shooting commandos marched their Jews to the crest of one of the mounds of waste material in the area of the gravel pits. The victims were lined up facing a six-foot drop. From a short distance behind, the policemen fired on order into the necks of the Jews. The bodies tumbled over the edge. Following each round, the next group of Jews was brought to the same spot and thus had to look down at the growing pile of corpses of their family and friends before they were shot in turn. Only after a number of rounds did the shooters change sites.

As the shooting proceeded, Sergeant Keller strolled down from his machine-gun nests to talk with Sergeant Jurich. While they watched the shooting at close range, Jurich complained about Wohlauf. After the captain had ordered this "shit," he had "sneaked off" to Serokomla and was sitting in the Polish police station.[5] Unable to show off to his new bride, who this time did not travel with him, Wohlauf apparently had no desire to be present at the killing. Subsequently, Wohlauf claimed that he did not have even the faintest memory of the Serokomla action. Perhaps his mind was already on his upcoming trip to Germany to take his bride home.

The shooting lasted until 3:00 p.m. Nothing was done about burial; the bodies of the dead Jews were simply left lying in the gravel pits. The policemen stopped in Kock, where they had an afternoon meal. When they returned to their respective lodgings that evening, they were given special rations of alcohol.[6]

Three days after the massacre at Serokomla, Sergeant Jobst* of First Company—dressed in civilian clothes and accompanied by a single Polish translator—departed from Kock for a rendezvous that had been arranged to entrap a member of the Polish resistance who was in hiding between the villages of Serokomla and Talcyn. The trap was successfully sprung, and Jobst captured his man. However, as Jobst was returning to Kock through Talcyn, he was ambushed and killed. The Polish interpreter escaped and reached Kock long after dark with news of the sergeant's death.[7]

Around midnight Sergeant Jurich telephoned battalion head-quarters in Radzyń to report the killing of Jobst.[8] When Keller talked with Jurich following the call, he got the impression that there was no inclination in battalion headquarters to punish the village. Major Trapp soon called back from Radzyń, however, and said that Lublin had ordered a retaliation shooting of 200 people.[9]

The same units that had descended upon Serokomla four days earlier now met at the same crossroads outside Kock early on the morning of September 26. Captain Wohlauf was not in command this time, for he was already on his way to Germany. Instead Major Trapp, accompanied by his adjutant, Lieutenant Hagen, and the battalion staff, was personally in charge.

Upon arrival in Talcyn the entire First Company was shown the body of Sergeant Jobst, which had been left lying in the street on the edge of town.[10] The town was sealed, and the Polish inhabitants were fetched from their homes and collected in the school. Many of the men had already fled the village,[11] but the remaining males were brought to the school gymnasium, where Trapp proceeded to carry out a selection.

Obviously anxious to alienate the local population as little as possible, Trapp and Lieutenant Hagen made the selection in consultation with the Polish mayor. Only two categories of Poles were involved: strangers and temporary residents in Talcyn on the one hand, and those "without sufficient means of existence" on the other.[12] Trapp sent at least one policeman to calm the women being held in nearby classrooms, who were crying and screaming in desperation.[13] Seventy-eight Polish men were selected by this process. They were taken outside of town and shot. As one German policeman recalled, they shot only "the poorest of the poor."[14]

Lieutenant Buchmann took some of the men directly back to Radzyń, but others stopped in Kock for lunch. They were in the middle of their meal when they learned that the killing for the day was not yet over. Still far short of his retaliation quota of 200, Trapp had apparently hit upon an ingenious way to meet it without further aggravating relations with the local population. Instead of shooting more Poles in Talcyn, his policemen would shoot Jews from the Kock ghetto.[15]

One German policeman, a driver who was on his way to Radzyń, claimed that he stopped at the ghetto on the edge of town to warn of the imminent action.[16] Such warnings, of course, were to no avail for a trapped population. Search squads of German police entered the ghetto and proceeded to grab anyone they could find, regardless of age or sex. Older Jews who could not march to the shooting site were gunned down on the spot. One policeman later testified, "Although I was supposed to take part in the search, here too I was able to mill around the streets. I disapproved of the Jewish actions in any form and thus did not deliver a single Jew to be shot."[17]

As usual, though, the few who shirked or evaded participation did not impede those intent upon their task. The Jews who had been caught in the dragnet were taken out of the ghetto to a large house that backed onto a walled courtyard. In groups of thirty, they were led into the courtyard and forced to lie down next to the wall. On the order of Lieutenant Brand, the Jews were shot by noncommissioned officers equipped with submachine guns. The bodies were left lying until the next day, when work Jews from the ghetto were fetched to bury their dead in a mass grave.[18] Major Trapp immediately reported to Lublin that 3 "bandits," 78 Polish "accomplices," and 180 Jews had been executed in retaliation for the ambush of Jobst in Talcyn.[19] Apparently the man who had wept through the massacre at Józefów and still shied from the indiscriminate slaughter of Poles no longer had any inhibitions about shooting more than enough Jews to meet his quota.

If Major Trapp was reconciling himself to his role in the murder of Polish Jewry, Lieutenant Buchmann was not. After Józefów he had informed Trapp that without a direct personal order he would not take part in Jewish actions. He had also asked for a transfer. In making such requests, Buchmann had an important advantage. Before being sent to officer training and becoming a reserve lieutenant, Buchmann had been a driver for Trapp during the battalion's first stint in Poland in 1939. He thus knew Trapp personally. He felt that Trapp "understood" him and was not "indignant" about the position he took.[20]

Trapp did not obtain an immediate transfer for Buchmann back to Germany, but he did protect him and accommodate his request not to participate in Jewish actions. Buchmann was stationed in Radzyń in the same building as the battalion staff, so it was not difficult to work out a procedure that avoided any "refusal to obey orders." Whenever a Jewish action was planned, orders were passed directly from headquarters to Buchmann's deputy, Sergeant Grund.* When Grund would ask Buchmann if he wished to accompany the platoon on its forthcoming action, Buchmann knew that it was a Jewish action and declined. Thus, he had not gone with First Company to either Międzyrzec or Serokomla. Talcyn did not begin as a Jewish action, however, and Buchmann was in the school when Trapp carried out the selection of the Poles, though it was no accident that Trapp sent him directly back to Radzyń before the killing of Jews from the Kock ghetto began.

In Radzyń Buchmann had made no effort to hide his feelings. On the contrary, he "was indignant about how the Jews were treated and openly expressed these views at every opportunity."[21] It was obvious to those around him that Buchmann was a very "reserved," "refined" man, a "typical civilian" who had no desire to be a soldier.[22]

For Buchmann, Talcyn was the final straw. On the afternoon he returned, the desk clerk tried to report to him, but he "had immediately gone to his room and locked himself in. For days Buchmann would not talk to me, although we knew each other well. He was very angry and complained bitterly, saying something to the effect, 'Now I won't do this shit any longer. I have a noseful.' "[23] Buchmann not only complained. In late September he also wrote directly to Hamburg, urgently requesting a transfer. He could not carry out those tasks "alien to the police" that his unit was being given in Poland.[24]

If Buchmann's behavior was tolerated and protected by Trapp, it received mixed reactions from his men. "Among my subordinates many understood my position, but others made disparaging remarks about me and looked down their noses at me."[25] A few men in the ranks followed his example, however, and told the company first sergeant, Kammer, "that they were neither able nor willing to take part in such actions anymore." Kammer did not report them. Instead he yelled at them, calling them "shitheads" who "were good for nothing." But for the most part he freed them from participating in further Jewish actions.[26] In so doing, Kammer was following the example Trapp had set from the beginning. As long as there was no shortage of men willing to do the murderous job at hand, it was much easier to accommodate Buchmann and the men who emulated him than to make trouble over them.

12

The Deportations Resume

BY THE END OF SEPTEMBER 1942 RESERVE POLICE BATTALION
101 had participated in the shooting of approximately 4,600 Jews
and 78 Poles and had helped deport approximately 15,000 Jews
to the extermination camp at Treblinka. These murderous
activities had involved eight separate actions stretched over
three months. On three occasions—the first deportation from
Parczew, the shooting at Łomazy, and the deportation from
Międzyrzec—the policemen had worked alongside Hiwi units
from Trawniki. On the other five—Józefów, the second Parczew
deportation, Serokomla, Talcyn, and Kock—the policemen had
worked alone.

The policemen were able to keep these actions distinct in their
memories; they could describe each in some detail and date

them fairly precisely. Between the beginning of October and early November, however, the activities of Reserve Police Battalion 101 intensified greatly. One action followed another in unremitting succession as tens of thousands of Jews were deported from the county of Radzyń in repeated ghetto-clearing operations. It is therefore very difficult to reconstruct the events of these deadly six weeks. The policemen's memories blurred as one action ran into another. They could still recall some particular incidents but could no longer fit them into a chronological sequence of distinct operations. My reconstruction of this rapid sequence of events, to which the confused memories of the policemen must be matched, is based above all upon the immediate postwar research of the Polish-Jewish historian Tatiana Brustin-Berenstein and the Jewish Historical Institute in Warsaw.[1]

In early September the disposition of Order Police in the Lublin district was modified. A fourth security zone was created, which included the three counties Biała Podlaska, Hrubieszów, and Chełm along the district's eastern border. This permitted the transfer of the First and Second Platoons of Gnade's Second Company from the county of Biała Podlaska to the towns of Międzyrzec and Komarówka in northern Radzyń county.[2]

In the last week of September most of the remaining Jews in Biała Podlaska followed Second Company; they were rounded up and transferred to the now nearly empty ghetto in Międzyrzec.[3] The Międzyrzec "transit ghetto" was also "restocked" in September and October from towns in the county of Radzyń, directly from Komarówka as well as from Wohyn and Czemierniki via Parczew.[4] Of all these transfers, the policemen remembered only the one from Komarówka, where Second Platoon of Second Company was regularly stationed.[5] Among the Jews in Komarówka was a woman from Hamburg who had formerly owned a movie theater—the Millertor-Kino—that one of the policemen had frequented.[6] The ghetto at Łuków served as a second "transit ghetto," receiving Jews from other small towns in the county of Radzyń.[7] This process of concentration was, of course, an ominous prelude to the renewed death transports to Treblinka and the systematic campaign to make the northern Lublin district *judenfrei*, or "free of Jews."

The coordinating center for the October "offensive" against the ghettos of Radzyń county was the branch office of the Security Police under Untersturmführer Fritz Fischer. Administration of the Radzyń, Łuków, and Międzyrzec ghettos had been taken over by Security Police officers in June 1942,[8] but local manpower was quite limited. The Radzyń branch office and its outpost in Łuków had perhaps a total of forty German Security Police and ethnic German "helpers" between them. Fischer also had a permanent unit of twenty Hiwis at his disposal. Międzyrzec, Łuków, and Radzyń had a total of forty to fifty Gendarmerie.[9] Clearly this limited force of Security Police and Gendarmerie, even with Fischer's own Hiwi unit, was utterly dependent on outside help for deporting the Jews from these ghettos. Once again, Reserve Police Battalion 101 provided the bulk of the manpower, without which the ghetto clearing could never have been carried out.

The deportations to Treblinka resumed on October 1, when 2,000 Jews were shipped from the ghetto of Radzyń. On October 5 5,000 Jews and on October 8 a further 2,000 Jews were deported to Treblinka from Łuków. In a parallel action, thousands of Jews were deported from Międzyrzec on October 6 and 9. Presumably the trains from Łuków and Międzyrzec were joined after loading, though no witnesses testified to this effect. Between October 14 and 16, the clearing of the Radzyń ghetto was completed by transferring its 2,000 to 3,000 Jews to Międzyrzec. Their stay was brief, for Jews were deported from Międzyrzec again on October 27 and November 7. On November 6, the 700 remaining Jews in Kock were taken to Łuków. The following day, as the ghetto in Międzyrzec was also being cleared, 3,000 Jews were deported to Treblinka from Łuków.[10] Interspersed with the deportations were occasional shootings to liquidate those Jews who had successfully evaded the ghetto clearing by hiding or had been deliberately left behind, either for lack of space in the trains or to work in cleanup details. When the six-week onslaught was over, the men of Reserve Police Battalion 101 had helped deport more than 27,000 Jews to Treblinka in eight actions and had killed perhaps 1,000 more during the roundups and in at least four "mopping up" shootings.

What the policemen remembered about each of these actions varied tremendously. The opening operation, the deportation of 2,000 Jews from Radzyń on October 1, was carried out jointly by men from First Company and twenty Hiwis under Untersturmführer Fischer. There was apparently little killing on the spot, though the Hiwis fired frequent warning shots to drive the Jews to the train station.[11] The following day, October 2, Sergeant Steinmetz's Third Platoon of Second Company completed the liquidation of the Parczew ghetto by shooting—on Gnade's orders—more than a hundred Jews who had apparently been brought there too late for the transfer to Międzyrzec.[12]

Thereafter simultaneous deportations were carried out from the two transit ghettos in Łuków and Międzyrzec by First and Second Companies respectively. Since early September, Lieutenant Gnade had made his new company headquarters in Międzyrzec. To avoid the difficult Polish pronunciation, the men of Second Company referred to it by the apt German nickname *Menschenschreck*, or "human horror." Gnade's driver, Alfred Heilmann,* remembered taking the lieutenant one evening to a five-hour meeting in a building on the main square in Międzyrzec that served as the Security Police headquarters and prison. During the meeting, a terrible cry arose from the cellar. Two or three SS officers came out of the building and emptied their submachine guns through the cellar windows. "So now we'll have quiet," one remarked as they reentered the building. Heilmann cautiously approached the cellar window, but the stench was terrible and he turned back. The noise from upstairs increased until Gnade emerged at midnight quite drunk and told Heilmann that the ghetto would be cleared the next morning.[13]

The men of Second Company who were stationed in Międzyrzec were awakened around 5:00 a.m. They were joined by Drucker's Second Platoon from Komarówka as well as a sizable contingent of Hiwis. Drucker's men apparently cordoned off the ghetto while the Hiwis and the rest of the Order Police drove the Jews into the main square. Gnade and others used their whips on the assembled Jews to enforce quiet. Some died from the beatings even before the march to the train station began.[14] Heilmann watched while the Jews who had been incarcerated in the cellar prison of Security Police headquarters were hauled out and led away. They were covered with excrement and obviously had not been fed in days. After the required number of Jews had been assembled, they were marched to the train station. Those who could not walk were shot on the spot, and the guards shot ruthlessly into the column of Jews whenever it slowed.[15]

A small contingent of policemen was already at the train station in order to keep Polish spectators away. Gnade supervised the loading of the arriving Jews onto the train. Shooting and beating were employed without restraint to maximize the number of Jews crammed into each cattle car. Twenty-two years later, Gnade's first sergeant made a very unusual confession, given the pronounced reluctance of the witnesses to criticize their former comrades. "To my regret, I must say that First Lieutenant Gnade gave me the impression that the entire business afforded him a great deal of pleasure."[16]

But even the most unfettered violence could not overcome the shortage of train cars, and when the doors were finally forced shut, about 150 Jews—mostly women and children but also some men—remained. Gnade summoned Drucker and told him to take these Jews to the cemetery. At the cemetery entrance the policemen chased away the "eager spectators"[17] and waited until First Sergeant Ostmann* arrived in a truck with a supply of vodka for the shooters. Ostmann turned to one of his men who had hitherto avoided shooting and chided him. "Drink up now, Pfeiffer.* You're in for it this time, because the Jewesses must be shot. You've gotten yourself out of it so far, but now you must go to it." An execution squad of about twenty men was sent into the cemetery. The Jews were brought in groups of twenty, men first and then women and children. They were forced to lie face down near the cemetery wall and then shot from behind in the neck. Each policeman fired seven or eight times.[18] At the cemetery gate one Jew sprang at Drucker with a syringe but was quickly subdued. The other Jews sat quietly awaiting their fate, even after the shooting began. "They were quite emaciated and looked half starved to death," one guard remembered.[19]

The number of victims of this Międzyrzec deportation of October 6 and a subsequent one three days later can not be ascertained. Witness accounts vary greatly.[20] In any case, the ghetto was restocked once again in mid-October, when 2,000 to 3,000 Jews were brought from Radzyń. These Jews were assembled early on the morning of October 14 and loaded onto a caravan of more than a hundred horse-drawn wagons. Guarded by Polish police, ethnic Germans of the Sonderdienst, and a few policemen from First Company, the caravan slowly made its way to Międzyrzec twenty-nine kilometers to the north, arriving after dark. The empty wagons were then returned to Radzyń.[21]

In subsequent actions on October 27 and November 7, the Międzyrzec ghetto was cleared of all but some 1,000 work Jews. These actions must have been smaller than those of early October, for neither Hiwi units nor Security Police from Radzyń were employed to assist the policemen. Gnade was now totally in charge. He apparently introduced one further step in the deportation procedure—the "strip search." After being assembled in the marketplace, the deportees were driven into two barracks where they were forced to undress and searched for valuables. They were allowed to put only their underclothing back on, despite the cold autumn weather. Scantily clad, they were marched to the train station and packed into cattle cars destined for Treblinka.[22] With the conclusion of the November 7 action, units of Reserve Police Battalion 101 had deported at least 25,000 Jews from the city of "human horror" to Treblinka since late August.

While Gnade was deporting Jews from Międzyrzec, First

Company was carrying out parallel actions in Łuków. Captain Wohlauf was no longer in charge, however. His relations with Trapp had steadily deteriorated, and the major spoke openly of his dismay over the Międzyrzec episode in which Wohlauf had taken his new bride to witness the ghetto clearing.[23] After the massacre at Serokomla, Wohlauf had accompanied his wife to Hamburg, where he remained for several days before returning. Back in Radzyń by mid-October, he became ill with jaundice. In early November his only brother, a Luftwaffe pilot, was killed, and several days later his father died in Dresden. Wohlauf returned to Dresden for the funeral, reported sick, and returned once again to Hamburg for treatment of his jaundice as an outpatient. While recuperating, he learned that his request to be recalled from frontline duty as the only surviving son had been approved. He returned to Radzyń only briefly in January 1943 to pick up his personal belongings.[24]

If Wohlauf had extricated himself from Reserve Police Battalion 101, his men enjoyed no similar respite. Joined by Steinmetz's men from Łomazy and Parczew (Third Platoon, Second Company) as well as a unit of Hiwis, they carried out two deportations from Łuków, of 5,000 and 2,000 on October 5 and 8. Memories of the deportations differed drastically. Some claimed that there had been only occasional shots and virtually no killing.[25] Others remembered much shooting.[26] Indeed, one policeman barely escaped being hit by a stray bullet.[27] The head of the Jewish council, along with other prominent Jews, was killed at the assembly point—the *Schweinemarkt*, or "hog market"—during the first deportation. Many who hid successfully during the first deportation were discovered and deported three days later.[28] The conclusion of one policeman that the deportation from Łuków was "decidedly more orderly and humane" than the August deportation from Międzyrzec reveals little, given the unmatched brutality of the latter.[29]

After the initial deportations, Steinmetz's platoon returned to Parczew, and the battalion headquarters was shifted from Radzyń to Łuków. On November 6, Lieutenant Brand and Sergeant

Jurich supervised the transfer to Łuków of the last 700 Jews in Kock. When Jurich discovered that many Jews were missing, he shot the head of the Jewish council on the spot. As in the transfer from Radzyń to Międzyrzec, horse-drawn wagons were used and reached Łuków only late at night.[30]

The concluding deportation of the 3,000 to 4,000 Jews from Łuków began the next morning (November 7), an operation that continued for several days.[31] No longer in any doubt about their fate, the Jews sang, "We are traveling to Treblinka," as they were marched away. In retaliation for the failure of the Jewish ghetto police to report hidden Jews, the Order Police carried out a shooting of forty to fifty Jews.[32]

During this final deportation many Jews had apparently been hiding tenaciously. After the trains left, the Security Police employed a ruse to lure the surviving Jews from their concealment. It was announced throughout the ghetto that new identity cards would be issued. Anyone who reported for his card would be spared; anyone found without one would be shot immediately. Hoping at least for another brief respite between deportations, desperate Jews emerged from their hiding places and reported. After at least 200 Jews had been collected, they were marched outside Łuków and shot on November 11. Another group was collected and shot on November 14.[33]

Members of Reserve Police Battalion 101 were caught up in at least one, if not both, of these final shootings. Because Trapp and the bulk of First Company were apparently elsewhere, Buchmann was temporarily without his protector. He and virtually every available man on the battalion staff—clerks, communications men, and drivers who had hitherto avoided direct participation in mass executions—suddenly found themselves pressed into service by the local Security Police. In contrast to the blurred recollections of those who by autumn were jaded veterans of many Jewish actions, the memories of shooting Jews in Łuków were quite vivid for these initiates.[34] One policeman recalled that word of an imminent shooting action had already spread the night before.

On this evening an entertainment unit of Berlin police—so-called welfare for the front—was our guest. This entertainment unit consisted of musicians and performers. The members of this unit had likewise heard of the pending shooting of the Jews. They asked, indeed even emphatically begged, to be allowed to participate in the execution of the Jews. This request was granted by the battalion.[35]

The following morning Buchmann returned from a meeting and led his men to the Security Police building near the entrance to the ghetto. The policemen took up guard posts along both sides of the street. The iron gate of the ghetto opened and several hundred Jews were driven out. The policemen marched them out of town.[36]

More guards were needed for yet another column of Jews. Members of the battalion staff were thereupon ordered to report to Security Police headquarters. A few days earlier they had watched from the windows of the school that had been turned into their lodgings as the Jews of Łuków were marched past on the way to the train station. Now it was their turn to take part. They received a contingent of fifty to a hundred Jews from the Security Police and followed the same route out of town.[37]

Meanwhile the first column had turned off the road and followed a path to an open meadow of sandy soil. A SS officer called a halt and told Buchmann's deputy, Hans Prutzmann,* to begin shooting the Jews. Prutzmann formed a firing squad of fifteen to twenty-five men, primarily volunteers from the entertainment unit who had been equipped with guns by the battalion. The Jews had to undress, the men entirely and the women down to their underclothing. They placed their shoes and clothing on a pile and were led off in groups to the execution spot some fifty meters away. Here they lay face down and, as usual, were shot from behind by policemen using fixed bayonets as aiming guides. Buchmann stood nearby with several SS officers.[38]

When the men from the battalion staff reached the sandy

meadow, the shooting was already underway. Buchmann approached and told them that they had to provide a firing squad to shoot the Jews they had brought with them. One staff clerk in charge of uniforms asked to be let out. "Because there were children among the Jews we had brought and at the time I myself was a father with a family of three children, I told the lieutenant something to the effect that I was unable to shoot and asked if he couldn't assign me to something else." Several others immediately made the same request.[39]

Buchmann thus found himself in the same position as Trapp at Józefów and basically reacted in the same way. Ordered directly by superior SS officers of the Security Police to carry out a mass shooting of Jews with the Order Police under his command, Buchmann complied. Faced with subordinates who explicitly requested a different assignment, just as he had done at Józefów, Buchmann consented and excused four men. As the shooting continued, Buchmann removed himself. In the company of the senior member of the staff contingent, a man whom he knew well and had excused from the firing squad upon request, he walked a considerable distance from the execution site.

Some time later communications men and drivers from the battalion staff were ordered to take part in another shooting of Jews collected by the Security Police in Łuków. This time Buchmann was not present.[40] His numerous requests for a recall to Hamburg had finally been granted. Upon his return he first took a position as an air defense officer. Between January and August 1943 he served as adjutant to the police president of Hamburg. He was then allowed to return to his lumber firm, whose business took him to France, Austria, and Czechoslovakia during the last years of the war. Just prior to his release from the Order Police, he had been promoted to the rank of reserve first lieutenant.[41] Clearly Trapp had not only protected him from Jewish actions in Poland (with the exception of the Łuków shooting) but also insured that his personnel file contained a very positive evaluation that in no way damaged his career.

13

The Strange Health
of Captain Hoffmann

UNTIL THE FALL OF 1942 THIRD COMPANY OF RESERVE POLICE
Battalion 101, under Captain and SS-Hauptsturmführer Wolfgang Hoffmann, had led a charmed existence, largely spared
from the killing that was becoming the predominant activity of
the other units in the battalion. At Józefów two platoons of Third
Company had initially been assigned to the outer cordon, and
none of its members had been sent to the firing squads in the
woods. When the battalion was transferred to the northern
security zone in the Lublin district, Second and Third Platoons
of Third Company were stationed in the county of Puławy. Third
Platoon was stationed in the town of Puławy itself, under
Hoffmann's direct command, and Lieutenant Hoppner's Second
Platoon nearby, first in Kurów and then in Wandolin. In the

county of Puławy the bulk of the Jewish population had already been deported to Sobibór in May 1942—the first Jews to be killed in that camp—and the remnants of the region's Jewish population were concentrated in a "collection ghetto" in the small town of Końskowola, about six kilometers east of Puławy. Thus, only Lieutenant Peters's First Platoon, stationed in the neighboring county of Radzyń, had been involved in the August deportations and late September shootings. Nor did the Polish resistance initially disturb Third Company's sojourn in Puławy. Hoffmann later reported that they had found the county "relatively quiet," and that before October not a single encounter with "armed bandits" had taken place.[1]

In early October, however, Third Company's luck ran out. The "collection ghetto" at Końskowola, containing some 1,500 to 2,000 Jews,[2] was scheduled to be cleared, like the ghettos in neighboring Radzyń. Northern Lublin was to be *judenfrei*. A considerable force was assembled for the task: all three platoons of Third Company, including Peters's from Czemierniki; the local Gendarmerie post of some twelve men under First Lieutenant Jammer* (whose main task was to supervise the work of the local Polish police); a roving motorized company of Gendarmerie under First Lieutenant Messmann*; and about a hundred Hiwis and three SS men from Lublin.[3] Third Company assembled in Puławy, where Hoffmann read his instructions from a piece of paper. The ghetto was to be combed and the Jews collected in the marketplace; those who could not move—the old, frail, and sick as well as infants—were to be shot on the spot. This had been standard procedure, he added, for quite some time.[4]

The policemen drove to Końskowola. Hoffmann, the senior police officer present, consulted with Jammer and Messmann and distributed the men. In contrast to the usual practice, the Hiwis were assigned to the cordon along with some of the police. The search commandos who initially entered the ghetto were composed of men from both Third Company and Messmann's motorized Gendarmerie. Each commando was assigned a particular block of houses.[5]

The ghetto had been afflicted by an epidemic of dysentery, and many of the Jews could not walk to the marketplace or even rise from their beds. Thus shooting was heard everywhere as the commandos conducted their first sweep through the ghetto. One policeman recalled, "I myself shot six old people in the dwellings; they were bedridden people who explicitly asked me to do it."[6] After the first sweep was completed and most of the surviving Jews were collected at the marketplace, the units assigned to the cordon were called in to carry out a search of the ghetto. They had heard the continuous shooting already. As they searched the ghetto, they encountered corpses strewn everywhere.[7]

Many of the men remembered in particular the building that had served as the ghetto hospital—in fact nothing more than a large room filled with three or four levels of bunk beds and emitting a terrible stench. A group of five or six policemen was assigned to enter the room and liquidate the forty or fifty patients, most of whom were suffering from dysentery. "In any case almost all of them were extremely emaciated and totally undernourished. One could say they consisted of nothing but skin and bones."[8] No doubt hoping to escape the smell as quickly as possible, the policemen opened fire wildly as soon as they entered the room. Under the hail of bullets, bodies toppled from the upper bunks. "This way of proceeding so disgusted me, and I was so ashamed, that I immediately turned around and left the room," reported one policeman.[9] Another remembered, "At the sight of the sick, it was not possible for me to shoot at one of the Jews, and I intentionally aimed all my shots wide." His sergeant, who had joined in the shooting, noticed his marksmanship, for "after the conclusion of the action he took me aside and reviled me as a 'traitor' and 'coward' and threatened to report the incident to Captain Hoffmann. However, he did not do that."[10]

At the marketplace the Jews were separated, men on one side, women and children on the other. There was a selection of men between eighteen and forty-five, particularly skilled workers. Possibly some women were selected for work as well. These Jews were marched out of the ghetto to the train station outside

Puławy, to be shipped to work camps in Lublin. They were in such a weakened condition that many could not make the five-kilometer march to the train station. Witnesses estimated that 500 to 1,000 Jews were selected for labor, but 100 were shot en route after collapsing from exhaustion. [11]

As the Jews deemed suitable for work were marched out of town, the remaining Jews—800 to 1,000 women and children as well as a large number of elderly men—were simultaneously led off to a shooting site in a woods beyond the edge of town. Peters's First Platoon and some of Messmann's Gendarmerie supplied the firing squads. First the Jewish men were taken into the woods, forced to lie face down, and shot. The women and children followed. [12] One of the policemen chatted with the head of the Jewish council, a German Jew from Munich, until he too was led away at the end. [13] When the policemen who had escorted the work Jews to the train station returned to the marketplace in Końskowola, they found it empty, but they could hear shooting from the woods. They were assigned to make one more sweep through the ghetto, after which they were allowed to break ranks and relax. By then it was late afternoon, and some of the men found a pleasant farmhouse and played cards. [14]

Twenty-five years later Wolfgang Hoffmann claimed to remember absolutely nothing of the Końskowola action, in which 1,100 to 1,600 Jews had been killed in a single day by policemen under his command. His amnesia may have been grounded not only in judicial expediency but also in the health problems he was experiencing during his assignment in Puławy. At the time Hoffmann blamed his illness on a dysentery vaccine that he had taken in late August. In the 1960s he found it more convenient to trace his illness to the psychological stress of the Józefów massacre. [15] Whatever the cause, Hoffmann began to suffer from diarrhea and severe stomach cramps in September and October 1942. By his own account, his condition—diagnosed as vegetative colitis—was terribly aggravated by bumpy movement, as on a bicycle or in a car, and thus he personally led few of his company's actions at this time. Nonetheless, out of "soldierly enthusiasm" and the hope of improvement, he refused to report his illness until the end of October. Only on November 2 did he enter the army hospital on doctor's orders.

Uniformly, Hoffmann's men offered a different perspective. By their observation his "alleged" bouts of stomach cramps, confining him safely to bed, coincided all too consistently with company actions that might involve either unpleasantness or danger. It became common for the men to predict, upon hearing the night before of a pending action, that the company chief would be bedridden by morning.

Hoffmann's behavior rankled his men even more because of two aggravating factors. First, he had always been strict and unapproachable—a typical "base officer" who liked his white collar and gloves, wore his SS insignia on his uniform, and demanded considerable deference. His apparent timidity in the face of action now seemed the height of hypocrisy, and they derided him as a *Pimpf*, the term for a member of the ten- to fourteen-year-old age group of the Hitler Youth—in effect a "Hitler cub scout."

Second, Hoffmann tried to compensate for his immobility by intensified supervision of his subordinates. He insisted on giving orders for everything from his bed, to all intents functioning not only as company commander but as platoon commander as well. Before every patrol or action, the noncommissioned officers reported to Hoffmann's bedroom for detailed instructions, and afterward they reported to him personally again. Third Platoon, stationed in Puławy, had no lieutenant and was led by the senior sergeant, Justmann.* He in particular was allowed to make no disposition of men without Hoffmann's approval. Justmann and the other sergeants felt they had been demoted to the rank of corporal.[16]

Hoffmann was hospitalized in Puławy from November 2 to November 25. He then returned to Germany for convalescent leave until after New Year's. He briefly led his company again, for one month, before returning to Germany for renewed treatment. During this second leave in Germany, Hoffmann learned that Trapp had had him relieved of his company command.

Hoffmann's relations with Trapp had already soured in January, when the battalion commander ordered all his officers, NCOs, and men to sign a special declaration pledging not to steal, plunder, or take goods without paying for them. Hoffmann wrote Trapp a blistering reply in which he explicitly refused to carry out this order because it deeply violated his "sense of honor."[17] Trapp had also heard unflattering accounts of Hoffmann's inactivity in Puławy from his temporary replacement, First Lieutenant Messmann, commander of the motorized Gendarmerie company that had taken part in the Końskowola massacre. Trapp consulted with First Sergeant Karlsen* of Third Company, who confirmed the pattern of Hoffmann's illness. On February 23, 1943, Trapp submitted his request that Hoffmann be dismissed from his post as company commander because he always reported sick before important actions and this "deficient sense of service" was not good for the morale of his men.[18]

The proud, touchy Hoffmann responded bitterly and energetically to his dismissal, claiming once again that his "honor as an officer and soldier had been most deeply hurt." He accused Trapp of acting out of personal spite.[19] Trapp responded in detail and was upheld. The commander of the Order Police for the Lublin district concluded that Hoffmann's behavior had been "in no way satisfactory," that if he really had been sick, he was irresponsible in not reporting according to regulations, and that he should be given an opportunity to prove himself with another unit.[20]

Hoffmann was in fact transferred to a police battalion that experienced frontline action in the fall of 1943 in Russia, where he earned the Iron Cross Second Class. He was later given command of a battalion of White Russian auxiliaries near Minsk, and then of a battalion of Caucasian "volunteers." He ended the war as first staff officer for the commanding police general in Poznań.[21] In short, from his subsequent career it would be difficult to conclude that Hoffmann's behavior in the fall of 1942 was a case of cowardice, as his men and Trapp suspected. Ill he was. Whether his illness was initially caused by the murderous activities of Reserve Police Battalion 101 cannot be established, but he had the symptoms of psychologically induced "irritable colon" or "adaptive colitis." Certainly, Hoffmann's duties aggravated his condition. Moreover, it is clear that rather than using his illness to escape an assignment that involved killing the Jews of Poland, Hoffmann made every effort to hide it from his superiors and to avoid being hospitalized. If mass murder was giving Hoffmann stomach pains, it was a fact he was deeply ashamed of and sought to overcome to the best of his ability.

14

The "Jew Hunt"

By MID-NOVEMBER 1942, FOLLOWING THE MASSACRES AT JÓZE-
fów, Łomazy, Serokomla, Końskowola, and elsewhere, and the
liquidation of the ghettos in Międzyrzec, Łuków, Parczew,
Radzyń, and Kock, the men of Reserve Police Battalion 101 had
participated in the outright execution of at least 6,500 Polish
Jews and the deportation of at least 42,000 more to the gas
chambers of Treblinka. Still their role in the mass murder
campaign was not finished. Once the towns and ghettos of the
northern Lublin district had been cleared of Jews, Reserve
Police Battalion 101 was assigned to track down and systematically eliminate all those who had escaped the previous roundups
and were now in hiding. In short, they were responsible for
making their region completely *judenfrei*.

One year earlier, on October 15, 1941, the head of the General Government, Hans Frank, had decreed that any Jew caught outside ghetto boundaries was to be hauled before a special court and sentenced to death. This decree was at least partly in response to the pleas of German public health officials in Poland, who realized that only the most draconian punishment could deter starving Jews from leaving the ghettos to smuggle food and thereby spreading the typhus epidemic that was ravaging the ghettos. For example, the head of public health for the district of Warsaw, Dr. Lambrecht, had argued for a law threatening Jews found outside the ghetto with "fear of death through hanging" that was "greater than fear of death through starvation."[1] Complaints soon arose concerning the implementation of Frank's decree, however. The manpower available to escort captured Jews was too limited, the distances to be covered too great, the judicial procedures of the special courts too cumbersome and time-consuming. The remedy was simple; all judicial procedures would be dispensed with, and Jews found outside the ghettos would be shot on the spot. At a meeting between the district governors and Frank on December 16, 1941, the deputy to the governor of the Warsaw district noted how "gratefully one had welcomed the shooting order of the commander of the Order Police, whereby Jews encountered in the countryside could be shot."[2]

In short, even before they were systematically deported to the death camps, the Jews of Poland were subject to summary execution outside the ghettos. This "shooting order," however, was loosely applied in the district of Lublin, for there—in comparison to the rest of the General Government— ghettoization was only partial. Jews living in the small towns and villages of northern Lublin were not concentrated in the transit ghettos of Międzyrzec and Łuków until September and October 1942. The predecessor to Trapp's unit in the northern Lublin district, Police Battalion 306, did indeed shoot Jews encountered outside of town on occasion.[3] But the systematic tracking down of Jews did not begin until ghetto-ization was complete. It truly intensified only after the ghettos were liquidated.

In late August Parczew became the first ghetto in the battalion's security zone to be completely cleared. According to Sergeant Steinmetz, whose Third Platoon of Second Company was stationed there, Jews continued to be found in the area. They were incarcerated in the local prison. Gnade ordered Steinmetz to shoot the imprisoned Jews. "This order of Lieutenant Gnade explicitly extended to all future cases as well. . . . I was given the task of keeping my territory free of Jews."[4] Lieutenant Drucker likewise remembered receiving orders from battalion headquarters in late August "that Jews wandering freely about the countryside were to be shot on the spot when encountered." But until the final deportations of Jews from the small villages to the transit ghettos, the order was not fully implemented.

By October the order was for real.[5] Placards announced that all Jews who did not go to the ghettos would be shot.[6] The "shooting order" was made part of regular company instructions to the men and given repeatedly, especially before they were sent on patrol.[7] No one could be left in any doubt that not a single Jew was to remain alive in the battalion's security zone. In official jargon, the battalion made "forest patrols" for "suspects."[8] As the surviving Jews were to be tracked down and shot like animals, however, the men of Reserve Police Battalion 101 unofficially dubbed this phase of the Final Solution the *Judenjagd*, or "Jew hunt."[9]

The "Jew hunt" took many forms. Most spectacular were two battalion sweeps through the Parczew forest in the fall of 1942 and the spring of 1943, the latter alongside army units. Not only Jews but partisans and escaped Russian prisoners of war were the targets of these sweeps, though Jews seem to have been the primary victims of the first one, in October 1942. Georg Leffler* of Third Company recalled:

We were told that there were many Jews hiding in the forest. We therefore searched through the woods in a skirmish line but could find nothing, because the Jews were obviously well hidden. We combed the woods a second time. Only then could we discover individual chimney pipes sticking out of the earth. We discovered that Jews had hidden themselves in underground bunkers here. They were hauled out, with resistance in only one bunker. Some of the comrades climbed down into this bunker and hauled the Jews out. The Jews were then shot on the spot. . . . the Jews had to lie face down on the ground and were killed by a neck shot. Who was in the firing squad I don't remember. I think it was simply a case where the men standing nearby were ordered to shoot them. Some fifty Jews were shot, including men and women of all ages, because entire families had hidden themselves there. . . . the shooting took place quite publicly. No cordon was formed at all, for a number of Poles from Parczew were standing directly by the shooting site. They were then ordered, presumably by Hoffmann, to bury the Jews who had been shot in a half-finished bunker.[10]

Other units of the battalion also remembered discovering bunkers and killing Jews in batches of twenty to fifty.[11] One policeman estimated the total body count for the October sweep at 500.[12]

By spring the situation had altered somewhat. The few Jews still alive had for the most part been able to join bands of partisans and escaped POWs. The spring sweep uncovered a "forest camp" of escaped Russians and Jews who offered armed resistance. Some 100 to 120 Jews and Russians were killed. The battalion suffered at least one fatality, for Trapp's adjutant, Lieutenant Hagen, was accidentally killed by his own men.[13]

A number of Jews had been sent as workers to various large agricultural estates that the German occupiers had confiscated and now administered. At Gut Jablon, near Parczew, a unit of Steinmetz's platoon loaded the thirty Jewish workers on trucks, drove them to the forest, and killed them with the now routine neck shot. The German administrator, who had not been informed of the impending liquidation of his work force, complained in vain.[14] The German administrator of Gut Pannwitz, near Puławy, encountered the opposite problem of too many Jewish workers. His estate became a refuge for Jews who had fled the ghettos to the nearby forest and then sought sanctuary and food among his work Jews. Whenever the Jewish worker population swelled noticeably, the estate administration phoned Captain Hoffmann, and a German police commando was sent to shoot the surplus Jews.[15] After Hoffmann's hospitalization, his successor, Lieutenant Messmann, formed a flying squadron that systematically eliminated small batches of Jewish workers in a fifty- to sixty-kilometer radius of Puławy. Messmann's driver, Alfred Sperlich,* recalled the procedure:

> In cases where the farmyard and the Jewish lodgings could be reached quickly, I drove into the farmyard at high speed, and the police sprang out and immediately rushed to the Jewish lodgings. Then all the Jews present at that time were driven out and shot in the farmyard near a haystack, potato pit, or dung heap. The victims were almost always naked and were shot in the neck while lying on the ground.

If the road into the farmyard was too visible, however, the police approached stealthily on foot to prevent their victims' escape. Routinely in workplaces near the woods the police found many more Jews than expected.[16]

Some Jews had survived by hiding in town rather than in the woods, but they too were tracked down.[17] The most memorable case was in Kock, where a cellar hiding place was reported by a Polish translator working for the Germans. Four Jews were captured. Under "interrogation," they revealed another cellar hiding place in a large house on the edge of town. A single German policeman and the Polish translator went to the second hiding place, expecting no difficulties. But this was a rare instance in which the Jews had arms, and the approaching policeman was fired upon. Reinforcements were summoned, and a fire fight broke out. In the end four or five Jews were killed in a breakout attempt, and eight to ten others were found dead or badly wounded in the cellar. Only four or five were captured unwounded; they were likewise "interrogated" and shot that evening.[18] The German police then went in search of the owner of the house, a Polish woman who had managed to flee in time. She was tracked to her father's house in a nearby village. Lieutenant Brand presented the father with a stark choice—his life or his daughter's. The man surrendered his daughter, who was shot on the spot.[19]

The most common form of the "Jew hunt" was the small patrol into the forest to liquidate an individual bunker that had been reported. The battalion built up a network of informers and "forest runners," or trackers, who searched for and revealed Jewish hiding places. Many other Poles volunteered information about Jews in the woods who had stolen food from nearby fields, farms, and villages in their desperate attempt to stay alive. Upon receiving such reports, the local police commanders dispatched small patrols to locate the hiding Jews. Time and again the same scenario was played out, with only minor variations. The policemen followed their Polish guides directly to the bunker hideouts and tossed grenades in the openings. The Jews who survived the initial grenade attack and emerged from the bunkers were forced to lie face down for the neck shot. The bodies were routinely left to be buried by the nearest Polish villagers.[20]

These patrols were "too frequent" for most policemen to remember how many they had participated in. "It was more or less our daily bread," said one.[21] The expression "daily bread" was applied to the "Jew hunts" by another policeman as well.[22] From the behavior of the patrol leaders, the men could quickly tell if they faced potential partisan action or were simply searching for reported Jews, who were assumed to be unarmed.[23] According to at least one policeman, the "Jew hunt" patrols predominated. "Such actions were our main task, and in comparison to real partisan actions they were much more numerous."[24]

With these small patrols hunting down surviving Jews, the men of Reserve Police Battalion 101 came almost full circle back to the experience at Józefów. During the large deportation operations, virtually all the policemen had to perform at least cordon duty. They herded masses of people onto the trains but could distance themselves from the killing at the other end of the trip. Their sense of detachment from the fate of the Jews they deported was unshakable.

But the "Jew hunt" was different. Once again they saw their victims face to face, and the killing was personal. More important, each individual policeman once again had a considerable degree of choice. How each exercised that choice revealed the extent to which the battalion had divided into the "tough" and the "weak." In the months since Józefów many had become numbed, indifferent, and in some cases eager killers; others limited their participation in the killing process, refraining when they could do so without great cost or inconvenience. Only a minority of nonconformists managed to preserve a beleaguered sphere of moral autonomy that emboldened them to employ patterns of behavior and stratagems of evasion that kept them from becoming killers at all.

Concerning the eager killers, the wife of Lieutenant Brand remembered vividly one event during a visit to her husband in Poland.

> I was sitting at breakfast one morning with my husband in the garden of our lodgings when an ordinary policeman of my husband's platoon came up to us, stood stiffly at attention, and declared, "Herr Leutnant, I have not yet had breakfast." When my husband looked at him quizzically, he declared further, "I have not yet killed any Jews." It all sounded so cynical that I indignantly reprimanded the man with harsh words and called him—if I remember correctly—a scoundrel. My husband sent the policeman away and then reproached me and told me that I'd get myself in deep trouble talking that way.[25]

Growing callousness can also be seen in the post-shooting behavior of the policemen. After Józefów and the early shootings, the men had returned to their quarters shaken and embittered, without appetite or desire to talk about what they had just done. With the relentless killing, such sensitivities were dulled. One policeman recalled, "At the lunch table some of the comrades made jokes about the experiences they'd had during an action. From their stories I could gather that they had just finished a shooting action. I remember as especially crass that one of the men said now we eat 'the brains of slaughtered Jews.' "[26] Only the witness found this "joke" less than hilarious.

In such an atmosphere it was quite easy for the officers and NCOs to form a "Jew hunt" patrol or firing squad simply by asking for volunteers. Most emphatic in this regard was Adolf Bittner.* "Above all I must categorically say that for the execution commandos basically enough volunteers responded to the request of the officer in charge. . . . I must add further that often there were so many volunteers that some of them had to be turned away."[27] Others were less categorical, noting that in addition to asking for volunteers, sometimes officers or NCOs picked from among those standing nearby, usually men whom they knew to be willing shooters. As Sergeant Bekemeier put it, "In summary one could perhaps say that in small actions, when not so many shooters were needed, there were always enough volunteers available. In larger actions, when a great many shooters were needed, there were also many volunteers, but if this did not suffice, others were also assigned."[28]

Like Bekemeier, Walter Zimmermann* also made a distinction between the large and small executions. Concerning the latter, he noted:

In no case can I remember that anyone was forced to continue participating in the executions when he declared that he was no longer able to. As far as group and platoon actions were concerned, here I must honestly admit that with these smaller executions there were always some comrades who found it easier to shoot Jews than did others, so that the respective commando leaders never had difficulty finding suitable shooters.[29]

Those who did not want to go on the "Jew hunts" or participate in firing squads followed three lines of action. They made no secret of their antipathy to the killing, they never volunteered, and they kept their distance from the officers and NCOs when "Jew hunt" patrols and firing squads were being formed. Some were never chosen simply because their attitude was well known. Otto-Julius Schimke, the first man to step out at Józefów, was frequently assigned to partisan actions but never to a "Jew hunt." "It is not to be excluded," he said, "that because of this incident I was freed from other Jewish actions."[30] Adolf Bittner likewise credited his early and open opposition to the battalion's Jewish actions with sparing him from further involvement.

> I must emphasize that from the first days I left no doubt among my comrades that I disapproved of these measures and never volunteered for them. Thus, on one of the first searches for Jews, one of my comrades clubbed a Jewish woman in my presence, and I hit him in the face. A report was made, and in that way my attitude became known to my superiors. I was never officially punished. But anyone who knows how the system works knows that outside official punishment there is the possibility for chicanery that more than makes up for punishment. Thus I was assigned Sunday duties and special watches.[31]

But Bittner was never assigned to a firing squad.

Gustav Michaelson,* who had lingered among the trucks at Józefów despite his comrades' taunts, also gained a certain immunity due to his reputation. About the frequent "Jew hunts," Michaelson recalled, "No one ever approached me concerning these operations. For these actions the officers took 'men' with them, and in their eyes I was no 'man.' Other comrades who displayed my attitude and my behavior were also spared from such actions."[32]

The tactic of keeping one's distance was invoked by Heinrich Feucht* to explain how he avoided shooting on all but one occasion. "One always had a certain freedom of movement of a few meters, and from experience I noticed very quickly that the platoon leader almost always chose the people standing next to him. I thus always attempted to take a position as far as possible from the center of events."[33] Others likewise sought to avoid shooting by staying in the background.[34]

Sometimes distance and reputation did not suffice, and outright refusal was required to avoid killing. In Second Platoon of Third Company, Lieutenant Hoppner became one of the most zealous practitioners of the "Jew hunt" and eventually tried to impose the policy that everyone had to shoot. Some men who had never shot before then killed their first Jews.[35] But Arthur Rohrbaugh* could not shoot defenseless people. "It was also known to Lieutenant Hoppner that I could not do it. He had already told me on earlier occasions that I must become tougher. In this sense he once said that I too would yet learn the neck shot." On patrol in the woods with Corporal Heiden* and five other policemen, Rohrbaugh encountered three Jewish women and a child. Heiden ordered his men to shoot the Jews, but Rohrbaugh simply walked away. Heiden grabbed his gun and shot the Jews himself. Rohrbaugh credited Trapp for his suffering no negative consequences. "On account of the old man, I think, I had no trouble."[36]

Others were more cautious and refrained from shooting only when no officer was present and they were among trusted comrades who shared their views. As Martin Detmold* recalled, "In small actions it often occurred that Jews whom we had picked up were let go again. That happened when one was sure that no superior could learn anything of it. Over time one learned how to evaluate one's comrades and if one could risk not shooting captured Jews contrary to standing orders but rather letting them go."[37] The battalion communications staff also claimed that they ignored Jews they encountered in the countryside when they were laying lines on their own.[38] When shooting at a distance rather than giving a neck shot, at least one policeman merely fired "into the air."[39]

How many hundreds of Jews—indeed, probably thousands—did Reserve Police Battalion 101 shoot in the course of the "Jew hunt"? No reports of such figures survive for this unit. However, we can get a sense of how important a component the "Jew hunt" was in the Final Solution from surviving reports of three other units operating in Poland.

From May to October 1943, long after the vast bulk of the Jews who had fled from the ghetto roundups and attempted to hide had already been tracked down and shot, the commander of the Order Police for the Lublin district (KdO)—these figures would therefore include the contributions of Reserve Police Battalion 101—reported to his superior in Kraków (BdO) the monthly body count of Jews shot by his men. For this six-month period, long past the killing peak in the Lublin district, the total was 1,695, or an average of nearly 283 per month. Two months were particularly prominent: August, when another large forest sweep was carried out, and October, when the escapees from the Sobibór death camp breakout were tracked down.[40]

More indicative of the killing rate for the "Jew hunt" during the peak period are the reports of the Gendarmerie platoon of Warsaw. This unit of only 80 men, responsible for patroling the nearby towns and countryside surrounding the city, was led by Lieutenant Liebscher, a notoriously energetic and eager participant in the Final Solution. His daily reports from March 26 to September 21, 1943, reflect a total of 1,094 Jews killed by his unit, for an average of nearly 14 Jews per policeman. The peak months, not unexpectedly, were April and May, when Jews were desperately seeking to escape the final liquidation of the Warsaw ghetto and had to pass through Liebscher's territory. Liebscher's reports contained detailed descriptions of a variety of daily incidents. They closed with the heading "Proceeded according to existing guidelines," followed simply by a date, place, and number of Jews, male and female. In the end, even the heading was dropped as superfluous, and only the date, place, and number of Jewish men and women were listed, without further explanation.[41]

Perhaps most relevant and most closely parallel to the situation of Reserve Police Battalion 101 was that of a company of Reserve Police Battalion 133 stationed in Rawa Ruska in the neighboring district of Galicia to the east of Lublin. According to six weekly reports for the period November 1 to December 12, 1942, this company executed 481 Jews who had either evaded deportation by hiding or jumped from trains on the way to Bełżec. For this brief six-week period, therefore, the company on average killed nearly three Jews per policeman in an area that had already been cleared by deportation and was being kept *judenfrei* by the "Jew hunt."[42]

Though the "Jew hunt" has received little attention, it was an important and statistically significant phase of the Final Solution. A not inconsiderable percentage of Jewish victims in the General Government lost their lives in this way. Statistics aside, the "Jew hunt" is a psychologically important key to the mentality of the perpetrators. Many of the German occupiers in Poland may have witnessed or participated in ghetto roundups on several occasions—in a lifetime, a few brief moments that could be easily repressed. But the "Jew hunt" was not a brief episode. It was a tenacious, remorseless, ongoing campaign in which the "hunters" tracked down and killed their "prey" in direct and personal confrontation. It was not a passing phase but an existential condition of constant readiness and intention to kill every last Jew who could be found.

15

The Last Massacres: "Harvest Festival"

ON OCTOBER 28, 1942, THE HSSPF FOR THE GENERAL GOVERN-ment, Wilhelm Krüger, decreed that eight Jewish ghettos could remain in the district of Lublin.[1] Four of the eight sites were within the security zone of Reserve Police Battalion 101: Łuków, Międzyrzec, Parczew, and Końskowola. In fact, only the first two remained as Jewish ghettos after the fall deportations, along with Piaski, Izbica, and Włodawa elsewhere in the Lublin district. Faced with the constant threat of death by starvation and exposure on the one hand, or betrayal and shooting on the other, many Jews who had fled to the forests during the deportations in October and November subsequently returned to the reinstated ghettos of Łuków and Międzyrzec. The winter weather made life in the forests increasingly difficult and precarious; any movement in the snow left tracks, and on at least one occasion frozen feces gave away a Jewish hiding place carved out within a haystack.[2] Thus, when it appeared that the deportations had come to an end, many Jews calculated that they stood a much better chance of survival within one of the permitted ghettos than as hunted prey in the forests.

In fact the deportations from the county of Radzyń had ended for the moment, but life in the ghettos of Łuków and Międzyrzec was not without continuing danger. In Łuków the SS ghetto administrator, Josef Bürger, had 500 to 600 Jews shot in December to reduce the ghetto population.[3] In Międzyrzec 500 Jewish workers in the brush factory who had been spared the fall deportation were deported to the work camp at Trawniki on December 30, 1942.[4] The following night, around 11:00 p.m. on New Year's Eve, Security Police from neighboring Biała Podlaska showed up at the Międzyrzec ghetto in inebriated condition and began shooting the remaining Jews "for sport" until the Radzyń Security Police arrived and chased them away.[5]

After four months of relative calm, the end came. On the night of May 1, the men of Second Company surrounded the ghetto in Międzyrzec, where they had carried out so many deportations the previous fall. Joined once again by a unit from Trawniki, they closed in on the ghetto in the morning and assembled the Jews in the marketplace. The policemen estimated the number of deportees in this action at 700 to 1,000, though one admitted it was said to have been as high as 3,000.[6] One Jewish witness estimated 4,000 to 5,000.[7] Once again the Jews were thoroughly searched and dispossessed in Gnade's undressing barracks and then stuffed into train cars so tightly that the doors would barely close. Some were sent to the Majdanek labor camp in Lublin, but most were deported to the gas chambers of Treblinka to conclude the so-called fifth action in Międzyrzec.[8] The "sixth action" occurred on May 26, when another 1,000 Jews were sent to the Majdanek camp.[9] At that point only 200 Jews remained. Some escaped, but the last 170 were shot by the Security Police on July 17, 1943, in the "seventh" and final action, after which Międzyrzec was proclaimed *judenfrei*. On May 2, simultaneously with the renewed deportations from Międzyrzec by Gnade's Second Company, SS units from Lublin along with Ukrainian auxiliaries from Trawniki liquidated the ghetto in Łuków, deporting an additional 3,000 to 4,000 Jews to Treblinka.[10]

Many of the men who had come to Poland with Reserve Police Battalion 101 in June 1942 were gradually reassigned to new tasks. During the winter of 1942–43, the older men—those born before 1898—were sent back to Germany.[11] At the same time men were culled from each platoon of the battalion and assembled in a special unit under Lieutenant Brand. They were sent back to Zamość in the southern part of the district to take part in the expulsion of Poles from villages as part of Himmler's and Globocnik's plan for a pure German settlement area deep in Poland.[12] In early 1943 a group of younger noncommissioned officers from the battalion was reassigned to the Waffen-SS and sent to specialized training.[13] Somewhat later Lieutenant Gnade was transferred to Lublin to form a special guard company. He took Sergeant Steinmetz as his deputy.[14] Gnade returned briefly to Międzyrzec to conduct the May deportations, however. Finally, Lieutenant Scheer was also reassigned to Lublin, to take command of one of two special "pursuit platoons" (*Jagdzüge*) especially formed to intensify the hunt for partisan bands. Some reinforcements were received to fill the void, especially a group of Berliners to help fill out depleted Second Company.[15] But for the most part, Reserve Police Battalion 101 remained understrength.

Because of the high rate of turnover and reassignment, only a portion of the policemen who had taken part in the first massacre at Józefów were still with the battalion in November 1943, when its participation in the Final Solution culminated in the great "harvest festival" (*Erntefest*) massacre, the single largest German killing operation against Jews in the entire war. With a victim total of 42,000 Jews in the Lublin district, *Erntefest* surpassed even the notorious Babi Yar massacre of more than 33,000 Jews outside Kiev. It was exceeded only by the Rumanian massacre of more than 50,000 Odessan Jews in October 1941.

Erntefest was the culmination of Himmler's crusade to destroy Polish Jewry. As the murder campaign gained momentum in 1942, Himmler had been plagued with complaints from industrial and military authorities about the removal of Jewish workers essential to the war effort. In response to such complaints, which he viewed as pure pretense, he agreed to spare some Jewish workers on the condition that they were lodged in camps and ghettos entirely under SS control. This allowed Himmler to parry pragmatic arguments based on the necessities of the war economy while insuring his ultimate control over the fate of all Jews. For in the end, the sanctuary of the labor camps and work ghettos was only temporary. As Himmler said, "There too the Jews shall likewise one day disappear in accordance with the wish of the Führer."[16]

In the Lublin district, work ghettos in Międzyrzec, Łuków, Piaski, Izbica, and Włodawa had been allowed to continue in existence through the winter of 1942–43. The latter three ghettos were eliminated in March and April 1943; as we have seen, Międzyrzec and Łuków suffered a similar fate in May.[17] Thereafter the only Jews in the Lublin district left alive by German consent were some 45,000 workers in the labor camp empire of Odilo Globocnik. These included a few survivors of the Lublin ghettos, as well as workers sent from the liquidated ghettos of Warsaw and Białystok.

By the fall of 1943, two things were apparent to Himmler. First, the work Jews in the camps would have to be killed if his mission were to be completed. Second, over the past six months Jewish resistance had arisen in Warsaw (April), Treblinka (July), Białystok (August), and Sobibór (October), when the Jews in those places saw no further hope of survival. Until the spring of 1943, the Jews of Poland had clung to the all too understandable but mistaken assumption that even the Nazis could not be so irrational by utilitarian standards as to kill work Jews making essential contributions to the German war economy. They had therefore pursued the desperate strategy of "salvation through labor" as the only hope that a remnant of Jews would survive. This strategy and hope were the crucial preconditions for continuing Jewish compliance. But the Jews were gradually being stripped of their illusions. The Germans encountered resistance when they tried to carry out the final liquidation of the Warsaw and Białystok ghettos, and revolts broke out in the death camps of Treblinka and Sobibór when the work Jews there realized that the camps were about to be closed. Himmler could not expect to liquidate the Lublin work camps gradually or one by one without encountering further Jewish resistance born of desperation. The inmates of the Lublin labor camps would therefore have to be killed in a single massive operation that would catch them by surprise. Such was the genesis of *Erntefest*.[18]

Mass killing on such a scale required planning and preparation. Globocnik's recent successor as SSPF, Jakob Sporrenberg, traveled to Kraków, where he consulted with his superior, Wilhelm Krüger. He returned with a special folder and began issuing instructions.[19] In late October Jewish prisoners were put to work digging trenches just outside the camps at Majdanek, Trawniki, and Poniatowa. Though the trenches were three meters deep and one and a half to three meters wide, the fact that they were dug in a zigzag pattern gave credence to the claim that they were intended as protection against air raids.[20] Mobilization of SS and police units from all over the General Government then began. On the evening of November 2, Sporrenberg met with the commanders of the various forces, which included Waffen-SS units from the districts of Kraków and Warsaw, Police Regiment 22 from Kraków, Lublin's own Police Regiment 25 (including Reserve Police Battalion 101), and the Lublin Security Police, as well as the commanders of the camps at Majdanek, Trawniki, and Poniatowa, and Sporrenberg's SSPF staff. The meeting room was full. Sporrenberg gave instructions from the special folder he had brought back from Kraków.[21] The massive killing operation began the next morning.

Members of Reserve Police Battalion 101 participated in virtually every phase of the *Erntefest* massacre in Lublin. They arrived in the district capital on November 2 (so Trapp presumably attended Sporrenberg's conference) and were lodged overnight. Early on the morning of November 3, they took up their stations. One group from the battalion helped to march Jews from various small work camps around Lublin to the Majdanek concentration camp several kilometers from the city center on the main road leading southeast.[22] The largest contingent of Reserve Police Battalion 101 took up positions five meters apart on both sides of the angled street that led from the main highway past the commandant's house to the entrance of the inner camp. Here they watched as an endless stream of Jews from various work sites in Lublin filed past.[23] Woman guards on bicycles escorted 5,000 to 6,000 women prisoners from the "old airport camp" where they had been employed sorting the warehouses of clothing collected at the death camps. Another 8,000 male Jews were also marched past in the course of the day. Together with the 3,500 to 4,000 Jews already in the camp, they swelled the victim pool to some 16,500 to 18,000.[24] As the Jews passed between the chain of reserve policemen into the camp, music blared from two loudspeaker trucks. Despite the attempt to drown out other noise, the sound of steady gunfire could be heard from the camp.[25]

The Jews were taken to the last row of barracks, where they undressed. Arms raised, hands clasped behind their necks, totally naked, they were led in groups from the barracks through a hole cut in the fence to the trenches that had been dug behind the camp. This route too was guarded by men from Reserve Police Battalion 101.[26]

Stationed only ten meters from the graves, Heinrich Bocholt* of First Company witnessed the killing procedure.

> From my position I could now observe how the Jews were driven naked from the barracks by other members of our battalion. . . . the shooters of the execution commandos, who

sat on the edge of the graves directly in front of me, were members of the SD. . . . Some distance behind each shooter stood several other SD men who constantly kept the magazines of the submachine guns full and handed them to the shooter. A number of such shooters were assigned to each grave. Today I can no longer provide details about the number of graves. It is possible that there were many such graves where shooting took place simultaneously. I definitely remember that the naked Jews were driven directly into the graves and forced to lie down quite precisely on top of those who had been shot before them. The shooter then fired off a burst at these prone victims. . . . How long the action lasted, I can no longer say with certainty. Presumably it lasted the entire day, because I remember that I was relieved once from my post. I can give no details about the number of victims, but there were an awful lot of them.[27]

Observing the killing from a greater distance was SSPF Sporrenberg, who circled above the camp in a Fieseler Storch airplane. Poles watched from the rooftops.[28]

On the same day and in the same way, other German units massacred the Jewish prisoners at the Trawniki work camp forty kilometers to the east of Lublin (estimates vary from 6,000 to 10,000 victims) and several smaller camps. Still alive were 14,000 Jews at Poniatowa, fifty kilometers west of Lublin, and 3,000 Jews at camps in Budzyn and Krasnik. The last two were to be spared; Budzyn was producing for the Heinkel aircraft company, and Krasnik for the personal needs of the SSPF Lublin. But the big labor camp at Poniatowa had not been liquidated on November 3 simply because the Germans lacked manpower. However, the camp had been sealed and telephone lines cut so that the events at Majdanek and Trawniki could give no forewarning of what was to happen the following day, November 4. Here too surprise was to be total.

In the memories of many of the men of Reserve Police Battalion 101, the two massacres in the two camps merged into a single operation of two to three days at a single camp, either

Majdanek or Poniatowa. But some witnesses—and at least one from each of the companies—did in fact remember shooting operations at two camps.[29] It seems clear, therefore, that early on the morning of November 4, the men of Reserve Police Battalion 101 traveled the fifty kilometers west from Lublin to Poniatowa.

This time the battalion was not dispersed. The men were stationed either between the undressing barracks and the zigzag graves of the shooting site or at the shooting site itself.[30] They formed the human cordon through which the 14,000 work Jews of Poniatowa, stark naked and hands behind their necks, marched to their deaths while the loudspeakers once again blared music in a vain attempt to cover up the noise of the shooting. The closest witness was Martin Detmold.

> I myself and my group had guard duty directly in front of the grave. The grave was a big zigzag-shaped series of slit trenches about three meters wide and three to four meters deep. From my post I could observe how the Jews . . . were forced to undress in the last barracks and surrender all their possessions and were then driven through our cordon and down sloped openings into the trenches. SD men standing at the edge of the trenches drove the Jews onward to the execution sites, where other SD men with submachine guns fired from the edge of the trench. Because I was a group leader and could move about more freely, I went once directly to the execution site and saw how the newly arriving Jews had to lie down on those already shot. They were then likewise shot with bursts from the submachine guns. The SD men took care that the Jews were shot in such a way that there were inclines in the piles of corpses enabling the newcomers to lie down on corpses piled as much as three meters high.
>
> . . . The whole business was the most gruesome I had ever seen in my life, because I was frequently able to see that after a burst had been fired the Jews were only wounded and those still living were more or less buried alive beneath the corpses of those shot later, without the wounded being given so-called

mercy shots. I remember that from out of the piles of corpses the SS [sic] men were cursed by the wounded.[31]

The other policemen were long inured to the mass killing of Jews, and few were as impressed as Detmold by the *Erntefest* massacres. What they did find new and impressive, however, was the problem—hitherto confined to the relative secrecy of the death camps—of disposing of so many corpses. Wilhelm Gebhardt,* who was part of Gnade's special guard company that remained in Lublin after the killing, recalled, "In Lublin itself it stank terribly for days. It was the typical smell of burned bodies. Anyone could imagine that a great number of Jews were burned in the camp at Majdanek."[32]

If the inhabitants of Lublin only had to smell the burning corpses at a distance, many members of Third Company had a much more immediate experience with the disposal of bodies at Poniatowa. As Poniatowa was a mere thirty-five kilometers south of Puławy, the men of the company sometimes had occasion to go there, and some were in fact assigned to guard the work Jews who had the gruesome task of disinterment and body burning. The policemen could observe in detail how the bodies were taken from the trenches, pulled to the burning site by horses, placed on a grill of iron rails by Jewish workers, and burned. A "bestial stench" dominated the area.[33] A truckload of policemen once stopped at the camp while the burning was in progress. "Some of our comrades got sick from the smell and sight of the half-decomposed corpses, so they had to throw up all over the truck."[34] When Third Company's new commander, Captain Haslach,* heard the reports from his returning men, he found them "unbelievable" and said to First Sergeant Karlsen, "Come, we'll go there and have a look for ourselves." When they arrived, the work was already done, but an obliging SS officer showed them the graves and "burning grill" of iron rails some four by eight meters.[35]

At the conclusion of the *Erntefest* massacres, the district of Lublin was for all practical purposes *judenfrei*. The murderous participation of Reserve Police Battalion 101 in the Final Solution came to an end. With a conservative estimate of 6,500 Jews shot during earlier actions like those at Józefów and Łomazy and 1,000 shot during the "Jew hunts," and a minimum estimate of 30,500 Jews shot at Majdanek and Poniatowa, the battalion had participated in the direct shooting deaths of at least 38,000 Jews. With the death camp deportation of at least 3,000 Jews from Międzyrzec in early May 1943, the number of Jews they had placed on trains to Treblinka had risen to 45,000. For a battalion of less than 500 men, the ultimate body count was at least 83,000 Jews.

16

Aftermath

WITH THE BATTALION'S CONTRIBUTION TO THE FINAL SOLU-
tion complete and the tide of war turning against Germany, the
men of Reserve Police Battalion 101 increasingly found themselves in action against armed partisans and enemy soldiers. In
the spring of 1943 the battalion experienced a rare casualty when
First Lieutenant Hagen was killed accidentally by police gunfire. In the last year of the war, the toll among the officers
rose dramatically; Lieutenants Gnade, Hoppner, and Peters fell
in action, and Lieutenant Drucker returned to Germany
wounded.[1] Major Trapp also returned to Germany, in early
1944.[2] A few of the men were captured by the advancing Russian
army, but most made their way back to Germany as the Third
Reich collapsed in defeat.

Many resumed their prewar occupations. For the two SS Hauptsturmführers, Hoffmann and Wohlauf, as well as twelve from the sample of thirty-two noncommissioned officers, this meant an ongoing career in the police. Another twelve policemen from the rank and file sample of 174 managed to put their reserve service to good use and made a postwar career in the police. Not surprisingly, the interrogations contained little information about the ease with which these twenty-six men continued in the police. While only two of the reservists had been Party members, nine of the NCOs had belonged, and three had been in the SS as well. Hoffmann and Wohlauf, of course, had also been in both the Party and the SS. Hoffmann mentioned a brief period of internment by the British due to his SS membership. Though interrogated by Polish authorities, he was released and immediately rejoined the Hamburg police.[3]

Ironically, it was not the hardcore SS officers who suffered postwar difficulties because of Reserve Police Battalion 101's actions in Poland, but Major Trapp and Lieutenant Buchmann. One policeman who had been in the firing squad at Talcyn was denounced by his estranged wife. Under interrogation, he named his battalion commander, Trapp, his company commander, Buchmann, and his first sergeant, Kammer. All of them were extradited to Poland in October 1947. On July 6, 1948, they had a one-day trial in the city of Siedlce. The trial focused solely on the reprisal shooting of seventy-eight Poles in Talcyn, not on any of the battalion's murderous and far more numerous actions against Polish Jews. The policeman and Trapp were sentenced to death and executed in December 1948. Buchmann was sentenced to eight years in prison and Kammer to three.[4]

Reserve Police Battalion 101 was not subjected to further judicial investigation until the 1960s. In 1958 the Zentrale Stelle der Landesjustizverwaltungen (Central Agency for the State Administrations of Justice), headquartered in the town of Ludwigsburg just north of Stuttgart, was formed to initiate and coordinate the prosecution of Nazi crimes. The staff of the Zentrale Stelle was organized into various task forces, each assigned to investigate various "crime complexes." Only after they had conducted the initial research into a particular crime complex and discovered the whereabouts of the highest-ranking suspects did they assign jurisdiction to the Office of the State Prosecutor of the federal state in which the prime suspect or suspects lived. It was in the course of investigating various crime complexes in the district of Lublin that Ludwigsburg investigators first encountered several witnesses from Reserve Police Battalion 101. In 1962 the case was turned over to police and judicial authorities in Hamburg, where most of the surviving battalion members still lived.

From late 1962 to early 1967, 210 former members of the battalion were interrogated, many of them more than once. Fourteen men were indicted: Captains Hoffmann and Wohlauf; Lieutenant Drucker; Sergeants Steinmetz, Bentheim, Bekemeier, and Grund; Corporals Grafmann* and Mehler*; and five reserve policemen. The trial began in October 1967, and the verdict was rendered the following April. Hoffmann, Wohlauf, and Drucker were sentenced to eight years, Bentheim to six, Bekemeier to five. Grafmann and the five reserve policemen were declared guilty, but at the judges' discretion—under a provision of the 1940 criminal code that governed the trial, so as to avoid the criticism leveled at the Nürnberg trials of applying *ex post facto* law—they were given no sentence. Grund, Steinmetz, and Mehler were not included in the verdict, as their cases had been separated during the trial because of their failing health. A lengthy appeals process finally concluded in 1972. The convictions of Bentheim and Bekemeier were upheld, but they also received no sentence. Hoffmann's sentence was reduced to four years, Drucker's to three and a half years. The case pending against other members of the battalion was dropped by the prosecution in light of its inability to get sentences against any but three defendants in the first trial.

However inadequate the postwar judicial outcome may seem at first sight, it must be kept in mind that the investigation of Reserve Police Battalion 101 was one of the few that led to the trial of any former members of the Order Police. Most of the investigations of police battalions did not even lead to indictments. In the few cases that did come to trial, only a handful of convictions were obtained. Comparatively speaking, the investigation and trial of Reserve Police Battalion 101 was a rare success for German judicial authorities attempting to deal with the police battalions.

The interrogations of 210 men from Reserve Police Battalion 101 remain in the archives of the Office of the State Prosecutor in Hamburg. They constitute the prime, indeed indispensable, source for this study. It is to be hoped that the admirable efforts of the prosecution in preparing this case will serve history better than they have served justice.

17

Germans, Poles, and Jews

THE PRETRIAL AND COURTROOM TESTIMONIES OF THE MEN OF Reserve Police Battalion 101 must, of course, be used with considerable caution. Problems of judicial calculation, involving both self-incrimination and incrimination of comrades, weighed heavily upon each witness. The effects of twenty-five years of memory loss and distortion, even when not feigned for judicial convenience, were equally important. Psychological defense mechanisms, especially repression and projection, crucially shaped the testimony as well. Nowhere do all these qualifications about the reliability of the testimonies become more problematic than in connection with the fateful triangle of German-Polish-Jewish relations. Simply put, the portrayal of German-Polish and

German-Jewish relations in these testimonies is extraordinarily exculpatory; in contrast, the portrayal of Polish-Jewish relations is extraordinarily damning. If we begin by examining the first two relationships as described by the former policemen, we can better see the asymmetry and distortion involved in their account of the third.

Concerning German-Polish relations, the most salient feature is the scarcity of any comment. The men make general references to partisans, bandits, and robbers, but the thrust of their comments is not the specifically anti-German character of such phenomena. On the contrary, they depict banditry as an endemic problem that predated the German occupation of Poland. Thus, they invoke the presence of partisans and bandits in two ways: on the one hand, to imply that the Germans were protecting Poles from an indigenous problem of lawlessness; and on the other hand, to obscure the frequency and intensity of the battalion's anti-Jewish activities by alleging that partisans and bandits, not Jews, were the chief preoccupation of the policemen.

Some of the witnesses referred to specific attempts at maintaining good German-Polish relations. Captain Hoffmann explicitly boasted of friendly relations between his company and the native population in Puławy. He claimed that he filed charges against Lieutenant Messmann because the "shoot on sight" tactics of the latter's marauding motorized Gendarmerie were embittering the Poles.[1] Lieutenant Buchmann noted that Major Trapp carried out the selection of victims for the Talcyn reprisal shootings in consultation with the Polish town mayor. Care was taken to shoot only strangers and the destitute, not citizens of good standing.[2]

This picture of a rather benign German occupation in Poland was contradicted by only two testimonies. Bruno Probst recalled early activities of the battalion in Poznań and Łódź in 1940–41, when the policemen carried out brutal expulsions and amused themselves with cruel harassments of the local population. He was even more critical of German treatment of Poles in 1942.

Even at that time denunciations or comments from envious neighbors sufficed for Poles to be shot along with their entire families on the mere suspicion of possessing weapons or hiding Jews or bandits. As far as I know, Poles were never arrested and turned over to the competent police authorities on these grounds. From my own observations and from the stories of my comrades, I recall that when the above-mentioned grounds for suspicion were at hand, we always shot Poles on the spot.[3]

The second witness to challenge the "rosy" view of German-Polish relations was not a surviving policeman but the wife of Lieutenant Brand, who had visited him briefly in Radzyń. At the time it was quite usual, she said, even for German civilians—to say nothing of uniformed policemen—to behave toward the Poles as a "master race." For instance, when Germans walked down a sidewalk in town, Poles were to step aside; when Germans entered a shop, Polish customers were expected to leave. One day her way was barred by some hostile Polish women in Radzyń; she and her companion got away only by threatening to call for the police. When Major Trapp heard of the incident, he was incensed. The Polish women should be shot in the public marketplace, he declared. According to Frau Brand, this incident was illustrative of the German attitude toward the Poles.[4]

In terms of sexual relations between German policemen and Polish women, there were only two references. Hoffmann claimed to have protected one of his men by not reporting a case of venereal disease contracted through forbidden intercourse with a Pole.[5] Another policeman was not so fortunate. He spent one year in a "punishment camp" for violating the ban on sexual relations with Poles.[6] The very existence of such a ban, of course, says a great deal about the reality of German-Polish relations so conveniently omitted from the bulk of the testimony.

Could the German policemen have done to the Poles what they did to the Jews? Though on a much smaller scale, the same process of growing callousness and indifference to Polish life seems to have set in. In September 1942 in Talcyn, the battalion was still cautious about the effect of reprisal shootings of large numbers of Poles. After killing seventy-eight "expendable" Poles, Trapp met his reprisal quota by shooting Jews instead. Bruno Probst recalled a different attitude prevailing by January 1943. As Hoppner's Second Platoon of Third Company was about to go to the movies in Opole, they received reports that a German policeman had been shot by Polish assailants. Hoppner took his men to the village of Niezdów to carry out a reprisal, only to discover that all but the most elderly inhabitants had fled. Even though word came in the middle of the action that the German policeman had only been wounded and not killed, Hoppner had all twelve to fifteen elderly Poles—mostly women—shot and the village burned down. The men then returned to the movie theater in Opole.[7]

The testimony is marked by similar omissions concerning German attitudes toward Jews. One reason for this is a stark legal consideration. According to German law, among the criteria for defining homicide as murder is the presence of a "base motive," such as racial hatred. Any member of the battalion who openly confessed to anti-Semitism would have seriously compromised his legal position; anyone who talked about the anti-Semitic attitudes of others risked finding himself in the uncomfortable position of witness against his former comrades.

But this reluctance to discuss anti-Semitism was also part of a much more general and pervasive reticence about the whole phenomenon of National Socialism and the policemen's own political attitudes or those of their comrades during that period. To admit an explicitly political or ideological dimension to their behavior, to concede that the morally inverted world of National Socialism—so at odds with the political culture and accepted norms of the 1960s—had made perfect sense to them at the time, would be to admit that they were political and moral eunuchs who simply accommodated to each successive regime. That was a truth with which few either wanted or were able to come to grips.

Captain Hoffmann—who joined the Nazi high school student organization at sixteen, the Hitler Youth at eighteen, and both the Party and the SS at nineteen—offered the usual denial of the political and ideological dimension. "My entry into the general SS in May 1933 is explained by the fact that at that time the SS was seen as a purely defensive formation. No special ideologically based attitude on my part lay at the root of my entry."[8] Considerably less dishonest, though still evasive, was the explanation of Lieutenant Drucker, the only defendant who seriously attempted to grapple with the problem of his past attitude.

> I received National Socialist ideological training only within the framework of training in the SA, and a certain influence was present from the propaganda of the time. Because I was a platoon leader in the naval SA and it was desirable at the time that platoon leaders were also Party members, I entered the Party shortly before the outbreak of the war. Under the influence of the times, my attitude to Jews was marked by a certain aversion. But I cannot say that I especially hated Jews—in any case it is my impression now that that was my attitude at that time.[9]

The few cases in which policemen testified to the brutality and anti-Semitism of others usually involved comments about particular officers by men from the ranks. With some reluctance, for instance, witnesses admitted that Gnade was a brutal, sadistic drunkard who was a Nazi and anti-Semite "out of conviction." Two sergeants were also the subject of quite negative comments in several testimonies. Rudolf Grund, who deputized for Buchmann when the latter was excused from participating in Jewish actions, was nicknamed the "poison dwarf" because he compensated for his short stature by screaming at his men. He was characterized as "especially harsh and loud," a "real go-getter," and a "one hundred and ten percent Nazi" who displayed a "great zeal for duty."[10] Heinrich Bekemeier was described as a "very unpleasant man" who proudly wore his Nazi insignia at all times. Disliked by his men, he was especially feared by Poles and Jews, toward whom he was "brutal and cruel." One of his men recounted how Bekemeier forced a group of Jews near Łomazy to crawl through a mud puddle while singing. When an exhausted old man collapsed and raised his hands to Bekemeier, begging for mercy, the sergeant shot him in the mouth. Heinrich Bekemeier, the witness concluded, was "a common dog."[11] But such denunciations by the policemen, even of unpopular superiors, much less of their comrades, were extremely rare.

A range of attitudes toward Jews is revealed in less direct and less guarded statements made during the interrogations. For instance, when asked how they could tell the difference between Poles and Jews in the countryside, some of the men cited clothing, hairstyle, and general appearance. Several, however, chose a vocabulary that still reflected the Nazi stereotype of twenty-five years earlier: the Jews were "dirty," "unkempt," and "less clean" in comparison to the Poles.[12] The comments of other policemen reflected a different sensibility that recognized the Jews as victimized human beings: they were dressed in rags and half starved.[13]

A similar dichotomy is reflected in descriptions of Jewish behavior at the shooting sites. Some stressed Jewish passivity, occasionally in a very exculpatory way that seemed to imply that the Jews were complicit in their own deaths. There was no resistance, no attempt to escape. The Jews accepted their fate; they practically lay down to be shot without waiting to be told.[14] In other descriptions the emphasis was clearly on the dignity of the victims; the composure of the Jews was "astonishing" and "unbelievable."[15]

The few references to sexual relations between Germans and Jews give a picture very different from forbidden romance or even quick sexual gratification between German policemen and Polish women. In cases involving German men and Jewish women, it was a question of domination over the powerless—of rape and voyeurism. The one policeman who was witnessed attempting to rape a Jewish woman was in fact the same man who was later denounced by his wife to Allied occupation authorities, extradited to Poland, and tried with Trapp, Buchmann, and Kammer. The witnessing NCO did not report the rapist.[16] The second case involved Lieutenant Peters, who would get drunk on vodka in the evening and make night patrols in the ghetto. "Booted and spurred," he entered Jewish dwellings, tore the bed covers off women, looked, and then left. By morning he was sober again.[17]

For the most part the Jews remained an anonymous collective in the German accounts. There were two exceptions. First, the policemen frequently mentioned encountering German Jews and were almost always able to remember exactly the hometown from which the Jew in question came: the decorated World War I veteran from Bremen, the mother and daughter from Kassel, the movie theater owner from Hamburg, the Jewish council head from Munich. The experience must have been quite unexpected and jarring—in sharp contrast to their usual view of the Jews as part of a foreign enemy—to have remained in their memories so vividly.

The other Jewish victims who took on a personal identity in the eyes of the German policemen were those who worked for them, particularly in the kitchen. One policeman remembered procuring extra rations for the Jewish work detail he supervised in Łuków, because "the Jews received practically nothing at all to eat, even though they had to work for us." The same man claimed to have allowed the wife of the head of the Jewish ghetto police to escape when the ghetto was being cleared.[18] In Międzyrzec, a kitchen worker begged another policeman to save her mother and sister during a ghetto clearing, and he let her bring them to the kitchen as well.[19] In Kock a policeman encountered a weeping Jewish woman during the late September shooting and sent her to the kitchen.[20]

But the tenuous relations that developed between the police and their Jewish kitchen helpers seldom saved lives in the end. When his two kitchen helpers did not come to work during a deportation from Łuków, one policeman went to the collection point. He found both, but the SS man in charge allowed only one to go. A short while later, she was taken too.[21]

Most vividly of all, the policemen remembered those occasions when they not only did not save their Jewish workers but in fact were supposed to carry out the executions themselves. In Puławy Captain Hoffmann summoned Corporal Nehring* to his bedroom, gave him a gift of good wine, and told him to go to the agricultural estate he had formerly guarded and shoot the Jewish workers. Nehring complained of the assignment because he "personally knew" many of the Jewish workers there, but to no avail. He and his unit shared the assignment with a Gendarmerie officer and four or five men also stationed in Puławy. Nehring told the officer that many of the Jews were well known to him and he could not take part in the shooting. More obliging than Hoffmann, the officer had his men shoot the fifteen to twenty Jews on their own so that Nehring did not have to be present.[22]

In Kock two Jewish kitchen workers, Bluma and Ruth, asked for help to escape. One policeman advised them that it was "pointless," but others helped them get away.[23] Two weeks later some of the policemen found Bluma and Ruth hiding in a bunker along with a dozen other Jews. One of the men who recognized them tried to leave because he knew what was coming. He was ordered to shoot them instead. He refused and left anyhow, but all the Jews in the bunker—including the former kitchen helpers—were shot.[24]

In Komarówka Drucker's Second Platoon of Second Company had two Jewish kitchen workers known as Jutta and Harry. One day Drucker said they could not stay any longer and there was nothing left to do but shoot them. Some of the policemen took Jutta to the woods and engaged her in conversation before she was shot from behind. Shortly thereafter, Harry was shot in the back of the head with a pistol while he was picking berries.[25] The policemen had clearly taken extra pains to shoot unawares victims who had prepared their food over the past months and whom they knew by name. By 1942 standards of German-Jewish relations, a quick death without the agony of anticipation was considered an example of human compassion!

While the policemen's testimonies offer scant information concerning German attitudes toward Poles and Jews, they contain very frequent and quite damning comment on Polish attitudes toward Jews. At least two factors must be kept in mind in evaluating this testimony. First, the German police quite naturally had considerable contact with Poles who collaborated in the Final Solution and helped them track down Jews. Indeed, such Poles attempted to curry favor with the German occupiers through their zealous anti-Semitism. Needless to say, Poles who helped Jews did their very best to remain totally unknown to the Germans. Thus there was an inherent bias in the sympathies and behavior of the Poles with whom the German policemen had firsthand experience.

This inherent one-sidedness is in my opinion further distorted by a second factor. It is fair to speculate that a great deal of projection was involved in German comments on Polish anti-Semitism. Often unwilling to make accusatory statements about their comrades or to be truthful about themselves, these men must have found considerable psychological relief in sharing blame with the Poles. Polish misdeeds could be spoken about quite frankly, while discussion about Germans was quite guarded. Indeed, the greater the share of Polish guilt, the less remained on the German side. In weighing the testimony that follows, these reservations must be borne in mind.

The litany of German accusation against the Poles began—like the mass murder itself—with the account of Józefów. The Polish mayor provided flasks of schnapps to the Germans on the marketplace, according to one policeman.[26] According to others, Poles helped roust Jews from their dwellings and revealed Jewish hiding places in garden bunkers or behind double walls. Even after the Germans had finished searching, Poles continued to bring individual Jews to the marketplace throughout the afternoon. They entered Jewish houses and began to plunder as soon as the Jews were taken away; they plundered the Jewish corpses when the shooting was over.[27]

The classic accusation was made by Captain Hoffmann, a man who claimed to remember absolutely nothing about the massacre his company had carried out at Końskowola. In contrast he remembered the following in exquisite detail. After the outer cordon had been lifted and his Third Company had moved into the town center at Józefów, two Polish students invited him into their house for a vodka. The young Poles exchanged Greek and Latin verses with Hoffmann but did not hide their political views. "Both were Polish nationalists who expressed themselves angrily over how they were treated and thought that Hitler had only one redeeming feature, that he was liberating them from the Jews."[28]

Virtually no account of the "Jew hunts" omitted the fact that hideouts and bunkers were for the most part revealed by Polish "agents," "informants," "forest runners," and angry peasants. But the policemen's word choice revealed more than just information about Polish behavior. Time and again they used the word "betrayed," with its unquestionable connotation of strong moral condemnation.[29] Most explicit in this regard was Gustav Michaelson. "I found it very disturbing at the time that the Polish population betrayed these Jews who had hidden themselves. The Jews had camouflaged themselves very well in the forest, in underground bunkers or in other hiding places, and would never have been found if they had not been betrayed by the Polish civilian population."[30] Michaelson belonged to the minority of "weak" policemen who never shot and could thus voice his moral criticism with less than total hypocrisy. The same cannot be said for most others who accused the Poles of "betrayal," never mentioning that it was German policy to recruit such people and reward such behavior.

Once again it was the ruthlessly honest Bruno Probst who put the matter in more balanced perspective. Often the "Jew hunts" were instigated by tips from Polish informants, he noted. But he added, "I further remember that at that time we also gradually began, more systematically than before, to shoot Poles who provided lodging to Jews. Almost always we burned down their farms at the same time."[31] Aside from the policemen who testified about the Polish woman who was surrendered by her father and shot for hiding Jews in her cellar in Kock, Probst was the sole man among 210 witnesses to acknowledge the existence of a German policy of systematically shooting Poles who hid Jews.

Probst also related another story. On one occasion Lieutenant Hoppner was leading a patrol that uncovered a bunker with ten Jews. A young man stepped forward and said that he was a Pole who had hidden there in order to be with his bride. Hoppner gave him the choice of leaving or being shot with his Jewish wife. The Pole stayed and was shot. Probst concluded that Hoppner never meant the offer seriously. The Pole would "certainly" have been shot "trying to escape" if he had decided to leave.[32]

The German policemen described other examples of Polish complicity. At Końskowola, one policeman in the cordon was approached by a woman dressed as a Polish peasant. The nearby Poles said that she was a Jew in disguise, but the policeman let her pass anyhow.[33] A number of policemen told of Poles arresting and holding Jews until the Germans could come and shoot them.[34] On several occasions the Jews had been beaten when the Germans arrived.[35] Only one witness, however, told of Polish policemen accompanying the German patrols and taking part in the shooting on two occasions.[36] In contrast, Toni Bentheim recounted what happened when the Polish police in Komarówka reported that they had captured four Jews. Drucker ordered Bentheim to shoot them. After he had taken the Jews to the cemetery, where he intended to shoot all four by himself, his submachine gun jammed. He thereupon asked the Polish policeman who had accompanied him "if he wanted to take care of it. To my surprise, however, he refused." Bentheim used his pistol.[37]

The German portrayals of Polish complicity are not false. Tragically, the kind of behavior they attributed to Poles is confirmed in other accounts and occurred all too often. The Holocaust, after all, is a story with far too few heroes and all too many perpetrators and victims. What is wrong with the German portrayals is a multifaceted distortion in perspective. The policemen were all but silent about Polish help to Jews and German punishment for such help. Almost nothing was said of the German role in inciting the Polish "betrayals" the policemen so hypocritically condemned. Nor was any note made of the fact that large units of murderous auxiliaries—the notorious Hiwis—were not recruited from the Polish population, in stark contrast to other nationalities in pervasively anti-Semitic eastern Europe. In some ways, therefore, the German policemen's comments about Poles reveal as much about the former as the latter.

18

Ordinary Men

WHY DID MOST MEN IN RESERVE POLICE BATTALION 101 become killers, while only a minority of perhaps 10 percent—and certainly no more than 20 percent—did not? A number of explanations have been invoked in the past to explain such behavior: wartime brutalization, racism, segmentation and routinization of the task, special selection of the perpetrators, careerism, obedience to orders, deference to authority, ideological indoctrination, and conformity. These factors are applicable in varying degrees, but none without qualification.

Wars have invariably been accompanied by atrocities. As John Dower has noted in his remarkable book, *War Without Mercy: Race and Power in the Pacific War*, "war hates" induce "war crimes."[1] Above all, when deeply embedded negative racial

159

stereotypes are added to the brutalization inherent in sending armed men to kill one another on a massive scale, the fragile tissue of war conventions and rules of combat is even more frequently and viciously broken on all sides. Hence the difference between more conventional war—between Germany and the Western allies, for example—and the "race wars" of the recent past. From the Nazi "war of destruction" in eastern Europe and "war against the Jews" to the "war without mercy" in the Pacific and most recently Vietnam, soldiers have all too often tortured and slaughtered unarmed civilians and helpless prisoners, and committed numerous other atrocities. Dower's account of entire American units in the Pacific openly boasting of a "take no prisoners" policy and routinely collecting body parts of Japanese soldiers as battlefield souvenirs is chilling reading for anyone who smugly assumes that war atrocities were a monopoly of the Nazi regime.

War, and especially race war, leads to brutalization, which leads to atrocity. This common thread, it could be argued, runs from Bromberg[2] and Babi Yar through New Guinea and Manila and on to My Lai. But if war, and especially race war, was a vital context within which Reserve Police Battalion 101 operated (as I shall indeed argue), how much does the notion of wartime brutalization explain the specific behavior of the policemen at Józefów and after? In particular, what distinctions must be made between various kinds of war crimes and the mind-sets of the men who commit them?

Many of the most notorious wartime atrocities—Oradour and Malmédy, the Japanese rampage through Manila, the American slaughter of prisoners and mutilation of corpses on many Pacific islands, and the massacre at My Lai—involved a kind of "battlefield frenzy." Soldiers who were inured to violence, numbed to the taking of human life, embittered over their own casualties, and frustrated by the tenacity of an insidious and seemingly inhuman enemy sometimes exploded and at other times grimly resolved to have their revenge at the first opportunity. Though atrocities of this kind were too often tolerated, condoned, or tacitly (sometimes even explicitly) encouraged by elements of the command structure, they did not represent official government policy.[3] Despite the hate-filled propaganda of each nation and the exterminatory rhetoric of many leaders and commanders, such atrocities still represented a breakdown in discipline and the chain of command. They were not "standard operating procedure."

Other kinds of atrocity, lacking the immediacy of battlefield frenzy and fully expressing official government policy, decidedly were "standard operating procedure." The fire-bombing of German and Japanese cities, the enslavement and murderous maltreatment of foreign laborers in German camps and factories or along the Siam-Burma railroad, the reprisal shooting of a hundred civilians for every German soldier killed by partisan attack in Yugoslavia or elsewhere in eastern Europe—these were not the spontaneous explosions or cruel revenge of brutalized men but the methodically executed policies of government.

Both kinds of atrocities occur in the brutalizing context of war, but the men who carry out "atrocity by policy" are in a different state of mind. They act not out of frenzy, bitterness, and frustration but with calculation. Clearly the men of Reserve Police Battalion 101, in implementing the systematic Nazi policy of exterminating European Jewry, belong in the second category. Except for a few of the oldest men who were veterans of World War I, and a few NCOs who had been transferred to Poland from Russia, the men of the battalion had not seen battle or encountered a deadly enemy. Most of them had not fired a shot in anger or ever been fired on, much less lost comrades fighting at their side. Thus, wartime brutalization through prior combat was not an immediate experience directly influencing the policemen's behavior at Józefów. Once the killing began, however, the men became increasingly brutalized. As in combat, the horrors of the initial encounter eventually became routine, and the killing became progressively easier. In this sense, brutalization was not the cause but the effect of these men's behavior.

The context of war must surely be taken into account in a more general way than as a cause of combat-induced brutalization and frenzy, however. War, a struggle between "our people" and "the enemy," creates a polarized world in which "the enemy" is easily objectified and removed from the community of human obligation. War is the most conducive environment in which governments can adopt "atrocity by policy" and encounter few difficulties in implementing it. As John Dower has observed, "The Dehumanization of the Other contributed immeasurably to the psychological distancing that facilitated killing."[4] Distancing, not frenzy and brutalization, is one of the keys to the behavior of Reserve Police Battalion 101. War and negative racial stereotyping were two mutually reinforcing factors in this distancing.

Many scholars of the Holocaust, especially Raul Hilberg, have emphasized the bureaucratic and administrative aspects of the destruction process.[5] This approach emphasizes the degree to which modern bureaucratic life fosters a functional and physical distancing in the same way that war and negative racial stereotyping promote a psychological distancing between perpetrator and victim. Indeed, many of the perpetrators of the Holocaust were so-called desk murderers whose role in the mass extermination was greatly facilitated by the bureaucratic nature of their participation. Their jobs frequently consisted of tiny steps in the overall killing process, and they performed them in a routine manner, never seeing the victims their actions affected. Segmented, routinized, and depersonalized, the job of the bureaucrat or specialist—whether it involved confiscating property, scheduling trains, drafting legislation, sending telegrams, or compiling lists—could be performed without confronting the reality of mass murder. Such a luxury, of course, was not enjoyed by the men of Reserve Police Battalion 101, who were quite literally saturated in the blood of victims shot at point-blank range. No one confronted the reality of mass murder more directly than the men in the woods at Józefów. Segmentation and routinization, the depersonalizing aspects of bureaucratized killing, cannot explain the battalion's initial behavior there.

The facilitating psychological effect of a division of labor for the killing process was not totally negligible, however. While members of the battalion did indeed carry out further shootings single-handed at Serokomla, Talcyn, and Kock, and later in the course of innumerable "Jew hunts," the larger actions involved joint ventures and splitting of duties. The policemen always provided the cordon, and many were directly involved in driving the Jews from their homes to the assembly point and then to the death trains. But at the largest mass shootings, "specialists" were brought in to do the killing. At Łomazy, the Hiwis would have done the shooting by themselves if they had not been too drunk to finish the job. At Majdanek and Poniatowa during *Erntefest*, the Security Police of Lublin furnished the shooters. The deportations to Treblinka had an added advantage psychologically. Not only was the killing done by others, but it was done out of sight of the men who cleared the ghettos and forced the Jews onto the death trains. After the sheer horror of Józefów, the policemen's detachment, their sense of not really participating in or being responsible for their subsequent actions in ghetto clearing and cordon duty, is stark testimony to the desensitizing effects of division of labor.

To what degree, if any, did the men of Reserve Police Battalion 101 represent a process of special selection for the particular task of implementing the Final Solution? According to recent research by the German historian Hans-Heinrich Wilhelm, considerable time and effort was expended by the personnel department of Reinhard Heydrich's Reich Security Main Office to select and assign officers for the Einsatzgruppen.[6] Himmler, anxious to get the right man for the right job, was also careful in his selection of Higher SS and Police Leaders and others in key positions. Hence his insistence on keeping the unsavory Globocnik in Lublin, despite his past record of corruption and objections to his appointment even within the Nazi Party.[7] In her book *Into That Darkness*, a classic study of Franz Stangl, the commandant of Treblinka, Gitta Sereny concluded that special care must have been taken to choose just 96 of some 400 people to be transferred from the euthanasia program in

Germany to the death camps in Poland.[8] Did any similar policy of selection, the careful choosing of personnel particularly suited for mass murder, determine the makeup of Reserve Police Battalion 101?

Concerning the rank and file, the answer is a qualified no. By most criteria, in fact, just the opposite was the case. By age, geographical origin, and social background, the men of Reserve Police Battalion 101 were least likely to be considered apt material out of which to mold future mass killers. On the basis of these criteria, the rank and file—middle-aged, mostly working-class, from Hamburg—did not represent special selection or even random selection but for all practical purposes negative selection for the task at hand.

In one respect, however, an earlier and more general form of selection may have taken place. The high percentage (25 percent) of Party members among the battalion's rank and file, particularly disproportionate for those of working-class origin, suggests that the initial conscription of reservists—long before their use as killers in the Final Solution was envisaged—was not entirely random. If Himmler at first thought of the reservists as a potential internal security force while large numbers of active police were stationed abroad, it is logical that he would have been leery of conscripting men of dubious political reliability. One solution would have been to draft middle-aged Party members for reserve duty in higher proportions than from the population at large. But the existence of such a policy is merely a suspicion, for no documents have been found to prove that Party members were deliberately drafted into the reserve units of the Order Police.

The case for special selection of officers is even more difficult to make. By SS standards, Major Trapp was a patriotic German but traditional and overly sentimental—what in Nazi Germany was scornfully considered both "weak" and "reactionary." It is certainly revealing that despite the conscious effort of Himmler and Heydrich to amalgamate the SS and the police, and despite the fact that Trapp was a decorated World War I veteran, career policeman, and *Alter Kämpfer* who joined the Party in 1932, he was never taken into the SS. He was certainly not given command of Reserve Police Battalion 101 and specifically assigned to the Lublin district because of his presumed suitability as a mass killer.

The remaining officers of the battalion scarcely evidence a policy of careful selection either. Despite their impeccable Party credentials, both Hoffmann and Wohlauf had been shunted into slow-track careers by SS standards. Wohlauf's career in the Order Police in particular was marked by mediocre, even negative, evaluations. Ironically, it was the relatively old (forty-eight) Reserve Lieutenant Gnade, not the two young SS captains, who turned out to be the most ruthless and sadistic killer, a man who took pleasure in his work. Finally, the assignment of Reserve Lieutenant Buchmann could scarcely have been made by anyone consciously selecting prospective killers.

In short, Reserve Police Battalion 101 was not sent to Lublin to murder Jews because it was composed of men specially selected or deemed particularly suited for the task. On the contrary, the battalion was the "dregs" of the manpower pool available at that stage of the war. It was employed to kill Jews because it was the only kind of unit available for such behind-the-lines duties. Most likely, Globocnik simply assumed as a matter of course that whatever battalion came his way would be up to this murderous task, regardless of its composition. If so, he may have been disappointed in the immediate aftermath of Józefów, but in the long run events proved him correct.

Many studies of Nazi killers have suggested a different kind of selection, namely self-selection to the Party and SS by unusually violence-prone people. Shortly after the war, Theodor Adorno and others developed the notion of the "authoritarian personality." Feeling that situational or environmental influences had already been studied, they chose to focus on hitherto neglected psychological factors. They began with the hypothesis that certain deep-seated personality traits made "potentially fascistic individuals" particularly susceptible to antidemocratic propaganda.[9] Their investigations led them to compile a list of the crucial traits (tested for by the so-called F-scale) of the "authoritarian personality": rigid adherence to conventional values; submissiveness to authority figures; aggressiveness toward outgroups; opposition to introspection, reflection, and creativity; a tendency to superstition and stereotyping; preoccupation with power and "toughness"; destructiveness and cynicism; projectivity ("the disposition to believe that wild and dangerous things go on in the world" and "the projection outward of unconscious emotional impulses"); and an exaggerated concern with sexuality. They concluded that the antidemocratic individual "harbors strong underlying aggressive impulses" and fascist movements allow him to project this aggression through sanctioned violence against ideologically targeted outgroups.[10] Zygmunt Bauman has summed up this approach as follows: "Nazism was cruel because Nazis were cruel; and the Nazis were cruel because cruel people tended to become Nazis."[11] He is highly critical of the methodology of Adorno and his colleagues, which neglected social influences, and of the implication that ordinary people did not commit fascist atrocities.

Subsequent advocates of a psychological explanation have modified the Adorno approach by more explicitly merging psychological and situational (social, cultural, and institutional) factors. Studying a group of men who had volunteered for the SS, John Steiner concluded that "a self-selection process for brutality appears to exist."[12] He proposed the notion of the "sleeper"—certain personality characteristics of violence-prone individuals that usually remain latent but can be activated under certain conditions. In the chaos of post–World War I Germany, people testing high on the F-scale were attracted in disproportionate numbers to National Socialism as a "subculture of violence," and in particular to the SS, which provided the incentives and support for the full realization of their violent potential. After World War II, such men reverted to law-abiding behavior. Thus Steiner concludes that "the situation tended to be the most immediate determinant of SS behavior" in rousing the "sleeper."

Ervin Staub accepts the notion that "some people become perpetrators as a result of their personality; they are 'self-selected'." But he concludes that Steiner's "sleeper" is a very common trait and that under particular circumstances most people have a capacity for extreme violence and the destruction of human life.[13] Indeed, Staub is quite emphatic that "ordinary psychological processes and normal, common human motivations and certain basic but not inevitable tendencies in human thought and feeling" are the "primary sources" of the human capacity for mass destruction of human life. "Evil that arises out of ordinary thinking and is committed by ordinary people is the norm, not the exception."[14]

If Staub makes Steiner's "sleeper" unexceptional, Zygmunt Bauman goes so far as to dismiss it as a "metaphysical prop." For Bauman "cruelty is social in its origin much more than it is characterological."[15] Bauman argues that most people "slip" into the roles society provides them, and he is very critical of any implication that "faulty personalities" are the cause of human cruelty. For him the exception—the real "sleeper"—is the rare individual who has the capacity to resist authority and assert moral autonomy but who is seldom aware of this hidden strength until put to the test.

Those who emphasize the relative or absolute importance of situational factors over individual psychological characteristics invariably point to Philip Zimbardo's Stanford prison experiment.[16] Screening out everyone who scored beyond the normal range on a battery of psychological tests, including one that measured "rigid adherence to conventional values and a submissive, uncritical attitude toward authority" (i.e., the F-scale for the "authoritarian personality"), Zimbardo randomly divided his homogeneous "normal" test group into guards and prisoners and placed them in a simulated prison. Though outright physical violence was barred, within six days the inherent structure of prison life—in which guards operating on three-man shifts had to devise ways of controlling the more numerous prisoner population—had produced rapidly escalating brutality, humiliation, and dehumanization. "Most dramatic and distressing to us was the observation of the ease with which sadistic behavior could be elicited in individuals who were not 'sadistic types'." The prison situation alone, Zimbardo concluded, was "a *sufficient* condition to produce aberrant, anti-social behavior."

Perhaps most relevant to this study of Reserve Police Battalion 101 is the spectrum of behavior that Zimbardo discovered in his sample of eleven guards. About one-third of the guards emerged as "cruel and tough." They constantly invented new forms of harassment and enjoyed their newfound power to behave cruelly and arbitrarily. A middle group of guards was "tough but fair." They "played by the rules" and did not go out of their way to mistreat prisoners. Only two (i.e., less than 20 percent) emerged as "good guards" who did not punish prisoners and even did small favors for them.[17]

Zimbardo's spectrum of guard behavior bears an uncanny resemblance to the groupings that emerged within Reserve Police Battalion 101: a nucleus of increasingly enthusiastic killers who volunteered for the firing squads and "Jew hunts"; a larger group of policemen who performed as shooters and ghetto clearers when assigned but who did not seek opportunities to kill (and in some cases refrained from killing, contrary to standing orders, when no one was monitoring their actions); and a small group (less than 20 percent) of refusers and evaders.

In addition to this striking resemblance between Zimbardo's guards and the policemen of Reserve Police Battalion 101, one other factor must be taken into account in weighing the relevance of "self-selection" on the basis of psychological predisposition. The battalion was composed of reserve lieutenants and men who had simply been conscripted after the outbreak of the war. The noncommissioned officers had joined the Order Police before the war because they hoped either to pursue a career in the police (in this case the metropolitan police of Hamburg, not the political police or Gestapo) or to avoid being drafted into the army. In these circumstances it is difficult to perceive any mechanism of self-selection through which the reserve battalions of the Order Police could have attracted an unusual concentration of men of violent predisposition. Indeed, if Nazi Germany offered unusually numerous career paths that sanctioned and rewarded violent behavior, random conscription from the remaining population—already drained of its most violence-prone individuals—would arguably produce even less than an average number of "authoritarian personalities." Self-selection on the basis of personality traits, in short, offers little to explain the behavior of the men of Reserve Police Battalion 101.

If special selection played little role and self-selection seemingly none, what about self-interest and careerism? Those who admitted being among the shooters did not justify their behavior on the basis of career considerations. In contrast, however, the issue of careerism was most clearly articulated by several of those who did not shoot. Lieutenant Buchmann and Gustav Michaelson, in explaining their exceptional behavior, noted that unlike their fellow officers or comrades, they had well-established civilian careers to return to and did not need to consider possible negative repercussions on a future career in the police.[18] Buchmann was clearly reluctant to have the prosecution use his behavior against the defendants and thus may have emphasized the career factor as constituting less of a moral indictment of men who acted differently. But Michaelson's testimony was not influenced by any such calculations or reticence.

In addition to the testimony of those who felt free of career considerations, there is the behavior of those who clearly did not. Captain Hoffmann is the classic example of a man driven by careerism. Crippled by stomach cramps—psychosomatically induced, at least in part, if not entirely, by the murderous actions of the battalion—he tenaciously tried to hide his illness from his superiors rather than use it to escape his situation. He risked his men's open suspicion of cowardice in a vain attempt to keep his company command. And when he was finally relieved, he bitterly contested that career-threatening development as well. Given the number of men from Reserve Police Battalion 101 who remained in the police after the war, career ambitions must have played an important role for many others as well.

Among the perpetrators, of course, orders have traditionally been the most frequently cited explanation for their own behavior. The authoritarian political culture of the Nazi dictatorship, savagely intolerant of overt dissent, along with the standard military necessity of obedience to orders and ruthless enforcement of discipline, created a situation in which individuals *had no choice*. Orders were orders, and no one in such a political climate could be expected to disobey them, they insisted. Disobedience surely meant the concentration camp if not immediate execution, possibly for their families as well. The perpetrators had found themselves in a situation of impossible "duress" and therefore could not be held responsible for their actions. Such, at least, is what defendants said in trial after trial in postwar Germany.

There is a general problem with this explanation, however. Quite simply, in the past forty-five years no defense attorney or defendant in any of the hundreds of postwar trials has been able to document a single case in which refusal to obey an order to kill unarmed civilians resulted in the allegedly inevitable dire punishment. [19] The punishment or censure that occasionally did result from such disobedience was never commensurate with the gravity of the crimes the men had been asked to commit.

A variation on the explanation of inescapable orders is "putative duress." Even if the consequences of disobedience would not have been so dire, the men who complied could not have known that at the time. They sincerely thought that they had had no choice when faced with orders to kill. Undoubtedly in many units zealous officers bullied their men with ominous threats. In Reserve Police Battalion 101, as we have seen, certain officers and NCOs, like Drucker and Hergert, tried to make everyone shoot initially, even if they subsequently released those not up to continuing. And other officers and NCOs, like Hoppner and

Ostmann, picked out individuals known as nonshooters and pressured them to kill, sometimes successfully.

But as a general rule, even putative duress does not hold for Reserve Police Battalion 101. From the time Major Trapp, with choked voice and tears streaming down his cheeks, offered to excuse those "not up to it" at Józefów and protected the first man to take up his offer from Captain Hoffmann's wrath, a situation of putative duress did not exist in the battalion. Trapp's subsequent behavior, not just excusing Lieutenant Buchmann from participation in Jewish actions but clearly protecting a man who made no secret of his disapproval, only made matters clearer. A set of unwritten "ground rules" emerged within the battalion. For small shooting actions, volunteers were requested or shooters were chosen from among those who were known to be willing to kill or who simply did not make the effort to keep their distance when firing squads were being formed. For large actions, those who would not kill were not compelled. Even officers' attempts to force individual nonshooters to kill could be refused, for the men knew that the officers could not appeal to Major Trapp.

Everyone but the most open critics, like Buchmann, did have to participate in cordon duty and roundups, but in such circumstances individuals could still make their own decisions about shooting. The testimonies are filled with stories of men who disobeyed standing orders during the ghetto-clearing operations and did not shoot infants or those attempting to hide or escape. Even men who admitted to having taken part in firing squads claimed not to have shot in the confusion and melee of the ghetto clearings or out on patrol when their behavior could not be closely observed.

If obedience to orders out of fear of dire punishment is not a valid explanation, what about "obedience to authority" in the more general sense used by Stanley Milgram—deference simply as a product of socialization and evolution, a "deeply ingrained behavior tendency" to comply with the directives of those positioned hierarchically above, even to the point of performing repugnant actions in violation of "universally accepted" moral norms.[20] In a series of now famous experiments, Milgram tested the individual's ability to resist authority that was not backed by any external coercive threat. Naive volunteer subjects were instructed by a "scientific authority" in an alleged learning experiment to inflict an escalating series of fake electric shocks upon an actor/victim, who responded with carefully programmed "voice feedback"—an escalating series of complaints, cries of pain, calls for help, and finally fateful silence. In the standard voice feedback experiment, two-thirds of Milgram's subjects were "obedient" to the point of inflicting extreme pain.[21]

Several variations on the experiment produced significantly different results. If the actor/victim was shielded so that the subject could hear and see no response, obedience was much greater. If the subject had both visual and voice feedback, compliance to the extreme fell to 40 percent. If the subject had to touch the actor/victim physically by forcing his hand onto an electric plate to deliver the shocks, obedience dropped to 30 percent. If a nonauthority figure gave orders, obedience was nil. If the naive subject performed a subsidiary or accessory task but did not personally inflict the electric shocks, obedience was nearly total. In contrast, if the subject was part of an actor/peer group that staged a carefully planned refusal to continue following the directions of the authority figure, the vast majority of subjects (90 percent) joined their peer group and desisted as well. If the subject was given complete discretion as to the level of electric shock to administer, all but a few sadists consistently delivered a minimal shock. When not under the direct surveillance of the scientist, many of the subjects "cheated" by giving lower shocks than prescribed, even though they were unable to confront authority and abandon the experiment.[22]

Milgram adduced a number of factors to account for such an unexpectedly high degree of potentially murderous obedience to a noncoercive authority. An evolutionary bias favors the survival of people who can adapt to hierarchical situations and organized social activity. Socialization through family, school, and military service, as well as a whole array of rewards and punishments within society generally, reinforces and internalizes a tendency toward obedience. A seemingly voluntary entry into an authority system "perceived" as legitimate creates a strong sense of obligation. Those within the hierarchy adopt the authority's perspective or "definition of the situation" (in this case, as an important scientific experiment rather than the infliction of physical torture). The notions of "loyalty, duty, discipline," requiring competent performance in the eyes of authority, become moral imperatives overriding any identification with the victim. Normal individuals enter an "agentic state" in which they are the instrument of another's will. In such a state, they no longer feel personally responsible for the content of their actions but only for how well they perform.[23]

Once entangled, people encounter a series of "binding factors" or "cementing mechanisms" that make disobedience or refusal even more difficult. The momentum of the process discourages any new or contrary initiative. The "situational obligation" or etiquette makes refusal appear improper, rude, or even an immoral breach of obligation. And a socialized anxiety over potential punishment for disobedience acts as a further deterrent.[24]

Milgram made direct reference to the similarities between human behavior in his experiments and under the Nazi regime. He concluded, "Men are led to kill with little difficulty."[25] Milgram was aware of significant differences in the two situations, however. Quite explicitly he acknowledged that the subjects of his experiments were assured that no permanent physical damage would result from their actions. The subjects were under no threat or duress themselves. And finally, the actor/victims were not the object of "intense devaluation" through systematic indoctrination of the subjects. In contrast, the killers of the Third Reich lived in a police state where the consequences of disobedience could be drastic and they were subjected to intense indoctrination, but they also knew they were not only inflicting pain but destroying human life.[26]

Was the massacre at Józefów a kind of radical Milgram

experiment that took place in a Polish forest with real killers and victims rather than in a social psychology laboratory with naive subjects and actor/victims? Are the actions of Reserve Police Battalion 101 explained by Milgram's observations and conclusions? There are some difficulties in explaining Józefów as a case of deference to authority, for none of Milgram's experimental variations exactly paralleled the historical situation at Józefów, and the relevant differences constitute too many variables to draw firm conclusions in any scientific sense. Nonetheless, many of Milgram's insights find graphic confirmation in the behavior and testimony of the men of Reserve Police Battalion 101.

At Józefów the authority system to which the men were responding was quite complex, unlike the laboratory situation. Major Trapp represented not a strong but a very weak authority figure. He weepingly conceded the frightful nature of the task at hand and invited the older reserve policemen to excuse themselves. If Trapp was a weak immediate authority figure, he did invoke a more distant system of authority that was anything but weak. The orders for the massacre had been received from the highest quarter, he said. Trapp himself and the battalion as a unit were bound by the orders of this distant authority, even if Trapp's concern for his men exempted individual policemen.

To what were the vast majority of Trapp's men responding when they did not step out? Was it to authority as represented either by Trapp or his superiors? Were they responding to Trapp not primarily as an authority figure, but as an individual—a popular and beloved officer whom they would not leave in the lurch? And what about other factors? Milgram himself notes that people far more frequently invoke authority than conformity to explain their behavior, for only the former seems to absolve them of personal responsibility. "Subjects deny conformity and *embrace* obedience as the explanation of their actions."[27] Yet many policemen admitted responding to the pressures of conformity—how would they be seen in the eyes of their comrades?—not authority. On Milgram's own view, such admission was the tip of the iceberg, and this factor must have been even more important than the men conceded in their testimony. If so, conformity assumes a more central role than authority at Józefów.

Milgram tested the effects of peer pressure in bolstering the individual's capacity to resist authority. When actor/collaborators bolted, the naive subjects found it much easier to follow. Milgram also attempted to test for the reverse, that is, the role of conformity in intensifying the capacity to inflict pain.[28] Three subjects, two collaborators and one naive, were instructed by the scientist/authority figure to inflict pain at the lowest level anyone among them proposed. When a naive subject acting alone had been given full discretion to set the level of electric shock, the subject had almost invariably inflicted minimal pain. But when the two collaborators, always going first, proposed a step-by-step escalation of electric shock, the naive subject was significantly influenced. Though the individual variation was wide, the average result was the selection of a level of electric shock halfway between no increase and a consistent step-by-step increase. This is still short of a test of peer pressure as compensation for the deficiencies of weak authority. There was no weeping but beloved scientist inviting subjects to leave the electric shock panel while other men—with whom the subjects had comradely relations and before whom they would feel compelled to appear manly and tough—stayed and continued to inflict painful shocks. Indeed, it would be almost impossible to construct an experiment to test such a scenario, which would require true comradely relations between a naive subject and the actor/collaborators. Nonetheless, the mutual reinforcement of authority and conformity seems to have been clearly demonstrated by Milgram.

If the multifaceted nature of authority at Józefów and the key role of conformity among the policemen are not quite parallel to Milgram's experiments, they nonetheless render considerable support to his conclusions, and some of his observations are clearly confirmed. Direct proximity to the horror of the killing significantly increased the number of men who would no longer comply. On the other hand, with the division of labor and removal of the killing process to the death camps, the men felt scarcely any responsibility at all for their actions. As in Milgram's experiment without direct surveillance, many policemen did not comply with orders when not directly supervised; they mitigated their behavior when they could do so without personal risk but were unable to refuse participation in the battalion's killing operations openly.

One factor that admittedly was not the focal point of Milgram's experiments, indoctrination, and another that was only partially touched upon, conformity, require further investigation. Milgram did stipulate "definition of the situation" or ideology, that which gives meaning and coherence to the social occasion, as a crucial antecedent of deference to authority. Controlling the manner in which people interpret their world is one way to control behavior, Milgram argues. If they accept authority's ideology, action follows logically and willingly. Hence "ideological justification is vital in obtaining willing obedience, for it permits the person to see his behavior as serving a desirable end."[29]

In Milgram's experiments, "overarching ideological justification" was present in the form of a tacit and unquestioned faith in the goodness of science and its contribution to progress. But there was no systematic attempt to "devalue" the actor/victim or inculcate the subject with a particular ideology. Milgram hypothesized that the more destructive behavior of people in Nazi Germany, under much less direct surveillance, was a consequence of an internalization of authority achieved "through relatively long processes of indoctrination, of a sort not possible within the course of a laboratory hour."[30]

To what degree, then, did the conscious inculcation of Nazi doctrines shape the behavior of the men of Reserve Police Battalion 101? Were they subjected to such a barrage of clever and insidious propaganda that they lost the capacity for independent thought and responsible action? Were devaluation of the Jews and exhortations to kill them central to this indoctrination?

The popular term for intense indoctrination and psychological manipulation, emerging from the Korean War experience of some captured American soldiers, is "brainwashing." Were these killers in some general sense "brainwashed"?

Unquestionably, Himmler set a premium on the ideological indoctrination of members of the SS and the police. They were to be not just efficient soldiers and policemen but ideologically motivated warriors, crusaders against the political and racial enemies of the Third Reich.[31] Indoctrination efforts embraced not only the elite organizations of the SS but also the Order Police, extending even to the lowly reserve police, though the reservists scarcely fit Himmler's notion of the new Nazi racial aristocracy. For instance, membership in the SS required proof of ancestry untainted by Jewish blood through five generations. In contrast, even "first-degree *Mischlinge*" (people with two Jewish grandparents) and their spouses were not banned from service in the reserve police until October 1942; "second-degree *Mischlinge*" (one Jewish grandparent) and their spouses were not banned until April 1943.[32]

In its guidelines for basic training of January 23, 1940, the Order Police Main Office decreed that in addition to physical fitness, use of weapons, and police techniques, all Order Police battalions were to be strengthened in character and ideology.[33] Basic training included a one-month unit on "ideological education." One topic for the first week was "Race as the Basis of Our World View," followed the second week by "Maintaining the Purity of Blood."[34] Beyond basic training, the police battalions, both active and reserve, were to receive continued military and ideological training from their officers.[35] Officers were required to attend one-week workshops that included one hour of ideological instruction for themselves and one hour of practice in the ideological instruction of others.[36] A five-part study plan of January 1941 included the subsections "Understanding of Race as the Basis of Our World View," "The Jewish Question in Germany," and "Maintaining the Purity of German Blood."[37]

Explicit instructions were issued on the spirit and frequency of this continuing ideological training, for which the National Socialist world view was to be the "plumb line." Every day, or at least every other day, the men were to be informed about current events and their proper understanding in ideological perspective. Every week officers were to hold thirty- to forty-five-minute sessions in which they delivered a short lecture or read an edifying excerpt from suggested books or specially prepared SS pamphlets. The officers were to choose some theme—loyalty, comradeship, the offensive spirit—through which the educational goals of National Socialism could be clearly expressed. Monthly sessions were to be held on the most important themes of the time and could feature officers and educational personnel of the SS and Party.[38]

The officers of Reserve Police Battalion 101 obviously complied with these directives on ideological education. In December 1942 Captains Hoffmann and Wohlauf and Lieutenant Gnade were recognized for their activities "in the area of ideological training and care for the troops." They were each awarded a book to be presented by their commanding officer.[39] Himmler's undoubted intentions aside, however, a look at the actual materials used to indoctrinate Reserve Police Battalion 101 raises serious doubts about the adequacy of SS indoctrination as an explanation for the men becoming killers.

Two kinds of Order Police educational materials are preserved in the German Federal Archives (Bundesarchiv) in Koblenz. The first are two series of weekly circulars issued by the department for "ideological education" of the Order Police between 1940 and 1944.[40] A few of the lead articles were written by such Nazi luminaries and noted ideological firebrands as Joseph Goebbels, Alfred Rosenberg (Hitler's minister for occupied Russia), and Walter Gross (the head of the Party's Office of Racial Politics). The general racist perspective was of course pervasive. Nonetheless, in some two hundred issues altogether, relatively little space was devoted *explicitly* to anti-Semitism and the Jewish question. One issue, "Jewry and Criminality"—exceptionally ponderous even by the quite undistinguished standards of the two series—concluded that alleged Jewish characteristics, such as "immoderateness," "vanity," "curiosity," "the denial of reality," "soullessness," "stupidity," "malice," and "brutality," were the exact characteristics of the "perfect criminal."[41] Such prose may have put readers to sleep; it certainly did not turn them into killers.

The only other article devoted entirely to the Jewish question, on the back page in December 1941, was entitled "A Goal of This War: Europe Free of Jews." It noted ominously that "the word of the Führer, that a new war instigated by the Jews would not bring about the collapse of anti-Semitic Germany but on the contrary the end of the Jews, was now being carried out." "The definitive solution of the Jewish problem, that is, not only depriving them of power but actually removing this parasitical race from the family of European peoples," was imminent. "What appeared impossible two years ago was now becoming reality step by step: at the end of this war there would exist a Europe free of Jews."[42]

Recalling Hitler's prophecy and invoking his authority in connection with the ultimate goal of a "Europe free of Jews" was not, of course, peculiar to SS indoctrination materials. On the contrary, the same message was widely circulated to the general public. How little these materials were directed at "brainwashing" the reserve police into becoming mass murderers, moreover, can be seen from another article of September 20, 1942, the single item in the entire two series devoted to the reserve police. Far from steeling them to be superhumanly inhuman to accomplish great tasks, the article assumed that the reserve police were doing nothing of noticeable importance. To boost their morale, presumably threatened above all by boredom, "older reservists" were assured that no matter how innocuous their jobs might seem, in total war "everyone is important."[43] By this time the "older reservists" of Reserve Police Battalion 101 had carried out the mass shootings at Józefów and Łomazy and the initial deportations from Parczew and Międzyrzec. They stood on the eve of a climactic and murderous six-week assault on the ghettos of northern Lublin. It is unlikely any of them would have found this article terribly relevant, much less inspiring.

A series of special pamphlets (four to six a year) "for the ideological education of the Order Police" constituted a second group of indoctrination materials. In 1941 one issue covered "The Blood Community of the German Peoples" and "The Great German Empire."[44] In 1942 there was an issue entitled "Germany Reorganizes Europe," and a "special issue" called "SS Man and the Question of Blood."[45] A large combined issue in 1943 was devoted to "The Politics of Race."[46] Beginning with the 1942 special issue on the question of blood but above all in the 1943 issue "The Politics of Race," the treatment of racial doctrine and the Jewish question became very thorough and systematic. The German "people" (*Volk*) or "blood community" (*Blutsgemeinschaft*) was comprised of a mixture of six closely related European races, the largest (50 to 60 percent) being the Nordic race. Shaped by a severe northern climate that ruthlessly eliminated weak elements, the Nordic race was superior to any other in the world, as could be seen from German cultural and military achievements. The German *Volk* faced a constant struggle for survival ordained by nature, according to whose laws "all weak and inferior are destroyed" and "only the strong and powerful continue to propagate." To win this struggle, the *Volk* needed to do two things: conquer living space to provide for further population growth and preserve the purity of German blood. The fate of peoples who did not expand their numbers or preserve their racial purity could be seen in the examples of Sparta and Rome.

The main threat to a healthy awareness of the need for territorial expansion and racial purity came from doctrines propagating the essential equality of mankind. The first such doctrine was Christianity, spread by the Jew Paul. The second was Liberalism, emerging from the French Revolution—"the uprising of the racially inferior"—instigated by the Jew-ridden Freemasons. The third and greatest threat was Marxism/Bolshevism, authored by the Jew Karl Marx.

"The Jews are a racial mixture, which in contrast to all other peoples and races, preserves its essential character first of all through its parasitical instinct." With no regard for either consistency or logic, the pamphlet then asserted that the Jew kept his own race pure while striking at the existence of his host race through race mixing. No coexistence was possible between a race-conscious people and the Jews, only a struggle that would be won when "the last Jew had left our part of the earth." The present war was just such a struggle, one that would decide the fate of Europe. "With the destruction of the Jews," the last threat of European collapse would be removed.

For what explicit purpose were these pamphlets written? What conclusions did this review of the basic tenets of National Socialist race thinking urge upon the reader? Neither "The Question of Blood" nor "The Politics of Race" ended with a call to eliminate the racial enemy. Rather they concluded with exhortations to give birth to more Germans. The racial battle was in part a demographic battle determined by the laws of "fertility" and "selection." War was "counterselection in pure form," for not only did the best fall on the field of battle, but they did so before having children. "The victory of arms" required a "victory of children." As the SS represented a selection of predominantly Nordic elements within the German people, SS men had an obligation to marry early, choose young, racially pure, and fertile brides, and have large numbers of children.

A number of factors must be kept in mind, therefore, in evaluating the indoctrination of the reserve police through pamphlets such as these. First, the most detailed and thorough pamphlet was not even issued until 1943, after the northern Lublin security zone of Reserve Police Battalion 101 was virtually "free of Jews." It appeared too late to have played a role in indoctrinating this battalion for mass murder. Second, the 1942 pamphlet was clearly directed at the family obligations of the young SS man and particularly irrelevant to middle-aged reservists who had long ago made their decisions about marriage partner and size of family. Thus, even though available, it would have seemed singularly inappropriate as the basis for one of the battalion's weekly or monthly indoctrination sessions.

Third, the age of the men affected their susceptibility to indoctrination in another way as well. Many of the Nazi perpetrators were very young men. They had been raised in a world in which Nazi values were the only "moral norms" they knew. It could be argued that such young men, schooled and formed solely under the conditions of the Nazi dictatorship, simply did not know any better. Killing Jews did not conflict with the value system they had grown up with, and hence indoctrination was much easier. Whatever the merits of such an argument, it clearly does not hold for the predominantly middle-aged men of Reserve Police Battalion 101. They were educated and spent their formative years in the pre-1933 period. Many came from a social milieu that was relatively unreceptive to National Socialism. They knew perfectly well the moral norms of German society before the Nazis. They had earlier standards by which to judge the Nazi policies they were asked to carry out.

Fourth, ideological tracts like those prepared for the Order Police certainly reflected the wider ambience within which the reserve policemen were trained and instructed as well as the political culture in which they had lived for the previous decade. As Lieutenant Drucker said with extraordinary understatement, "Under the influence of the times, my attitude to the Jews was marked by a certain aversion." The denigration of Jews and the proclamation of Germanic racial superiority was so constant, so pervasive, so relentless, that it must have shaped the general attitudes of masses of people in Germany, including the average reserve policeman.

Fifth and last, the pamphlets and materials that dealt with the Jews justified the necessity of a *judenfrei* Europe, seeking support and sympathy for such a goal, but they did not explicitly urge personal participation in achieving that goal through killing Jews. This point is worth mentioning, because some of the Order Police instructional guidelines concerning partisan warfare stated quite plainly that each individual must be tough enough to kill partisans and, more important, "suspects."

> The partisan struggle is a struggle for Bolshevism, it is not a people's movement. . . . The enemy must be *totally destroyed*. The incessant decision over life and death posed by the partisans and suspects is difficult even for the toughest soldier. But it must be done. He behaves correctly who, by setting aside all possible impulses of personal feeling, proceeds ruthlessly and mercilessly. [47]

In all the surviving indoctrination materials of the Order Police, there is no parallel set of guidelines that attempts to prepare policemen to kill unarmed Jewish women and children. Certainly in Russia large numbers of Jews were murdered in the framework of killing "suspects" during antipartisan sweeps. In the Polish territories garrisoned by Reserve Police Battalion 101 in 1942, however, there simply was no major overlap between killing partisan suspects and killing Jews. For this unit, at least, the killing of Jews cannot be explained by brutal exhortations to kill partisans and "suspects."

One other comparison is pertinent here. Before the Einsatzgruppen entered Soviet territory, they underwent a two-month training period. Their preparation included visits and speeches by various SS luminaries who gave them "pep talks" about the coming "war of destruction." Four days before the invasion, the officers were recalled to Berlin for an intimate meeting with Reinhard Heydrich himself. In short, considerable effort was made to prepare these men for the mass murder they were going to perpetrate. Even the men of the police battalions that followed the Einsatzgruppen into Russia in the summer of 1941 were partially prepared for what awaited them. They were informed of the secret directive for the execution of captured Communists (the "commissar order") and the guidelines for the treatment of the civilian population. Some battalion commanders also attempted to inspire their troops through speeches, as did Daluege and Himmler when visiting. In contrast, both officers and men of Reserve Police Battalion 101 were singularly unprepared for and surprised by the murderous task that awaited them.

In summary, the men of Reserve Police Battalion 101, like the rest of German society, were immersed in a deluge of racist and anti-Semitic propaganda. Furthermore, the Order Police provided for indoctrination both in basic training and as an ongoing practice within each unit. Such incessant propagandizing must have had a considerable effect in reinforcing general notions of Germanic racial superiority and "a certain aversion" toward the Jews. However, much of the indoctrination material was clearly not targeted at older reservists and in some cases was highly inappropriate or irrelevant to them. And material specifically designed to harden the policemen for the personal task of killing Jews is conspicuously absent from the surviving documentation. One would have to be quite convinced of the manipulative powers of indoctrination to believe that any of this material could have deprived the men of Reserve Police Battalion 101 of the capacity for independent thought. Influenced and conditioned in a general way, imbued in particular with a sense of their own superiority and racial kinship as well as Jewish inferiority and otherness, many of them undoubtedly were; explicitly prepared for the task of killing Jews they most certainly were not.

Along with ideological indoctrination, a vital factor touched upon but not fully explored in Milgram's experiments was conformity to the group. The battalion had orders to kill Jews, but each individual did not. Yet 80 to 90 percent of the men proceeded to kill, though almost all of them—at least initially— were horrified and disgusted by what they were doing. To break ranks and step out, to adopt overtly nonconformist behavior, was simply beyond most of the men. It was easier for them to shoot.

Why? First of all, by breaking ranks, nonshooters were leaving the "dirty work" to their comrades. Since the battalion had to shoot even if individuals did not, refusing to shoot constituted refusing one's share of an unpleasant collective obligation. It was in effect an asocial act vis-à-vis one's comrades. Those who did not shoot risked isolation, rejection, and ostracism—a very uncomfortable prospect within the framework of a tight-knit unit stationed abroad among a hostile population, so that the individual had virtually nowhere else to turn for support and social contact.

This threat of isolation was intensified by the fact that stepping out could also have been seen as a form of moral reproach of one's comrades: the nonshooter was potentially indicating that he was "too good" to do such things. Most, though not all, nonshooters intuitively tried to diffuse the criticism of their comrades that was inherent in their actions. They pleaded not that they were "too good" but rather that they were "too weak" to kill.

Such a stance presented no challenge to the esteem of one's comrades; on the contrary, it legitimized and upheld "toughness" as a superior quality. For the anxious individual, it had the added advantage of posing no moral challenge to the murderous policies of the regime, though it did pose another problem, since the difference between being "weak" and being a "coward" was not great. Hence the distinction made by one policeman who did not dare to step out at Józefów for fear of being considered a coward, but who subsequently dropped out of his firing squad. It was one thing to be too cowardly even to try to kill; it was another, after resolutely trying to do one's share, to be too weak to continue.[48]

Insidiously, therefore, most of those who did not shoot only reaffirmed the "macho" values of the majority—according to which it was a positive quality to be "tough" enough to kill unarmed, noncombatant men, women, and children—and tried not to rupture the bonds of comradeship that constituted their social world. Coping with the contradictions imposed by the demands of conscience on the one hand and the norms of the battalion on the other led to many tortured attempts at compromise: not shooting infants on the spot but taking them to the assembly point; not shooting on patrol if no "go-getter" was along who might report such squeamishness; bringing Jews to the shooting site and firing but intentionally missing. Only the very exceptional remained indifferent to taunts of "weakling" from their comrades and could live with the fact that they were considered to be "no man."[49]

Here we come full circle to the mutually intensifying effects of war and racism noted by John Dower, in conjunction with the insidious effects of constant propaganda and indoctrination. Pervasive racism and the resulting exclusion of the Jewish victims from any common ground with the perpetrators made it all the easier for the majority of the policemen to conform to the norms of their immediate community (the battalion) and their society at large (Nazi Germany). Here the years of anti-Semitic propaganda (and prior to the Nazi dictatorship, decades of shrill German nationalism) dovetailed with the polarizing effects of war. The dichotomy of racially superior Germans and racially inferior Jews, central to Nazi ideology, could easily merge with the image of a beleaguered Germany surrounded by warring enemies. If it is doubtful that most of the policemen understood or embraced the theoretical aspects of Nazi ideology as contained in SS indoctrination pamphlets, it is also doubtful that they were immune to "the influence of the times" (to use Lieutenant Drucker's phrase once again), to the incessant proclamation of German superiority and incitement of contempt and hatred for the Jewish enemy. Nothing helped the Nazis to wage a race war so much as the war itself. In wartime, when it was all too usual to exclude the enemy from the community of human obligation, it was also all too easy to subsume the Jews into the "image of the enemy," or *Feindbild*.

In his last book, *The Drowned and the Saved*, Primo Levi included an essay entitled "The Gray Zone," perhaps his most profound and deeply disturbing reflection on the Holocaust.[50] He maintained that in spite of our natural desire for clear-cut distinctions, the history of the camps "could not be reduced to the two blocs of victims and persecutors." He argued passionately, "It is naive, absurd, and historically false to believe that an infernal system such as National Socialism sanctifies its victims; on the contrary, it degrades them, it makes them resemble itself." The time had come to examine the inhabitants of the "gray zone" between the simplified Manichean images of perpetrator and victim. Levi concentrated on the "gray zone of *protekcya* [corruption] and collaboration" that flourished in the camps among a spectrum of victims: from the "picturesque fauna" of low-ranking functionaries husbanding their minuscule advantages over other prisoners; through the truly privileged network of Kapos, who were free "to commit the worst atrocities" at whim; to the terrible fate of the Sonderkommandos, who prolonged their lives by manning the gas chambers and crematoria. (Conceiving and organizing the Sonderkommandos was in Levi's opinion National Socialism's "most demonic crime".)

While Levi focused on the spectrum of victim behavior within the gray zone, he dared to suggest that this zone encompassed perpetrators as well. Even the SS man Muhsfeld of the Birkenau crematoria—whose "daily ration of slaughter was studded with arbitrary and capricious acts, marked by his inventions of cruelty"—was not a "monolith." Faced with the miraculous survival of a sixteen-year-old girl discovered while the gas chambers were being cleared, the disconcerted Muhsfeld briefly hesitated. In the end he ordered the girl's death but quickly left before his orders were carried out. One "instant of pity" was not enough to "absolve" Muhsfeld, who was deservedly hanged in 1947. Yet it did "place him too, although at its extreme boundary, within the gray band, that zone of ambiguity which radiates out from regimes based on terror and obsequiousness."

Levi's notion of the gray zone encompassing both perpetrators and victims must be approached with a cautious qualification. The perpetrators and victims in the gray zone were not mirror images of one another. Perpetrators did not become fellow victims (as many of them later claimed to be) in the way some victims became accomplices of the perpetrators. The relationship between perpetrator and victim was not symmetrical. The range of choice each faced was totally different.

Nonetheless, the spectrum of Levi's gray zone seems quite applicable to Reserve Police Battalion 101. The battalion certainly had its quota of men who neared the "extreme boundary" of the gray zone. Lieutenant Gnade, who initially rushed his men back from Minsk to avoid being involved in killing but who later learned to enjoy it, leaps to mind. So do the many reserve policemen who were horrified in the woods outside Józefów but subsequently became casual volunteers for numerous firing squads and "Jew hunts." They, like Muhsfeld, seem to have experienced that brief "instant of pity" but cannot be absolved by it. At the other boundary of the gray zone, even Lieutenant Buchmann, the most conspicuous and outspoken critic of the battalion's murderous actions, faltered at least once. Absent his protector, Major Trapp, and facing orders from the local Security Police in Łuków, he too led his men to the killing fields shortly before his transfer back to Hamburg. And at the very center of the perpetrators' gray zone stood the pathetic figure of Trapp himself, who sent his men to slaughter Jews "weeping like a child," and the bedridden Captain Hoffmann, whose body rebelled against the terrible deeds his mind willed.

The behavior of any human being is, of course, a very complex phenomenon, and the historian who attempts to "explain" it is indulging in a certain arrogance. When nearly 500 men are involved, to undertake any general explanation of their collective behavior is even more hazardous. What, then, is one to conclude? Most of all, one comes away from the story of Reserve Police Battalion 101 with great unease. This story of ordinary men is not the story of all men. The reserve policemen faced choices, and most of them committed terrible deeds. But those who killed cannot be absolved by the notion that anyone in the same situation would have done as they did. For even among them, some refused to kill and others stopped killing. Human responsibility is ultimately an individual matter.

At the same time, however, the collective behavior of Reserve Police Battalion 101 has deeply disturbing implications. There are many societies afflicted by traditions of racism and caught in the siege mentality of war or threat of war. Everywhere society conditions people to respect and defer to authority, and indeed could scarcely function otherwise. Everywhere people seek career advancement. In every modern society, the complexity of life and the resulting bureaucratization and specialization attenuate the sense of personal responsibility of those implementing official policy. Within virtually every social collective, the peer group exerts tremendous pressures on behavior and sets moral norms. If the men of Reserve Police Battalion 101 could become killers under such circumstances, what group of men cannot?

AFTERWORD

Since *Ordinary Men* first appeared six years ago, it has been relentlessly scrutinized and criticized by another author, Daniel Jonah Goldhagen, who not only wrote on the same topic—the motivation of the "ordinary" Germans who became Holocaust perpetrators—but also chose to develop his own work in part by researching the same documents concerning the same unit of Holocaust killers, namely the postwar judicial interrogations of members of Reserve Police Battalion 101.[1] It is not unusual, of course, for different scholars to ask different questions of, apply different methodologies to, and derive different interpretations from the same sources. But the differences are seldom so stridently argued and cast in such an adversarial framework as in this case. And seldom in academic controversies has the work of one of the adversaries become both an international best-seller and the subject of countless reviews ranging from the euphorically positive to harshly negative.[2] Professor Goldhagen, so critical of my work, has become a target in turn. In short, Goldhagen's critique of this book and the subsequent controversy surrounding his own work merit a retrospective "afterword" in subsequent editions of *Ordinary Men*.

On several issues Goldhagen and I do not disagree: first, the participation of numerous "ordinary" Germans in the mass murder of Jews, and second, the high degree of voluntarism they exhibited. The bulk of the killers were not specially selected but drawn at random from a cross-section of German society, and they did not kill because they were coerced by the threat of dire punishment for refusing. However, neither of these conclusions is a new discovery in the field of Holocaust studies. It was one of the fundamental conclusions of Raul Hilberg's magisterial and pathbreaking study *The Destruction of the European Jews*, which first appeared in 1961, that the perpetrators "were not different in their moral makeup from the rest of the population. The German perpetrator was not a special kind of German." The perpetrators represented "a remarkable cross-section of the German population," and the machinery of destruction "was structurally no different from organized German society as a whole."[3] And it was the German scholar Herbert Jäger[4] and the German prosecutors of the 1960s who firmly established that no one could document a single case in which Germans who refused to carry out the killing of unarmed civilians suffered dire consequences. Goldhagen does credit Jäger and the German prosecutors in this regard, but he is utterly dismissive of Hilberg.

Aside from the differences in the tone that we employ in writing about the Holocaust and in the attitude that we display toward other scholars who have worked in this field of study, Goldhagen and I disagree significantly in two major areas of historical interpretation. The first is our different assessments of the role of anti-Semitism in German history, including the National Socialist era. The second is our different assessments of the motivation(s) of the "ordinary" German men who became Holocaust killers. These are the two topics that I would like to discuss at some length.

In his book *Hitler's Willing Executioners*, Daniel Goldhagen asserts that anti-Semitism "more or less governed the ideational life of civil society" in pre-Nazi Germany,[5] and when the Germans "elected" [sic] Hitler to power, the "centrality of antisemitism in the Party's worldview, program, and rhetoric . . . mirrored the sentiments of German culture."[6] Because Hitler and the Germans were "of one mind" about the Jews, he had merely to "unshackle" or "unleash" their "pre-existing, pent-up" anti-Semitism to perpetrate the Holocaust.[7]

To buttress his view that the Nazi regime should be seen merely as allowing or encouraging Germans to do what they wanted to do all along and not basically shaping German attitudes and behavior after 1933, Goldhagen formulates a thesis that he proclaims is "new" to the study of anti-Semitism. Anti-Semitism "does not appear, disappear, then reappear in a given society. Always present, antisemitism becomes more or less manifest." Not anti-Semitism itself, but merely its "expression," either "increases or decreases" according to changing conditions.[8]

Then in Goldhagen's account this picture of underlying permanency and superficial fluctuation changes abruptly after 1945. The pervasive and permanent eliminationist German anti-Semitism that was the sole and sufficient motivation of the Holocaust killers suddenly disappeared. Given reeducation, a change in public conversation, a law banning anti-Semitic expression, and the lack of institutional reinforcement, a German culture dominated by anti-Semitism for centuries was suddenly transformed.[9] Now, we are told, the Germans are just like us.

That anti-Semitism was a very significant aspect of Germany's political culture before 1945 and that Germany's political culture is both profoundly different and dramatically less anti-Semitic today are two propositions that I can easily support. But if Germany's political culture in general and anti-Semitism in particular could be transformed after 1945 by changes in education, public conversation, law, and institutional reinforcements, as Goldhagen suggests, then it seems to me equally plausible that they could have been equally transformed in the three or four decades preceding 1945 and especially during the twelve years of Nazi rule.

In his introductory chapter Goldhagen provides a useful model for a three-dimensional analysis of anti-Semitism, even if he does not employ his own model in the subsequent chapters. Anti-Semitism, he argues, varies according to the alleged source or cause (for example, race, religion, culture, or environment) of the Jews' alleged negative character. It varies in degree of preoccupation or priority, or how important is anti-Semitism to the anti-Semite. And it varies in degree of threat, or how endangered the anti-Semite feels.[10] That anti-Semitism can vary in its diagnosis of the alleged Jewish threat and along continuums of priority and intensity would suggest not only that anti-Semitism changes over time as any or all of these dimensions change, but that it can exist in infinite variety. Even for a single country like Germany, I think we should speak and think in the plural—of anti-Semitisms rather than anti-Semitism.

The actual concept Goldhagen employs, however, produces the opposite effect; it erases all differentiation and subsumes all manifestations of anti-Semitism in Germany under a single rubric. All Germans who perceived Jews as different and viewed this difference as something negative that should disappear—whether through conversion, assimilation, emigration, or extermination— are classed as "eliminationist" anti-Semites, even if by Goldhagen's prior model they differ as to cause, priority, and intensity. Such differences that do exist are analytically insignificant in any case, for, according to Goldhagen, variations on eliminationist solutions "tend to metastasize" into extermination.[11] By using such an approach, Goldhagen moves seamlessly from a variety of anti-Semitic manifestations in Germany to a single German "eliminationist antisemitism" that, taking on the properties of organic malignancy, naturally metastasized into extermination. Thus all Germany was "of one mind" with Hitler on the justice and necessity of the Final Solution.

If one adopts the analytical model that Goldhagen proposes rather than the concept he actually uses, what then can one say about the changing variety of anti-Semitisms in German political culture and their role in the Holocaust? And where to begin?

Let us begin with nineteenth-century German history, or more precisely with various interpretations of Germany's alleged "special path" or *Sonderweg*. According to the traditional social/structural approach, Germany's failed liberal revolution of 1848 derailed simultaneous political and economic modernization. Thereafter, the precapitalist German elites maintained their privileges in an autocratic political system, while the unnerved middle classes were bought off with the prosperity of rapid economic modernization, gratified by a national unification they had been unable to achieve through their own revolutionary efforts, and ultimately manipulated by an escalating "social imperialism."[12] According to the cultural/ideological approach, the distorted and incomplete embrace of the Enlightenment by some German intellectuals, followed by their despair over an increasingly endangered and dissolving traditional world, led to a continuing rejection of liberal-democratic values and traditions on the one hand, and a selective reconciliation with aspects of modernity (such as modern technology and ends-means rationality) on the other, producing what Jeffrey Herf termed a peculiarly German "reactionary modernism."[13] A third approach, exemplified by John Weiss and Daniel Goldhagen, asserts a German *Sonderweg* in terms of the singular breadth and virulence of anti-Semitism in Germany, though the former paints with a less broad brush than the latter and is careful to identify the late nineteenth-century loci of this German anti-Semitism in populist political movements and among the political and academic elites.[14]

It seems to me that Shulamit Volkov's interpretation of late nineteenth-century German anti-Semitism as a "cultural code" constitutes an admirable synthesis of major elements of these different, though not totally mutually exclusive, notions of a German *Sonderweg*.[15] German conservatives, dominating an illiberal political system but feeling their leading role increasingly imperiled by the changes unleashed by modernization, associated anti-Semitism with everything they felt threatened by—liberalism, democracy, socialism, internationalism, capitalism, and cultural experimentation. To be a self-proclaimed anti-Semite was also to be authoritarian, nationalist, imperialist, protectionist, corporative, and culturally traditional. Volkov concludes, "Antisemitism was by then strongly associated with everything the conservatives stood for. It became increasingly inseparable from their antimodernism. . . ." But insofar as the conservatives co-opted the anti-Semitic issue from populist, single-issue anti-Semitic political parties and enlisted pseudo-scientific and Social Darwinist racial thinking in its support, the conservatives were embracing an issue in defense of reaction that had a peculiarly modern cast to it (not unlike the simultaneous embrace of naval building).

By the turn of the century a German anti-Semitism increasingly racial in nature had become an integral part of the conservative political platform and penetrated deeply into the universities. It had become more politicized and institutionalized than in the western democracies of France, Britain, and the United States. But this does not mean that late nineteenth-century German anti-Semitism dominated either politics or ideational life. The conservatives and single-issue anti-Semitic parties together constituted a minority. While majorities could be found in the Prussian Landtag to pass discriminatory legislation against Catholics in the 1870s and in the Reichstag against socialists in the 1880s, the emancipation of Germany's Jews, who constituted less than 1 percent of the population and were scarcely capable of defending themselves against a Germany united in hostile obsession against them, was not revoked. If the left did not exhibit a philo-Semitism comparable to the right's anti-Semitism, it was primarily because for the left anti-Semitism was a nonissue that did not fit into its own class analysis, not because of its own anti-Semitism.

Even for the openly anti-Semitic conservatives, the Jewish issue was but one among many. And to suggest that they felt more threatened by the Jews than, for example, by the Triple Entente abroad or Social Democracy at home would be a serious distortion. If anti-Semitism was neither the priority issue nor the greatest threat even for conservatives, how much less was this the case for the rest of German society. As Richard Levy has noted, "One can make a convincing case that [Jews] were of very little interest to most Germans most of the time. Putting them at the center of German history in the nineteenth and twentieth centuries is a highly unproductive strategy."[16]

For some Germans, of course, Jews were the top priority and source of greatest fear. The turn-of-the-century anti-Semitism of German conservatives fits well Gavin Langmuir's notion of "xenophobic" anti-Semitism—a negative stereotype comprised of various assertions that did not describe the real Jewish minority but rather symbolized various threats and menaces that anti-Semites could not and did not want to understand.[17] Langmuir notes as well that "xenophobic" anti-Semitism provides the fertile soil for the growth of fantastic or "chimeric" anti-Semitism—or what Saul Friedländer has recently dubbed "redemptive" anti-Semitism.[18] If Germany's xenophobic anti-Semitism was an important piece of the political platform of an important segment of the political spectrum, the "redemptive" anti-Semites with their chimeric accusations—from Jewish poisoning of Aryan blood to a secret Jewish world conspiracy behind the twin threats of Marxist revolution and plutocratic democracy—were still a fringe phenomenon.

The succession of traumatic experiences in Germany between 1912 and 1929—loss of control of the Reichstag by the right, military defeat, revolution, runaway inflation, and economic collapse—transformed German politics. The right grew at the expense of the center, and within the former the radicals, or New Right, grew at the expense of the traditionalists, or Old Right. Chimeric anti-Semitism grew commensurately from a fringe phenomenon to the core idea of a movement that became Germany's largest political party in the summer of 1932 and its ruling party six months later.

That fact alone makes the history of Germany and German anti-Semitism different from that of any other country in Europe. But even this must be kept in perspective. The Nazis never gained more than 37 percent of the vote in a free election, less than the combined socialist-communist vote. Daniel Goldhagen is right to remind us "that individuals' attitudes on single issues cannot be inferred from their votes."[19] But it is highly unlikely that he is correct in his related assertion that large numbers of Germans who voted for the Social Democratic Party for economic reasons were nonetheless of one mind with Hitler and the Nazis about Jews. While I cannot prove it, I strongly suspect far more Germans voted Nazi for reasons other than anti-Semitism than Germans who considered anti-Semitism a priority issue but nonetheless voted for a party other than the Nazis. Neither the election returns nor any plausible spin put on them suggest that in 1932 the vast majority of Germans were "of one mind" with Hitler about the Jews or that the "centrality of antisemitism in the Party's worldview, program, and rhetoric . . . mirrored the sentiments of German culture."[20]

Beginning in 1933 all the factors that Goldhagen credits with dismantling German anti-Semitism after 1945—education, public conversation, law, and institutional reinforcement—were operating in the opposite direction to intensify anti-Semitism among the Germans, and indeed in a far more concerted manner than in the postwar period. Can one seriously doubt that this had significant impact, particularly given the rising popularity of Hitler and the regime for its economic and foreign policy successes? As William Sheridan Allen succinctly concluded, even in a highly Nazified town like Northeim, most people "were drawn to anti-Semitism because they were drawn to Nazism, not the other way around."[21] Moreover, the 1936 Sopade underground report to which Goldhagen repeatedly refers—"antisemitism has no doubt taken root in wide circles of the population. . . . The general antisemitic psychosis affects even thoughtful people, our comrades as well"[22]—is evidence of change in German attitudes following the Nazi seizure of power in 1933, not the prior situation.

Even in the post–1933 period, however, it is best to speak in the plural of German anti-Semitisms. Within the party, there was indeed a large core of Germans for whom the Jews were a dire racial threat and central priority. The hardcore "chimeric" or "redemptive" anti-Semites of the Nazi movement differed in style and preferred response, however. At one end of the spectrum were the SA and Streicher types lusting for pogroms; at the other end were the cool and calculating, intellectual anti-Semites described by Ulrich Herbert in his new biography of Werner Best, who advocated a more systematic but dispassionate persecution.[23]

Hitler's conservative allies favored deemancipation and segregation of the Jews as part of the counterrevolution and movement of national renewal. They strove to end the allegedly "inordinate" Jewish influence on German life, though this was scarcely a priority equal to dismantling the labor unions, Marxist parties, and parliamentary democracy, or to rearmament and the restoration of Germany's great-power status. They often spoke the language of racial anti-Semitism, but not consistently. Some, like President Hindenburg, wanted exemptions for Jews who had proved themselves worthy through loyal service to the fatherland, and the churches, of course, wanted exemptions for converted Jews. In my opinion, it is unlikely that the conservatives on their own would have proceeded beyond the initial discriminatory measures of 1933–34 that drove the Jews out of the civil and military services, the professions, and cultural life.

What the conservatives conceived of as sufficient measures overlapped with what were for the Nazis scarcely the first steps. The Nazis understood far better than the conservatives the distance that separated them. As complicitous in the first anti-Jewish measures as they were in the wrecking of democracy, however, the conservatives could no more oppose radicalization of the persecution of the Jews than they could demand for themselves rights under the dictatorship that they had denied others. And while they may have lamented their own increasing loss of privilege and power at the hands of the Nazis whom they helped into power, with few exceptions they had no remorse or regret for the fate of the Jews. To argue that the Nazis' conservative allies were not of one mind with Hitler does not deny that their behavior was despicable and their responsibility considerable. As before, xenophobic anti-Semitism provided fertile soil for the chimeric anti-Semites.

What can be said of the German population at large in the 1930s? Was the bulk of the German population swept along by the Nazis' anti-Semitic tide? Only in part, according to the detailed research of historians like Ian Kershaw, Otto Dov Kulka, and David Bankier, who have reached a surprising degree of consensus on this issue.[24] For the 1933–39 period, these three historians distinguish between a minority of party activists, for whom anti-Semitism was an urgent priority, and the bulk of the German population, for whom it was not. Apart from the activists, the vast majority of the general population did not clamor or press for anti-Semitic measures. But the majority of "ordinary Germans"—whom Saul Friedländer describes as "onlookers" in contrast to "activists"[25]— nonetheless accepted the legal measures of the regime, which ended emancipation and drove the Jews from public positions in 1933, socially ostracized the Jews in 1935, and completed the expropriation of their property in 1938–39. Yet this majority was critical of the hooliganistic violence of party radicals toward the same German Jews whose legal persecution they approved. The boycott of 1933, the vandalistic outbreaks of 1935, and above all the *Kristallnacht* pogrom of November 1938 produced a negative response among much of the German population.

Most important, however, a gulf had opened up between the Jewish minority and the general population. The latter, while not mobilized around strident and violent anti-Semitism, were increasingly "apathetic," "passive," and "indifferent" to the fate of the former. Anti-Semitic measures—if carried out in an orderly and legal manner—were widely accepted for two main reasons: such measures sustained the hope of curbing the violence most Germans found so distasteful, and most Germans now accepted the goal of limiting, and even ending, the role of Jews in German society. This was a major accomplishment for the regime, but it still did not offer the prospect that most "ordinary Germans" would approve of, much less participate in, the mass murder of European Jewry, that the "onlookers" of 1938 would become the genocidal killers of 1941–42.

Concerning the war years, Kershaw, Kulka, and Bankier disagree on some issues but generally concur that the anti-Semitism of the "true believers" was not identical to the anti-Semitic attitudes of the general population, and that the anti-Semitic priorities and genocidal commitment of the regime were still not shared by ordinary Germans. Bankier, who in no way downplays German anti-Semitism, wrote: "Ordinary Germans knew how to distinguish between an acceptable discrimination . . . and the unacceptable horror of genocide. . . . The more the news of mass murder filtered through, the less the public wanted to be involved in the final solution of the Jewish question."[26] Nonetheless, as Kulka put it, "a strikingly abysmal indifference to the fate of the Jews as human beings" gave "the regime the freedom of action to push for a radical 'Final Solution.'"[27] Kershaw emphasized the same point with his memorable phrase that "the road to Auschwitz was built by hatred, but paved with indifference."[28]

Kulka and Rodrigue are uneasy about the term "indifference," which they as well as Kershaw use, feeling that it does not sufficiently capture the internalization of Nazi anti-Semitism among the population at large, particularly concerning the acceptance of a solution to the Jewish question through some unspecified kind of "elimination." They suggest a more morally weighted term such as "passive complicity" or "objective complicity."[29] Goldhagen is more emphatic, declaring the very concept of "indifference"— which he equates with having "no views" on and being "utterly morally neutral to mass slaughter"—to be conceptually flawed and psychologically impossible. For Goldhagen, Germans were not apathetic and indifferent but "pitiless," "unsympathetic," and "callous," and their silence should be interpreted as approval.[30] I have no problem with the desire of Kulka, Rodrigue, and Goldhagen to employ more powerful, morally condemnatory language to describe German behavior. But I do not think that choice of language here alters the basic point made by Kershaw, Kulka, and Bankier, namely that in terms of the priority of anti-Semitism and commitment to killing Jews a useful and important distinction can be made between the Nazi core and the population at large. In my opinion, Goldhagen is setting up a straw man in his definition of indifference and misinterprets the meaning of silence under a dictatorship. He also seems oblivious to the fact that Kershaw's notion of indifference anticipates the continuums in Goldhagen's own analytical model, when Kershaw notes that during the war years Germans may well have disliked Jews more while caring about them less.

There are two additional points on which Goldhagen and I agree. First, one must look at the attitudes and behavior of ordinary Germans not only on the home front but also in occupied eastern Europe, and second, when faced with the task of killing Jews, most ordinary Germans there became "willing" executioners. If ordinary Germans at home were indifferent and apathetic, complicitous and callous, in the east they were killers.

We differ, however, on context and motive for this murderous behavior. For Goldhagen, these ordinary Germans, "equipped with little more than the cultural notions current in Germany" before 1933 and now at last given the opportunity, simply "wanted to be genocidal executioners."[31] In my opinion, ordinary Germans in eastern Europe brought with them a set of attitudes that included not only the different strands of anti-Semitism found in German society and fanned by the regime since 1933, but much else as well. As the Treaty of Brest-Litovsk, the *Freikorps* campaigns, and the almost universal rejection of the Versailles Treaty demonstrate, refusal to accept the verdict of World War I, imperial aspirations in eastern Europe underpinned by notions of German racial superiority, and virulent anticommunism were broadly held sentiments in German society. I would argue that they provided more common ground for the bulk of the German population and the Nazis than did anti-Semitism.

And in eastern Europe ordinary Germans were transformed even more by the events and situation of 1939–41 than they had been by their experience of the domestic dictatorship of 1933–39. Germany was now at war; moreover, this was a "race war" of imperial conquest. These ordinary Germans were stationed in the territory where the native populations were proclaimed inferior and occupying Germans were constantly exhorted to behave as the master race. And the Jews encountered in these territories were the strange and alien *Ostjuden*, not assimilated, middle-class German Jews. In 1941 two more major factors, the ideological crusade against Bolshevism and "war of destruction," were added. Is it even plausible to suggest that this wartime change in situation and context did not alter the attitudes and behavior of ordinary Germans in eastern Europe, and that only a common cognitive image of Jews predating 1933 and held by virtually all Germans accounts for their willingness, and for some even eagerness, to kill Jews?

In this regard, it is important to note that before the Final Solution was implemented (beginning on Soviet territory in the second half of 1941 and in Poland and the rest of Europe in the spring of 1942), the Nazi regime had already found willing executioners for 70,000 to 80,000 mentally and physically handicapped Germans, tens of thousands of Polish intelligentsia, tens of thousands of noncombatant victims of reprisal shootings, and more than 2 million Russian POWs. Clearly, as of September 1939, the regime was increasingly capable of legitimizing and organizing mass murder on a staggering scale that did not depend on the anti-Semitic motivation of the perpetrators and the Jewish identity of the victims.

Daniel Goldhagen has recently written that even if he is "not entirely correct about the scope and character of German anti-Semitism, it does not follow that this would invalidate" his "conclusions about the . . . perpetrators and their motives."[32] Central to Goldhagen's interpretation is that these men were not only "willing executioners" but in fact "*wanted* to be genocidal executioners" of Jews (italics mine).[33] They "slaked their Jewish blood-lust" with "gusto"; they had "fun"; they killed "for pleasure."[34] Moreover, "the quantity and quality of personalized brutality and cruelty that the Germans perpetrated upon Jews was also distinctive" and "unprecedented"; indeed, they "stand out" in the "long annals of human barbarism."[35] Goldhagen concludes emphatically that "with regard to the motivational cause of the Holocaust, for the vast majority of the perpetrators, a monocausal explanation does suffice"—namely the "demonological antisemitism" that "was the common structure of the perpetrators' cognition and of German society in general."[36]

In support of this interpretation, Goldhagen constantly invokes the conscious use of rigorous social science methodology as one of the factors that sets his book above the work and beyond the reproach of other scholars in the field.[37] I would like to focus on two aspects of Goldhagen's argument for this interpretation and measure them against the very standard of rigorous social science that he himself sets: first, the design and structure of his argument, and second, his methodology concerning use of evidence.

While the bulk of Goldhagen's book focuses on anti-Semitism in German history and German treatment of Jews during the Holocaust, crucial to the design of his argument are two comparisons.[38] First, Germans are compared with non-Germans in their respective treatment of Jews. Second, German treatment of Jewish victims is compared with their treatment of non-Jewish victims. The purpose is to establish that only a pervasive, eliminationist anti-Semitism specific to German society can account for the stark differences that allegedly emerge from these comparisons.

The problems with the design are manifold. For the second comparison to adequately support his argument, Goldhagen must prove not only that Germans treated Jewish and non-Jewish victims differently (on which virtually all historians agree), but also that the different treatment is to be explained fundamentally by the anti-Semitic motivation of the vast majority of the perpetrators and not by other possible motivations, such as compliance with different government policies for different victim groups. The second and third case studies of *Hitler's Willing Executioners* are aimed at meeting the burden of proof on these two points. Goldhagen argues that the case of the Lipowa and Flughafen Jewish labor camps in Lublin demonstrates that in contrast to other victims, only Jewish labor was treated murderously by the Germans without regard for and indeed even counter to economic rationality. And the Helmbrechts death march case, he argues, demonstrates that Jews were killed even when orders have been given to keep them alive, and hence the driving motive for the killing was not compliance to government policy or obedience to orders but the deep personal hatred of the perpetrators for their Jewish victims that had been inculcated by German culture. And from all his cases, Goldhagen argues that the unprecedented, continuous, and pervasive cruelty with which the German perpetrators treated their Jewish victims is only explicable for the same reason.

Bringing wider attention to the death marches is one of the redeeming merits of Goldhagen's book, but his attempt to generalize from the one case of the Helmbrechts death march is unpersuasive. His powerful description of this horrific event must not obscure the fact that in terms of proof of a widespread eagerness to kill Jews even contrary to orders, he has established neither its representativeness for other death marches nor that the same phenomenon did not occur in Germans' treatment of other victims. And even in his own case Goldhagen admits that the guards had to prevent the local German population from providing food and lodging and German soldiers from providing medical care to the Jews, without ever considering whether these other Germans were not just as typical of German society at large as the murderous death march guards. Indeed, the stark difference in behavior of these different groups of Germans would suggest the importance of situational and institutional factors that he dismisses.[39]

Likewise one can find a counterexample concerning the ongoing killing of non-Jewish victims despite a top-level change of policy and the irrational misuse of non-Jewish labor. Having just decided to murder all the Jews of Europe, in October 1941 the Nazi regime reversed its earlier position concerning Soviet prisoners of war and ordered that henceforth they were to be used for labor rather than simply left to die from hunger, disease, and exposure. Rudolph Höss at Auschwitz was informed that he would receive a large contingent of Soviet POWs for the purpose of constructing a new camp at Birkenau—a project high on Himmler's list of priorities. In short, both economic rationale and superior orders mandated that the Soviet POWs be kept alive and put to useful labor. Nearly 10,000 Soviet POWs arrived in Auschwitz in October 1941 and were sent to Birkenau. By the end of February, four months later, only 945 were alive—a survival rate of 9.5 percent.[40] Himmler's order to use Soviet POWs for a priority construction project did not immediately reverse either the habitual and ingrained behavior of concentration camp personnel of using labor for torture and extermination or the deadly conditions at Birkenau.

Indeed, as Michael Thad Allen has pointed out in his recent Ph.D. dissertation on the Business Administration Main Office (Wirtschaftsverwaltungshauptamt) of the SS,[41] within the concentration camp system the use of labor to punish and torture inmates rather than for production was part of the institutional culture long before Jews were a significant portion of the inmate population. Moreover, attempts to harness concentration camp labor productively continued to founder throughout the war on the resistance of concentration camp personnel stubbornly hostile to economic rationality. The concentration camp culture proved difficult to alter in this regard, whatever the ethnic identity of the prisoners involved.

What about the treatment of Jewish labor in Birkenau at this time? In comparison, 7,000 young Slovak Jewish women were sent to the Auschwitz main camp or *Stammlager* in the spring of 1942, also for labor. In mid-August, the 6,000 who were still alive were moved to Birkenau. At the end of December, just over four months later, only 650 had not yet died—a comparable survival rate of 10.8 percent.[42] In short, institutional and situational factors and an ideology whose murderous potential was not derived solely from anti-Semitism produced nearly identical fatality rates among the Soviet POWs and Slovak Jewish women over the same period of time in the same camp, and this despite a change in government policy concerning the fate of Soviet POWs and the urgency of the economic task they were to perform.

Goldhagen is indeed correct that in the long run the murderous treatment of Soviet POWs did change while the murderous treatment of Jewish labor, except in minor ways, did not. But this simply indicates that, despite institutional inertia and the initial persistence of murderous patterns of behavior toward Soviet POWs, compliance with government policy ultimately prevailed in both cases. It does not demonstrate, as Goldhagen suggests,[43] that the fate of Slavs, such as the Soviet POWs, and Jews differed primarily because of different culturally induced attitudes toward the two sets of victims. The Germans presided over the death of some 2 million Soviet POWs in the first nine months of the war—far more than the number of Jewish victims up to that point. The death rate in these POW camps far exceeded the death rates in the Polish ghettos *prior* to the Final Solution. The fact that the Nazi regime changed its policy to murder all Jews and changed its policy not to starve all Soviet POWs is more a measure of the ideology, priorities, and obsessions of Hitler and the Nazi leadership than of the attitudes of German society. The staggering fatality rate of Soviet POWs in the first months suggests above all the regime's capacity to harness ordinary Germans to murder limitless numbers of Soviet POWs if that had remained its goal. The continuing mass death of Soviet POWs into the spring of 1942 demonstrates that killing institutions are not turned off and the attitudes and behavior of their personnel are not altered instantly, even when policy changes.

There are, in short, a number of conceivable variables—government policy and past patterns of behavior as well as culturally induced cognitive images—that are important. Yet, in accounting for differential German behavior toward Jewish and non-Jewish victims, Goldhagen's argument does not adequately separate the variety of possible causal factors. His insistence on the German cognitive image of Jews as the "only" adequate framework is bolstered above all by his emphasis on the cruelty of the perpetrators.

However, the argument from unprecedented, singular German cruelty toward Jews is problematic on two counts. First, Goldhagen's claim of singularity is grounded on the emotional impact of his narrative rather than actual comparison. He offers numerous graphic and chilling descriptions of German cruelty toward Jews and then simply asserts to the numbed and horrified reader that such behavior is clearly unprecedented. If only that were the case. Unfortunately, accounts of Romanian and Croatian killings would readily demonstrate that these collaborators not only equaled but routinely surpassed the Germans in cruelty. And that leaves myriad possible non-Holocaust examples from Cambodia to Rwanda totally aside.

Conversely, he downplays the cruelty in the Nazi murder of

other victims, particularly the German handicapped in which Germans allegedly were "coldly involved" in inflicting "painless" death without celebration.[44] Yet the mentally handicapped were first gunned down by the firing squads of the Eimann commando before the development of the gas vans and gas chambers, and many infants were simply not fed and left to starve to death. Screaming and fleeing patients were hunted down and dragged away from asylums to the waiting buses. And at Hadamar the killers threw a party to celebrate the milestone of 10,000 victims![45]

Secondly, Goldhagen simply asserts as intuitively self-evident that such cruelty can be explained only by a cognitive image of the Jew peculiar to German culture.[46] Goldhagen is quite correct that cruelty in the Holocaust—so salient in the memories of survivors—is an issue that scholars have not dealt with at length, but that does not mean his own ungrounded assertion concerning motivation is correct. Interestingly, the eloquent survivor Primo Levi agreed at least in part with Franz Stangl, the notorious Treblinka commandant, on a different, quite functional explanation for perpetrator cruelty, namely that the total debasement and humiliation of the victim facilitated the victim's dehumanization so essential to the actions of the perpetrator—"to condition those who actually had to carry out the policies. To make it possible for them to do what they did." But we can share Levi's frustration that such an explanation in itself, if not entirely wrong, is nonetheless inadequate. "This is an explanation not devoid of logic," he continues, "but it shouts to heaven; it is the sole usefulness of useless violence."[47]

Indeed, too many instances of cruelty transcend a purely functional explanation. Another approach is taken by Fred E. Katz, who argues that in a killing environment the creation of "a culture of cruelty" is a "powerful phenomenon" that provides many satisfactions—individualized reputation and enhanced standing among one's peers, alleviation of boredom, and a sense of joy and festivity, of artistry and creativity—to those who flaunt their gratuitous and inventive cruelties.[48] But we are still left with an unresolved question that cannot be solved by simple assertion: Is a culture of hatred the necessary precondition for such a culture of cruelty? Goldhagen has posed an important question. I do not believe that we have as yet found a satisfactory answer.

Let us turn to the other comparison, namely that of German and non-German treatment of Jews. To be valid by accepted social science standards, German behavior would have to be compared with behavior in the complete set, or at least an unbiased random sample, of countries involved in the Final Solution. Instead Goldhagen suggests the behavior of Danes and Italians as the standard of comparison, which is neither random nor unbiased.[49] Indeed, his suggestion merely begs the question of the rarity of Danish and Italian behavior vis-à-vis the ability of the Germans to find murderous collaborators virtually everywhere else in Europe. It does not demonstrate the singularity of German treatment of Jews, much less that this was due to a culturally specific German anti-Semitism. Elsewhere Goldhagen acknowledges the participation of east Europeans in the killing squads and calls for a study of the "combination of cognitive and situational factors" that brought such perpetrators to the Holocaust.[50] He does not explain why a multicausal explanation is suddenly acceptable for east European but not for German perpetrators.

Moreover, as I noted at the April 1996 symposium at the U.S. Holocaust Memorial Museum,[51] the example of the Luxemburgers in Reserve Police Battalion 101 offers the rare opportunity of comparing people in the same situation but of different cultural background. While the evidence is suggestive rather than conclusive, I noted that the fourteen Luxemburgers seem to have behaved very much like their German comrades, implying that situational factors were very strong indeed. Goldhagen replied that the 14 Luxemburgers were only a small number, from which one could not draw sweeping conclusions, though he has not been reluctant to draw sweeping conclusions from the small numbers of guards in the Lipowa and Flughafen labor camps or on the Helmbrechts death march.

My objections to the design of Goldhagen's argument do not disprove his interpretation as such. They merely demonstrate that he has not met the standard of proof of rigorous social science that he has not only set for himself but also repeatedly claimed that others have so ignominiously failed even to understand. To demonstrate not only the lack of conclusive proof on behalf of his interpretation but flaws that render it unpersuasive, we must examine his use of evidence.

Goldhagen admits that he began with the hypothesis "that the perpetrators were motivated to take part in the lethal persecution of the Jews because of their beliefs about the victims."[52] The primary source of evidence for the behavior and motivation of the men of Reserve Police Battalion 101 by which to measure this hypothesis is the postwar testimony gathered through judicial investigation. It is not a matter of contention among scholars that postwar perpetrator testimony is highly problematic; it is shaped both by the questions posed by the investigators and by the forgetfulness, repression, distortion, evasion, and mendacity of the witnesses.

It is my position, however, that the judicial testimonies of Reserve Police Battalion 101 are qualitatively different from the vast bulk of such testimony. The roster of the unit survived, and more than 40 percent of the battalion members (most of them rank and file reservists rather than officers) were interrogated by able and persistent investigative attorneys. The large amount of unusually vivid and detailed testimony stands in stark contrast to the formulaic and transparently dishonest testimony so often encountered. Aware of the subjective and fallible nature of the judgments I will be making, I feel nonetheless that, used carefully, this body of testimony offers the historian a unique opportunity to probe issues in a way that is not possible from the records of other cases. It is no accident, after all, that among the hundreds of postwar German trials, both Goldhagen and I found our ways independently to the very same court records.

To deal with the problem of the evidentiary value of perpetrator testimony, Goldhagen argues in contrast that "the only methodological position that makes sense is to discount *all* self-exculpating testimony that finds no corroboration from other sources."[53] Goldhagen is also aware that "the temptation to pick and choose propitious material from a large number of cases should be resisted so as to avoid bias in the conclusions."[54] And he asserts that in his methodology "such bias is negligible."[55]

But does Goldhagen's methodology avoid bias? What in practice is Goldhagen's standard for judging testimony as self-exculpating and thus to be excluded unless corroborated? For Goldhagen testimonies are "in all likelihood" self-exculpating if the witnesses deny giving "their souls, their inner will and moral assent" to the killing.[56] In short, testimony about any state of mind or motivation at odds with his initial hypothesis is excluded unless corroborated, and finding corroborating evidence concerning state of mind—given the absence of contemporary letters and diaries—is nearly impossible. As a result, Goldhagen is left only with a residue of testimony compatible with his hypothesis, and the conclusions are for all practical purposes predetermined. A methodology that can scarcely do other than confirm the hypothesis that it was designed to test is not valid social science.

The problem of a deterministic methodology is compounded by another flaw in Goldhagen's use of evidence, namely a double standard in which he does not apply the same evidentiary standards and high exclusionary threshold when the victims are Poles rather than Jews. The cumulative effect of these problems in Goldhagen's use of evidence can be dramatically illustrated in comparing our respective accounts of Reserve Police Battalion 101's initial massacres of Jews and Poles at Józefów and Talcyn.

According to Goldhagen, at Józefów Major Wilhelm Trapp delivered a "pep talk," inciting his men to murder by activating the demonic view of the Jews that virtually all of them held. Though Trapp was "conflicted" and "uneasy," his speech betrayed "his Nazified conception of the Jews." Goldhagen concedes that "many of the men were shaken, even momentarily depressed by the killings," but warns against "the temptation" of reading into the testimonies about the men's negative reaction more than visceral weakness when faced with too much blood and gore.[57]

What is left out of this portrayal? Goldhagen acknowledges in one footnote, though not in the main text, that one witness described Trapp as "weeping." There is no mention of the other seven witnesses who described Trapp as weeping or otherwise displaying visible physical distress.[58] He does not mention the testimony of two policemen who recalled that Trapp explicitly said the orders did not come from him,[59] nor four of the five who noted that Trapp openly distanced himself from the orders when transmitting them to his men.[60] He does not mention the testimony of Trapp's chauffeur: "Concerning the events in Józefów, he later told me more or less: 'If this Jewish business is ever avenged on earth, then have mercy on us Germans.'"[61] The "pep talk" allegedly activating a demonic view of the Jews turns out, on examination, to be a rather pathetic attempt to rationalize the imminent massacre of Jews as a wartime action against Germany's enemies, similar to the bombs falling on German women and children at home. The repeated testimony of the men that they felt shaken, depressed, embittered, despondent, dejected, stricken, angered, and burdened is dismissed by Goldhagen out of hand as self-exculpatory or reflecting "momentary" visceral weakness.

Describing the first execution of Poles in a reprisal shooting at Talcyn, Goldhagen argues: "This illustrative episode juxtaposes the Germans' attitudes towards Poles and Jews." As proof, he cites just two witnesses—one witness to the effect that at Talcyn Trapp "wept," and another that "Some of the men expressed afterwards their desire not to undertake any more missions of this sort."[62] In short, precisely the kinds of repeated testimony that Goldhagen excludes or dismisses when discussing the battalion's murder of Jews at Józefów is suddenly embraced—even when voiced by just two individuals—to prove how differently the battalion felt about murdering Poles.

Moreover, this double standard in the selection of evidence can also be seen in Goldhagen's analysis of the men's motives. The failure of the policemen to opt out at Talcyn is not construed as evidence of a desire to kill Poles, while not opting out at Józefów is cited as evidence that they "wanted to be genocidal executioners" of the Jews. Nothing more than "momentary" visceral weakness is seen in the mountain of testimony about the men's distress at Józefów, while the statement of a single witness at Talcyn is cited as valid evidence of the men's "obvious distaste and reluctance" to kill Poles.[63]

The double standard concerning Jewish and Polish victims can be seen in yet another way. Goldhagen cites numerous instances of gratuitous and voluntaristic killing of Jews as relevant to assessing the attitudes of the killers. But he omits a similar case of gratuitous, voluntaristic killing by Reserve Police Battalion 101 when the victims were Poles. A German police official was reported killed in the village of Niezdów, whereupon policemen about to visit the cinema in Opole were sent to carry out a reprisal action. Only elderly Poles, mostly women, remained in the village, as the younger Poles had all fled. Word came, moreover, that the ambushed German policeman had been only wounded, not killed. Nonetheless, the men of Reserve Police Battalion 101 shot all the elderly Poles and set the village on fire before returning to the cinema for an evening of casual and relaxing entertainment.[64] There is not much evidence of "obvious distaste and reluctance" to kill Poles to be seen in this episode. Would Goldhagen have omitted this incident if the victims had been Jews and an anti-Semitic motivation could have easily been inferred?

A pattern of tendentious selection of evidence[65] can also been seen in Goldhagen's portrayal of near total uniformity among the men. Lieutenant Heinz Buchmann was the one member of the battalion who articulated a principled opposition to the mass murder and refused to take part in any aspect of the anti-Jewish actions. Concerning the difference in behavior between himself and the SS captains Julius Wohlauf and Wolfgang Hoffmann, Buchmann testified reluctantly that promotion was unimportant to him because he owned a successful business, while Wohlauf and Hoffmann were ambitious career policemen "who wanted to become something." Moreover, he added, "Through my business experience, especially because it extended abroad, I had gained a better overview of things."[66] Goldhagen quickly glosses over the importance Buchmann himself gives to careeristic motives and construes the second portion of the statement as evidence that Buchmann alone in the battalion was not in the grip of German hallucinatory anti-Semitism.[67]

But if Buchmann is to be cited as a prime witness providing evidence for a uniform anti-Semitism within the battalion, ought not the following statements also be included? Concerning the differing reactions of the men to Buchmann's own refusal to take part in the anti-Jewish actions, he said: "Among my subordinates many understood my position, but others made disparaging remarks about me and looked down their noses at me."[68] Concerning their attitude to the killing itself, he stated that "the men did not carry out the Jewish actions with enthusiasm. . . . The men were all very depressed."[69]

One final example of tendentious selectivity of evidence. Goldhagen consistently emphasizes that the perpetrators "had fun" killing Jews, and that these "men's accounts of conversations that they had while in the killing fields suggest . . . that these men in principle approved of the genocide and of their own deeds."[70] A typical example of this is his account of Sergeant Heinrich Bekemeier's squad carrying out the "Jew hunt" in Łomazy after the massacre. Goldhagen writes:

> When Bekemeier's men did find Jews, they not only killed them but, in one instance that has been described, they, or at least Bekemeier, also had fun with them beforehand:

He then quotes directly from the policeman's testimony.

> One episode has been preserved in my memory to this day. Under the command of Sergeant Bekemeier we had to convey a transport of Jews to some place. He had the Jews crawl through a water hole and sing as they did it. When an old man could not walk anymore, which was when the crawling episode was finished, he shot him at close range in the mouth. . . .

At this point Goldhagen breaks off the quote and resumes the description of this same incident from testimony given at a later interrogation.

After Bekemeier had shot the Jew, the latter raised his hand as if to appeal to God and then collapsed. The corpse of the Jew was simply left lying. We did not concern ourselves with it.

How different this testimony sounds if the witness's account is not broken off, for after describing Bekemeier's shooting of the old Jew in the mouth, he continues: "I said to Heinz Richter, who was walking next to me, 'I'd like to bump off this trash.'" Indeed, according to the same witness, within the "circle of comrades" Bekemeier was deemed "vile trash" and "a dirty dog." He was notorious for being "violent and cruel" to both "Poles and Jews" and even for kicking his own men.[71] In short, by tendentious selectivity Goldhagen portrays this event as part of a pattern of generalized and uniform cruelty and approval, when the full testimony provides a picture instead of the cruelty of an especially vicious and disliked SS officer, whose behavior evoked disapproval among his men.

In contrast to Goldhagen, I offered a portrayal of the battalion that was multilayered. Different groups within the battalion behaved in different ways. The "eager killers"—whose numbers increased over time—sought the opportunity to kill, and celebrated their murderous deeds. The smallest group within the battalion comprised the nonshooters. With the exception of Lieutenant Buchmann, they did not make principled objections against the regime and its murderous policies; they did not reproach their comrades. They took advantage of Trapp's policy within the battalion of exempting from shooting those who "didn't feel up to it" by saying that they were took weak or that they had children.

The largest group within the battalion did whatever they were asked to do, without ever risking the onus of confronting authority or appearing weak, but they did not volunteer for or celebrate the killing. Increasingly numb and brutalized, they felt more pity for themselves because of the "unpleasant" work they had been assigned than they did for their dehumanized victims. For the most part, they did not think what they were doing was wrong or immoral, because the killing was sanctioned by legitimate authority. Indeed, for the most part they did not try to think, period. As one policeman stated: "Truthfully, I must say that at the time we didn't reflect about it at all. Only years later did any of us become truly conscious of what had happened then."[72] Heavy drinking helped: "most of the other men drank so much solely because of the many shootings of Jews, for such a life was quite intolerable sober."[73]

That these policemen were "willing executioners" does not mean that they "wanted to be genocidal executioners." This, in my opinion, is an important distinction that Goldhagen consistently blurs. He also repeatedly poses the interpretational dispute in the form of a false dichotomy: either the German killers must have been "of one mind" with Hitler about the demonological nature of the Jews and hence believed in the necessity and justice of the mass murder, or they must have believed that they were committing the greatest crime in history. In my view the majority of the killers could not be described by either of these polar-opposite views.

In addition to a multilayered portrayal of the battalion, I offered a multicausal explanation of motivation. I noted the importance of conformity, peer pressure, and deference to authority, and I should have emphasized more explicitly the legitimizing capacities of government. I also emphasized the "mutually intensifying effects of war and racism," as "the years of anti-Semitic propaganda . . . dovetailed with the polarizing effects of war." I argued that "nothing helped the Nazis to wage a race war so much as the war itself," as the "dichotomy of racially superior Germans and racially inferior Jews, central to Nazi ideology, could easily merge with the image of a beleaguered Germany surrounded by enemies." Ordinary Germans did not have to be "of one mind" with Hitler's demonological view of the Jews to carry out genocide. A combination of situational factors and ideological overlap that concurred on the enemy status and dehumanization of the victims was sufficient to turn "ordinary men" into "willing executioners."

Goldhagen claims that we have "no choice but to adopt" his own explanation, because he has "irrefutably" and "resoundingly" disproved the "conventional explanations" (coercion, obedience, social-psychological observations about human behavior, self-interest, and attenuation or fragmentation of responsibility). Several problems emerge. First, these "conventional explanations" are not invoked by scholars as sole and sufficient causes of perpetrator behavior but are usually part of a multicausal approach, what Goldhagen derides as a "laundry list."[74] Thus they do not have to meet the same high test of allegedly accounting for everything that Goldhagen sets for his own explanation. Second, to claim that one has disproved something irrefutably sets a high test that Goldhagen does not meet. And third, even a comprehensive refutation of the "conventional explanations" would not necessitate accepting Goldhagen's thesis.

Let us look more closely at Goldhagen's alleged refutation of two of the so-called conventional explanations: a German propensity to follow orders, and general attributes of human behavior studied by social psychologists (deference to authority, role adaptation, conformity to peer pressure). Goldhagen abruptly dismisses the notion that a propensity to follow orders and unthinking obedience to authority were prominent elements of German political culture. After all, he notes that Germans battled in the streets of Weimar and were openly disdainful of the Republic.[75] But one incident does not make a country's history or characterize its political culture. To claim that German political culture displayed no tendency to obedience because of opposition to Weimar is no more valid than to claim that anti-Semitism was not a part of German political culture by citing Jewish emancipation in nineteenth-century Germany—a notion Goldhagen emphatically resists.

More important is the historical context of Weimar disobedience. Goldhagen notes that Germans were obedient only to government and authority that they deemed "legitimate." This is indeed vital to the issue, for it was precisely the democratic, nonauthoritarian character of Weimar that delegitimized it in the eyes of those who disdained and attacked it. It was precisely the Nazis' demolition of democracy and the restoration of an authoritarian political system, emphasizing communal obligations over individual rights, that gave them legitimacy and popularity among significant segments of the German population. Indeed, many historians have argued that Germany's incomplete and halfhearted democratic revolutions in 1848 and 1918 opened the door for successful authoritarian counterrevolution and restoration, and that failed democratization—not anti-Semitism—decisively distinguished Germany's political culture from that of France, England, and the United States.

The same kinds of evidence and arguments that Goldhagen cites as proof of the pervasiveness of anti-Semitism inculcating hatred of Jews in Germany can also be found in support of the notion that Germany had a strong tradition of authoritarianism inculcating habits of obedience and antidemocratic attitudes. All the elements that Goldhagen himself cites as decisive for shaping political culture—education, public conversation, law, and institutional reinforcement[76]—were at work inculcating authoritarian values in Germany long before the Nazis also used them to incessantly disseminate anti-Semitism.

Moreover, the most outspoken anti-Semites in Germany were also antidemocratic and authoritarian. To deny the importance of authoritarian traditions and values in German political culture while arguing for the pervasiveness of anti-Semitism is to insist that the glass is half-full while denying that it is half-empty. To the extent that Goldhagen's arguments about German political culture and anti-Semitism are valid, they are even more so for German political culture and obedience to authority.

Goldhagen claims that the social-psychological interpretation is "ahistorical" and that its adherents "imply that any group of people, regardless of their socialization and their beliefs, could be parachuted into the same circumstances and would act in exactly the same way toward any arbitrarily selected group of victims."[77] This is a serious mischaracterization that confuses the experimental setting with scholars' subsequent application of the insights derived. For example, the point of the Milgram and Zimbardo experiments was to isolate the variables of deference to authority and role adaptation precisely so that the dynamic of these factors in human behavior could be examined and better understood. To have run either of these experiments pitting Serbs against Bosnian Muslims or Hutus against Tutsis would have been ludicrous, for the very reason that the historically specific ethnic animosities would have introduced a second powerful variable, totally skewing the results.

It was precisely because the experiments were kept ahistorical that the insights from them have validity, and that scholars now know that deference to authority and role adaptation are powerful factors shaping human behavior. For scholars studying motivation in concrete historical situations, in which variables cannot be isolated and historical actors are not themselves fully conscious of the complex interaction of factors that shape their behavior, such insights can in my opinion be invaluable for sifting through problematic evidence.

Goldhagen has repeatedly claimed that his interpretation alone correctly assumes that the perpetrators believed that the slaughter of Jews was necessary and just, while the "conventional explanations" suffer from the false assumption that the killers believed that what they were doing was wrong and had to be induced to kill against their will. This both mischaracterizes the position of others and poses the issue as a false dichotomy. Employing a social-psychological approach in investigating the historically specific instance of "crimes of obedience" in Vietnam, Kelman and Hamilton have noted a spectrum of response to authority. Between those who acted out of conviction because they shared the values of the regime and its policies on the one hand, and nominal compliers who acted against their will under supervision but did not obey orders when not being watched, there were other possibilities. Many accepted and internalized the role expectation that soldiers must be tough and obedient and carry out state policies regardless of the content of specific orders.[78] Soldiers and police can willingly obey orders and implement policy that they do not identify as commensurate with their own personal values, even when not supervised, in the same way that soldiers and police often willingly follow orders and are killed in the line of duty, though they do not want to die. They can commit acts in their capacity of soldiers and police that they would deem wrong if done of their own volition, but which they do not consider wrong if sanctioned by the state.[79] And people can change their values, adopting new ones that do not conflict with their actions, thus becoming killers out of conviction as the killing becomes routine. The relationship between authority, belief, and action is not only complex, but it is also unstable and can change over time.[80]

The social-psychological approach does not assume, as Goldhagen claims, that the perpetrators' ideology, moral values, and conception of the victims do not matter.[81] But the approach is certainly not congenial to the simplistic reduction of the perpetrators' ideology, moral values, and conception of the victim to a single factor, such as anti-Semitism. I agree with Goldhagen when he states that "'crimes of obedience' . . . depend upon the existence of a propitious social and political context."[82] But the social and political context invariably introduces a plurality of factors beyond the cognition of the perpetrators and identity of the victims, and it produces a complex and changing spectrum or range of response.

In short, Goldhagen has not come even close to accurately explicating and then "irrefutably" disproving several of the key "conventional explanations,"[83] neither of which is claimed to be a total explanation in itself. Even if the five conventional explanations noted by Goldhagen had been "irrefutably" disproved, it is not the case that we are left with "no choice but to adopt" Goldhagen's own interpretation. The search for understanding the motivations of the Holocaust perpetrators is not confined to a limited set. The scholar's quest is not a multiple-choice exam. Or at the very least there must always be another choice: "None of the above."

Throughout the controversy, Goldhagen has claimed that his approach has restored a moral dimension missing from the accounts of previous historians. For instance, in his recent reply to his critics in *The New Republic*, Goldhagen asserts that he has recognized "the humanity" of the perpetrators. His analysis is "predicated upon the recognition that each individual made choices about how to treat Jews," which "restores the notion of individual responsibility." On the other hand, he claims that scholars like myself have "kept the perpetrators at a comfortable arm's length" and treated them as "automatons or puppets."[84]

These claims by Goldhagen are untenable. First, the social-psychological insights he cavalierly dismisses do not treat individuals as mechanically interchangeable parts, nor do they dismiss cultural and ideological factors.[85] As noted above, Goldhagen's assertion that the psycho-sociological approach is "demonstrably false"[86] is based on crude caricature. Second, concerning the "humanity" of the perpetrators and not keeping them "at a comfortable arm's length," it is Goldhagen himself who admonishes other scholars to rid themselves of the notion that Germans in the Third Reich were "more or less like us" and that "their sensibilities had remotely approximated our own."[87] And his claim to treat perpetrators as "responsible agents who make choices" is difficult to reconcile with his deterministic conclusion: "During the Nazi period, and even long before, most Germans could no more emerge with cognitive models foreign to their society . . . than they could speak fluent Romanian without ever having been exposed to it."[88]

It is my position, in contrast, that psycho-sociological theories—based upon the assumption of inclinations and propensities common to human nature but not excluding cultural influences—provide important insights into the behavior of the perpetrators. I believe that the perpetrators not only had the capacity to choose but exercised that choice in various ways that covered the spectrum from enthusiastic participation, through dutiful, nominal, or regretful compliance, to differing degrees of evasion. Which of our two approaches, I would ask, is predicated upon the humanity and individuality of the perpetrators and allows for a moral dimension in the analysis of their choices?

Goldhagen and I agree that Reserve Police Battalion 101 was representative of "ordinary Germans," and that "ordinary Germans" randomly conscripted from all walks of life became "willing executioners." But I do not think that his portrayal of the battalion is representative. He is certainly right that there were numerous enthusiastic killers who sought the opportunity to kill, found gratification in inflicting terrible cruelties, and celebrated their deeds. All too many frightening examples of such behavior can be found in both this book and his. But Goldhagen minimizes or denies other layers of behavior that are important to understanding the dynamics of genocidal killing units and that cast doubt on his assertion that the battalion was uniformly pervaded by "pride" in and "principled approval" of the mass murder it perpetrated. His portrayal is skewed because he mistakes the part for the whole.

This is a flaw that appears repeatedly throughout the book. For instance, I agree that anti-Semitism was a strong ideological current in nineteenth-century Germany, but I do not accept Goldhagen's assertion that anti-Semitism "more or less governed the ideational life of civil society" in pre-Nazi Germany.[89] I agree that by 1933 anti-Semitism had become part of the "common sense" of the German right without thereby concluding that all German society was "of one mind" with Hitler about the Jews, and that the "centrality of antisemitism in the Party's worldview, program, and rhetoric . . . mirrored the sentiments of German culture."[90] I agree that anti-Semitism—negative stereotyping, dehumanization, and hatred of the Jews—was widespread among the killers of 1942, but I do not agree that this anti-Semitism is primarily to be seen as a "pre-existing, pent-up" anti-Semitism that Hitler had merely to "unleash" and "unshackle."[91]

In short, the fundamental problem is not to explain why ordinary Germans, as members of a people utterly different from us and shaped by a culture that permitted them to think and act in no other way than to want to be genocidal executioners, eagerly killed Jews when the opportunity offered. The fundamental problem is to explain why ordinary men—shaped by a culture that had its own particularities but was nonetheless within the mainstream of western, Christian, and Enlightenment traditions—under specific circumstances willingly carried out the most extreme genocide in human history.

Why does it matter which of our portrayals of and conclusions about Reserve Police Battalion 101 are closer to the truth? It would be very comforting if Goldhagen were correct, that very few societies have the long-term, cultural-cognitive prerequisites to commit genocide, and that regimes can only do so when the population is overwhelmingly of one mind about its priority, justice, and necessity. We would live in a safer world if he were right, but I am not so optimistic. I fear that we live in a world in which war and racism are ubiquitous, in which the powers of government mobilization and legitimization are powerful and increasing, in which a sense of personal responsibility is increasingly attenuated by specialization and bureaucratization, and in which the peer group exerts tremendous pressures on behavior and sets moral norms. In such a world, I fear, modern governments that wish to commit mass murder will seldom fail in their efforts for being unable to induce "ordinary men" to become their "willing executioners."

ACKNOWLEDGMENTS

I am extremely grateful to Theodore Raphael, Michael Marrus, Saul Friedländer, Lawrence Langer, Aaron Asher, E. Wayne Carp, and Mark Jensen for their many thoughtful suggestions to improve the manuscript. The shortcomings that remain are, of course, my own responsibility.

TWENTY-FIVE YEARS LATER

Ordinary Men WAS FIRST PUBLISHED IN 1992. FOLLOWING THE publication of Daniel Goldhagen's *Hitler's Willing Executioners* in 1996 and the ensuing debate over our differing interpretational approaches and methodologies concerning the use of problematic evidence, a second edition of *Ordinary Men* was published in 1998 with an afterword that summarized my arguments in this controversy. Now, twenty-five years after its first publication, it seems fitting to take stock once again. I will examine four areas in which fruitful historical research has added to our knowledge and insight about the issues raised by the initial publication of *Ordinary Men*. First, there have been numerous studies of other battalions of the Order Police, which allows for a much fuller comparative context of the ways in which Reserve Police Battalion 101 was typical or representative and the ways in which its singularity was illuminating.

Second, there have been further contributions to the study of the motivation of "ordinary" participants in the Final Solution. Third, there has been an exemplary study of the contingent of Luxembourg police in the battalion that allows for a comparison of the German and non-German members of the unit. And fourth, there has been a more careful study of photographic evidence—both old and new—concerning RPB 101.

OTHER BATTALIONS OF THE ORDER POLICE

In chapters three and four of *Ordinary Men*, I made brief mention of the role of Police Battalions 309 and 322 in Bialystok, Reserve Police Battalion 45 in the Ukraine, Police Battalion 11 in Slutsk, and Reserve Police Battalion 133 in Eastern Galicia. Daniel Goldhagen also discussed Police Battalions 309 in Bialystok and 65 in the Baltic in 1941 and southern Poland in 1942. Beginning in the 1990s, further studies of some of these units as well as many others finally began to be published. First was the journalist Heiner Lichtenstein's *Himmlers grüne Helfer: Die Schutz-und Ordnungspolizei im "Dritten Reich,"* that reviewed the judicial investigations of various Order Police units, especially battalions, and the failure of the German courts to achieve anything but a handful of convictions.[1] This was quickly followed by two different studies of Police Battalion 322 that were based upon the rare surviving "war diaries" of the battalion and its third company that were among a collection of SS documents held in the Military Archive in Prague.[2] This battalion began its murderous activities in Bialystok in July 1941, and then moved across present-day Belarus, engaging in major killing actions in Minsk and Mogilew as well as many other smaller mass killings.

In 1996, Winfried Nachtwei looked at five different police battalions that were primarily recruited from Rhineland cities. In addition to the two battalions touched upon by Goldhagen, namely 65 and 309, he also examined 307 and 316 (like 322, members of the police regiment under the command of Colonel Mantua during the July 1941 killings in Bialystok), and finally Reserve Police Battalion 61, notorious for its role in guarding the Warsaw ghetto.[3] Richard Breitman, in his book *Official Secrets,* briefly touched on Police Battalions 322 and 11 as well as Police Regiment South (comprised of 45, 303, and 314).[4]

These rather cursory sketches were followed by two particularly important studies. In 1998, Edward Westermann published his study of Police Battalion 310, in which he focused on the "striking dissimilarities" between that unit and Reserve Police Battalion 101.[5] Police Battalion 310 spent sixteen months in Poland (October 1941 to February 1942) learning to behave like an occupying master race before being transferred to Soviet territory and suffering heavy casualties on the Leningrad front. Its rank and file, mostly born between 1905 and 1912, were drawn from a much more nazified age cohort: over 40 percent held party membership and some 10 percent SS membership. At the core of Westermann's study is his account, based on both surviving reports and judicial interrogations, of the battalion's pacification actions from August through October 1942, in which the battalion engaged in the casual "equal opportunity" killing of Jews, Slavs (*Ostmenschen*), "Gypsies," and various categories of "asocials"—in short, the entire spectrum of National Socialism's ideologically targeted enemies. Arguing that the historian can "infer" motivation from the words, deeds, party membership, age cohort, and experiences of indoctrination and brutalization of the men of Police Battalion 310, Westermann concludes that they should be thought of as "ideological soldiers" rather than "ordinary men."

Just one year later (1999) Klaus-Michael Mallmann published a study of Police Battalion 307 from Lübeck.[6] Following nine months of occupation duty in Poland, it was involved in a mass killing of adult male Jews in Brest-Litovsk in July 1941 and then in subsequent killings in Belarus. Ghetto-clearing in the Lublin district in the spring and summer of 1942 was then followed by anti-partisan campaigns in Belarus from fall 1942 to summer 1944. In the initial massacre at Brest-Litovsk, Mallmann noted, all the shooters were drawn from an ample supply of volunteers. He dismissed coercion, brutalization, and propaganda as adequate explanations. Employing (like Goldhagen) the notion of a "cognitive model" through which the policemen viewed and understood their world, Mallmann invoked what he called "a situational radicalization of the image of the enemy." The biological, political, ideological, and now real enemy were blended into a "virtual reality" that legitimized killing Jews as "necessary self-defense." A prior anti-Semitic attitude combined with the situational inversion of the German offense into perceived self-defense drove the qualitative leap to mass murder.

Two books that appeared in 2000 and 2001, each containing a series of articles by various authors on various Order Police units, returned the focus to the failure of the German judicial system even to bring to trial much less convict more than a handful of Holocaust perpetrators who wore the green uniform.[7] Most important in expanding scholarly knowledge of the role of the Order Police in the Holocaust were two articles by Stefan Klemp that dealt with two battalions that were dispersed across the eastern front. Four companies of Police Battalion 9 were assigned one each to the four Einsatzgruppen. In this case 247 members of this battalion were delivered by the British to Soviet authorities in January 1947. They typically received twenty-five-year sentences but were released in 1956.[8] Klemp also studied Reserve Police Battalion 69, which was divided into small detachments that were distributed across the eastern front in August 1941 for the purpose of guarding construction work sites of Organisation Todt but were also frequently employed to kill nearby Jews.[9]

After this spate of articles on different police battalions, most of which focused on establishing the facts of their killing activities during the war and near total lack of judicial consequences after the war, five books have been more recently published that merit special mention. In 2005, Harald Welzer published *Täter: Wie aus ganz normalen Menschen Massenmörder werden*, a social-psychological study of how ordinary men become mass murderers, that used the judicial interrogations of Reserve Police Battalion 45 as its empirical basis.[10] In the same year, Edward Westermann published *Hitler's Police Battalions: Enforcing Racial War in the East*, which examined the "organizational culture" of the German Order Police and how this was reflected in its members' subsequent behavior in Eastern Europe.[11] In 2011, Karl Schneider published *Auswärts eingesetzt: Bremer Polizeibataillone und der Holocaust*, a dense study of the two Police Battalions, 105 and 303, from the city of Bremen.[12] And finally, Wolfgang Curilla published two massive compendia that contained entries on all of the Order Police units stationed in the Baltic states and Belarus on the one hand and in Poland on the other and their respective contributions to the Holocaust.[13] I will return to the Welzer and Westermann books later for their contributions to the debate over motivation and will focus now on the works of Schneider and Curilla for what they add to the comparative framework concerning RPB 101.

Karl Schneider's careful reconstruction of the formation of both Reserve Police Battalion 105 and Police Battalion 303 shows how both were significantly different from RPB 101. What was initially designated Police Battalion 105 was formed in the fall of 1939. Its rank and file were drawn from the 1902–1909 cohorts (i.e., thirty-to thirty-seven-year-olds) who had already served as reserve policemen in the 1937–1939 period. Roughly two-thirds of the rank and file were working class; one-third middle or lower-middle class. Having already been at least partially indoctrinated and socialized into the German police during weekend training sessions in the prewar period as reservists waiting to be mobilized, they received extensive military training and some additional ideological schooling in late 1939 and early 1940 before taking up rather pleasant and fondly remembered occupation duty in Norway and being renamed a Reserve Police Battalion in January 1941. The battalion then went on to serve in the Baltic in summer/fall 1941 (where it conducted numerous anti-partisan operations) and in the Netherlands from 1942 to 1944 (where it helped send transports of Dutch Jews to Auschwitz).[14]

After the outbreak of war, the rank and file of Police Battalion 303 was drawn from a pool of volunteers from the 1909–1912 cohorts (i.e., twenty-seven-to thirty-year-olds) made available to the SS and police in exchange for the large numbers of trained policemen who had been transferred to the army. As Westermann has pointed out, this was a highly nazified age group, and both the SS and police could exercise selectivity concerning whom among the oversupply of volunteers they chose. They received extensive training and were then sent for nine months of occupation duty in Poland before invading the Ukraine in June 1941, where they participated in numerous massacres of Jews including Babi Yar.[15]

Reserve Police Battalion 101 during its first and second tours of duty in Poland in 1939 and 1940 was constructed much the same way as RPB 105 or other murderous reserve battalions on Soviet territory in 1941, such as RPB 45 in the Ukraine and 133 in East Galicia. But after RPB 101 returned to Hamburg in 1941, its first generation of now highly experienced reserve police men were reassigned, and the rank and file were reconstituted from cohorts in which the maximum age was pushed back to forty-five (i.e., born as early as 1896), and the average age shifted from the low-thirties to nearly forty years old. There was no luxury of selectivity. Schneider quotes the Bremen Police president concerning the manpower shortage as the war progressed, stating that the city was "fully pumped out."[16] Hamburg was no different. And at this stage training and indoctrination also became much more perfunctory. In short, those who wish to explain the murderous record of police battalions as a product of highly nazified age cohorts, selectivity in recruiting, intense training and indoctrination, and the corrupting influence of months of imposing Nazi racial policy in Poland prior to service on Soviet territory—all factors that correlate with most police battalions—must confront the fact that these factors were absent for RPB 101, and thus are neither necessary nor sufficient factors in explaining its killing record.

How did the killing record of RPB 101 compare with other battalions? The exhaustive studies of Wolfgang Curilla now permit us to construct a chart that ranks the battalions' killing records.[17] The top twelve were the following:

RPB 61	1,100 killed, 300,000 deported to death camps
RPB 9	187,600 killed
RPB 133	31,900 killed; 74,000 deported
RPB 101	38,000 killed; 45,200 deported
RPB 53	13,200 killed; 65,000 deported
PB 320	66,700 killed
RPB 45	65,000 killed
RPB 3	62,500 killed
RPB 41	36,800 killed; 18,500 deported
RPB 131	14,900 killed; 35,500 deported
PB 304	44,300 killed
PB 303	41,600 killed

Given that RPB 61 and 53 were involved in the massive deportations from the Warsaw ghetto, and RPB 9 and 3 were attached to the Einsatzgruppen, the killing record attained by RPB 101 stands out even more and exceeds any of the "elite" 300-level battalions composed of carefully selected, highly nazified, intensively trained and indoctrinated young men. In short, part of the significance of RPB 101 as an illuminating case study is not that it was a typical or representative police battalion, but precisely the contrary. It was atypical in terms of age, selectivity, nazification, training and indoctrination, but nevertheless obtained the fourth highest killing record among all police battalions.

MOTIVATION

If many of the publications concerning the police battalions sought first to document their involvement in the Holocaust and second to expose the utter inadequacy of postwar judicial reckoning, another cluster of publications has focused on the ongoing debate over motivation.[18] How can a historian best explain why the Order Policemen behaved as they did? If the policemen were not coerced to act against their will, why did they choose to kill? In what ways did their actions make sense to them as unpleasant but necessary on the one hand, or justified and even praiseworthy on the other?

In *Ordinary Men* I cited the classic works of Stanley Milgram concerning obedience or deference to authority and Philip Zimbardo concerning role adaptation. Additionally I placed considerable emphasis on conformity as a key factor in trying to make sense of the behavior of the men of RPB 101 and explaining the group dynamics of the battalion, and I should have cited the work of Solomon Asch as well. This invoking of social psychology was deemed by Daniel Goldhagen to be of marginal significance on the one hand and exculpatory of the policemen's moral responsibility on the other. In the aftermath of that debate, several social psychologists have made contributions that I have found particularly important in advancing our ability to explain the behavior of genocidal killers. In *Becoming Evil: How Ordinary People Commit Genocide and Mass Killing*, James

Waller sought to explain how "ordinary people" committed "extraordinary evil" through a "four-pronged model."[19] First are innate and universal aspects of human nature that have emerged through the evolutionary process, designated by Waller as ethnocentrism, xenophobia, and desire of social dominance. Second are the factors that shape the dispositions of the perpetrators: cultural belief systems, moral disengagement, and rational self-interest. Third are factors that create an immediate social context: professional socialization, group binding, and merger of role and person. And fourth are factors that shape how perpetrators define or perceive their victims: us-them thinking, dehumanization, and blaming the victim. Clearly this is a broad and universalistic approach, but one that allows also for historical specificity. It is a comprehensive rejection of any monocausal approach that would place undue explanatory weight on a single aspect of either a perpetrator nation's cultural belief system (such as anti-Semitism) on the one hand or of social context (such as conformity in group binding) on the other. And it is a model that considers cultural and situational factors as complementary and mutually reinforcing rather than as dichotomous or mutually exclusive explanations for human behavior.

The second key contribution by a social psychologist was, in my opinion, made by Leonard S. Newman.[20] He specifically addressed Goldhagen's dismissive treatment of social psychology, but at the same time he articulated that discipline's wider contributions to explaining perpetrator behavior. Like Waller, Newman rejected the "false dichotomy" of cognitive versus situational or dispositional versus contextual explanations. Goldhagen's cognitive explanation was simply an assertion of "attitude-behavior consistency," which accounts for some but certainly not all human behavior and cannot be the sufficient explanation for something as complex as the actions of Holocaust perpetrators. There is, Newman notes, a dynamic relationship between persons/dispositions and situations. If attitude can shape behavior, the opposite is also the case. According to cognitive dissonance theory, discomfort occurs when people are engaged in activities that contradict their beliefs and attitudes. Particularly when people are in a position that makes it difficult to alter their behavior, they tend to reduce the discrepancy between action and belief by altering the latter through devising justifications and rationalizations for what they are doing. People are more susceptible to this when in a position of "induced compliance" (through subtle pressures like conformity and comradeship) rather than outright coercion.

Particularly when the behavior in question involves harming others, the harm-doer is likely to perceive the victim as deserving of punishment—a psychological response known as the "just world phenomenon." This process in turn creates a vicious circle in the form of an escalation in cruelty and brutality in harm-doing and dehumanization/devaluation of the victim. Through "fundamental attribution error" people tend to ignore the impact of their own actions on others and attribute the degraded and miserable status of the victim as further proof of the victim's inherent inferiority or even sub-humanity.

In addition to the fact that behavior can change attitude, another aspect of the dynamic relationship between disposition and situation is that situations themselves are not static or objective but rather subjective, because they are perceived, construed, and interpreted by the people in them. In particular, Newman notes that through a phenomenon he calls "pluralistic ignorance," numerous individuals could conform to an "illusory norm" that almost everyone else in the battalion endorsed the killing of Jews, even if most individuals would never have harmed Jews acting on their own. The collective behavior of a group is not simply the sum of its individual dispositions but is shaped by how group members perceive the group as a whole, as well as one another and the situation they collectively find themselves in.

The issues of how policemen perceived the institutional norms of the Order Police and the situations in which they found themselves as occupiers and enforcers of Nazi racial policy in Eastern Europe have been taken up by two scholars in particular, Edward Westermann and Jürgen Matthäus. They have examined the "organizational culture" and indoctrination practices of the Order Police. According to Westermann, "organizational culture sets the boundaries for accepted behavior, establishes institutional goals, and defines the standards of group membership."[21] With the centralization of all German police under Himmler in 1936, he and Order Police chief Kurt Daleuge sought to establish both an institutional merger of the Order Police with the SS as well as the transformation of its organizational culture through the dual processes of militarization and nazification. Central to nazification were the establishment of anti-Semitism and anti-Bolshevism as institutional norms, while militarization created an ethos of duty, comradeship, and absolute obedience. Together they transformed policemen into "ideological warriors" through broadening "the boundaries of acceptable and desired behavior" and making mass murder of ideological enemies both "acceptable and desirable."[22] In short, while Goldhagen attributed the creation of "willing executioners" to centuries of the systemic inculcation of eliminationist anti-Semitism inherent in German culture, Westermann saw these "ideological warriors" as the calculated short-term product of the institutional culture of a nazified and militarized German police.

Jürgen Matthäus also argued that indoctrination of the Order Police has been insufficiently examined and too quickly dismissed as a factor in explaining police behavior.[23] However, after actually examining the indoctrination materials used, he ultimately comes to a more complex conclusion about their effects than the basic "attitude-behavior consistency" model of Westermann, in which "ideological warriors" acted out institutionally implanted ideological beliefs.

Matthäus notes that there already existed an "ideological affinity" between the police and the new regime in 1933, and the police generally refused to provide German Jews with protection against the various assaults they faced from party activists. Following the centralization of the German police in 1936, the Order Police were schooled with indoctrination materials prepared within the SS that portrayed the Jews as the most dangerous enemy of the German people and attributed to this *Feindbild* (image of the enemy) responsibility for liberalism, Marxism/Bolshevism, exploitive capitalism, free masonry, pacifism, and the "politicized" churches. The "cool objectivity" of racial principles, not emotion, dictated Nazi Jewish policy as a matter of "self-defense." By late 1938 and early 1939, SS publications pointed to a "total solution" of the Jewish question through either *Umsiedlung* or *Vernichtung* (resettlement or annihilation). By December 1941 one such publication predicted a Europe free of Jews by the end of the war. At the same time other training materials sought to maintain the police self-image of correctness, professionalism, incorruptibility, idealism, and decency.

Matthäus argues that a "direct causal relationship" between indoctrination and participation in mass killing is difficult for the historian to prove in all but a few notorious cases, such as the initial atrocities committed by Police Battalion 309 in Bialystok. But he does think indoctrination "facilitated" the policemen's participation in many ways. It lowered "inhibitions" and provided "legitimization" for those seeking to rationalize or justify the brutal mass killing, as it portrayed their actions as a "difficult duty" and a "historic mission" that objective racial principles showed to be necessary self-defense. For those for whom this was not sufficient, it linked killing Jews with other legitimate missions, such as waging anti-partisan warfare or defeating communism. And it provided a "façade" or cover for other motives—greed, sadism, the opportunity to torture and kill with impunity—that they wanted to hide from themselves. In short, these indoctrination materials provided a buffet of anti-Semitic slogans and assertions from which policemen could choose to help them mitigate and counter the cognitive dissonance that many experienced with the onset of mass killing.

In a seminal article on the Order Police as the "foot soldiers" of the Final Solution in the East, Klaus-Michael Mallmann also argued for a close relationship between the situation in which the policemen found themselves on Soviet territory and the enactment of Nazi racial ideology.[24] Order Police indoctrination, according to Mallmann, has been "overvalued." Its impact was seen less in the production of ideological fanaticism or what he terms "ideological fundamentalism" than in a more diffuse change in the mentality and attitude of the men through a denigration of Christian values as humanitarian drivel and traditional notions of soldierly chivalry as weak and unmanly. It encouraged policemen to think in racial categories of "master race" and "sub-humans," of German superiority and native inferiority, which could encompass a spectrum of anti-Jewish attitudes from aversion and contempt to hate and the desire to destroy, but facilitated the policemen's mass killing of non-Jewish victims in the east as well.

Mallmann also emphasized the group dynamics, which shaped the policemen's lives. Notions of manliness based on toughness and an overriding fear of being perceived as weak or cowardly were part of their shared mental world, the origins of which predated National Socialism. As members of a unit or primary group that constituted their social world, they feared isolation and craved comradeship and community, the price of which was conformity to brutality, or more specifically shooting alongside the others. "Moral unburdening" was found in collective identity. For Mallmann, only a "complex combination of cognitive and situational factors," complementary and mutually reinforcing, can explain the policemen's behavior as Holocaust perpetrators. But ultimately, like Matthäus, he concluded that "The ideological factor . . . was not the original driving force, but rather a subsequent sedative, not the actual impulse, but rather a narcotic after the fact."[25]

If Westermann looked at the organizational culture of the Order Police and its presumed impact on police behavior, and Matthäus and Mallmann focused on how anti-Semitic ideology functioned within the situational context of Operation Barbarossa, Harald Welzer and Thomas Kühne sought to articulate broader, societal-wide frameworks that enabled or caused the policemen to value and embrace what they were doing. They in effect argued that Goldhagen posed the right question but provided the wrong answer concerning why, for Germans, participation as a society (and not just Order Police units subject to indoctrination and particular situational factors) in the Final Solution made sense.

Harald Welzer, combining a case study of Reserve Police Battalion 45 with social-psychological theorizing and historical background, posed two big questions: how and why did the "normative frames of reference" in Germany change so quickly and totally after 1933, and why were almost all "ordinary men" in units like RPB 45 willing to kill, even if they did so with varying degrees of enthusiasm, indifference, or distaste?[26] For Welzer the centerpiece of the Nazi revolution was the redefining of the community of human obligation, from one of inclusion based on Enlightenment notions of humanity to one of exclusion based on racism and anti-Semitism. This radical restructuring of membership in the German community was possible in part because the exclusion and denigration of Jews inherently provided the psychic gratification of enhanced status as well as opportunities for material gain for all included in the *Volksgemeinschaft*, "racial community," even for those from the lowest rungs of the social ladder. For Welzer, 1933, not 1939 or 1941, was the key turning point for establishing these new social norms. The degree to which everyday social practice (beyond any conscious acceptance of

Nazi ideology and propaganda) incorporated exclusion of the Jews from the community of human obligation meant broad acceptance of a new "Nazi morality." The key elements of this "Nazi morality" were that is was "good and meaningful" to solve the Jewish question, even through radical means, that "work" in that direction was difficult but rewarding, and that the ultimate goal was the creation of a community without Jews. However unimagined at the beginning, in the end this exclusion allowed ordinary Germans to decouple the dispossession and murder of Jews on the one hand from any sense of criminality or immorality on the other.

Welzer then examined how "ordinary men" in Reserve Police Battalion 45 became willing killers. Like Goldhagen, Welzer argued that the perpetrators, when confronted with their killing task, did not have to overcome moral scruples or inhibitions, because they had already internalized the new "frame of reference" that decoupled the killing of Jews from criminality. Their killing actions were essentially a reflection of the beliefs they had adopted in previous years. But they still had to become acclimatized to what they were doing. Here he invoked both situation and process. These men, when confronted with the task of the mass murder of Jews, passed through a professionalizing and normalizing process that transformed mass murder into "work." Many of them considered their "work" unpleasant but nonetheless a necessary historic task about which they did not feel guilt either then or later.

Thomas Kühne argued for a synthesis of anthropological-social and ideological factors in explaining the widespread participation of rank-and-file German soldiers and policemen in the Holocaust.[27] He did not deny that anti-Semitism, anti-Bolshevism, and anti-Slavism were factors, but he considered them an insufficient explanation. Crucial to understanding the behavior of the ordinary Germans in uniform, he argued, were the "myths" of *Kameradschaft* and *Volksgemeinschaft* (comradeship and community). These powerful "myths" must be understood as the Germans knew them, for they were the lenses through which Germans saw the world, constructed their reality, and derived the moral framework that in turn shaped their behavior.

The myth of the *Volksgemeinschaft* derived from Germany's euphoric sense and collective memory of unity transcending class, party, and confession, as proclaimed by the Kaiser in August 1914. With Germans traumatized by the defeat of 1918 and the Great Depression, the Nazis were able to appropriate the emotive power of the myth while transforming its essence from political, social, and religious inclusivity to racial exclusivity. Not only were Jews and other racial aliens excluded, but so were those whose behavior constituted an internal threat or potential treason against the German race. In short, conformity was an essential component of belonging. And the Nazis also appropriated the myth of *Kameradschaft* based on the ideal of German national unity in the trenches, not the international brotherhood of all soldiers victimized by the war as articulated by E. M. Remarque in *All Quiet on the Western Front*. The emotional power and need for belonging embodied in these two myths enabled the Nazis to preside over a "moral revolution," in which the western tradition of universalism, humanity, and individual responsibility based on a guilt culture was replaced by a shame culture that elevated loyalty to and standing within the group to be the new moral fulcrum of German society. Whether it be the *Volksgemeinschaft* as a whole, or the small unit within which a German fought, "the group claimed moral sovereignty."[28]

The shame culture, making conformity a prime virtue, impelled ordinary Germans in uniform to commit terrible crimes rather than suffer the stigma of cowardice and weakness and the "social death" of isolation and alienation vis-à-vis their comrades. This dynamic was intensified by several other factors. The first was that the "pleasures" of comradeship and the "joy of togetherness" derived from a heightened sense of belonging could be enhanced even further through transgression against the norms of members outside the group. "Nothing makes people stick together better than committing a crime together," Kühne noted.[29] And second was the pernicious Nazi invention that Kühne dubbed the "morality of immorality."[30] Both Hitler and various military commanders made the coercive zero-sum moral argument that pity and lenience toward the enemy and failure to overcome one's personal scruples was a "sin" against one's comrades and future generations. The combination of all these factors created a "competition for mercilessness" and a "culture of brutality" within units.[31] For Germans at large, the "outcome was the national brotherhood of mass murder—Hitler's community."[32]

Kühne qualifies this grim portrayal of uniformity, conformity, and criminality in an important way. "Ethics do not change within just a couple of years" for everyone, he noted. Thus "uncertainty and dissenting convictions seethed in the culture of cruelty," and "pangs of conscience" persisted.[33] Kühne cited the testimony of a member of the Security Police and SD in Warsaw concerning the spectrum and distribution of attitudes and participation among the perpetrators: "Absolute executioners about 30 percent, the anti-group about 20 percent, and then a group between, which stuck to the methods of the hellraisers."[34] Because "two different value systems" continued to coexist alongside one another, some Germans in uniform felt doubt, shame, and embarrassment. Many, nonetheless, joined in the mass killing and masked their feelings to avoid conspicuous nonconformity. Others who did not take part accepted the stigma of weakness and unmanliness, thereby validating the ethic of toughness of their comrades. Virtually no one dared show solidarity with the victims, reproach their comrades, or criticize the regime, though one could complain about the "dirty business" that the unit had been assigned.[35]

Though differing in some ways, virtually all of these scholars agree that any attempt to explain the motivation of the killers must be complex and multifaceted, not monocausal. They combine and synthesize situational and dispositional with cultural and ideological factors rather than oppose them in a false dichotomy. In much the same way as the artificially polarized "intentionalist-functionalist" debate led to fruitful scholarship and various forms of a "consensus model" concerning Nazi decision- and policy-making, so too the stark polarization of positions in the so-called Goldhagen Debate has been superseded by more complex attempts at synthesis.

THE LUXEMBOURGERS

On April 8, 1996, Daniel Goldhagen presented his book *Hitler's Willling Executioners* to a symposium held at the United States Holocaust Memorial Museum (USHMM), and I was one of four respondents.[36] In my comments I noted that the presence of fourteen Luxembourg policemen in Reserve Police Battalion 101—young men in their early twenties who had been incorporated into the German police after the annexation of Luxembourg to the Third Reich—offered the opportunity to measure the impact of similar situational factors on men of differing cultural and national background. Unfortunately, only one German witness described the participation of the Luxembourgers in the battalion's activities in any detail. As members of Lieutenant Buchmann's first company, they were present at Józefów but escorted the Jews taken to Lublin for labor. While present for Trapp's speech, the roundup of the Jews, and the process of selection, they did not act as shooters on that occasion. Thereafter, according to this witness, the Luxembourgers were not only not exempt, but were intentionally chosen for assignments because of their youth and professional training. "In general the old men remained behind," but "the Luxembourgers were in fact present at every action. With these people it was a matter of career police officials from the state of Luxembourg, who were all young men in their twenties."[37]

The Luxembourg historian Paul Dostert called to my attention the postwar accounts to two of these fourteen Luxembourg members of RPB 101, which had been published in 1986. Several aspects of their accounts stand out. First, they portrayed themselves as victims of both German conscription and the horrors of war. Second, they portrayed the actions of the Luxembourgers as consistently non-supportive of the German cause. Roger Vietor claimed to have provided the Polish resistance with both information about impending searches and arrests as well as guns and ammunition, at great risk to himself.[38] Jean Heinen claimed that the Luxembourgers assigned to machine-gun duty did not shoot in action and feigned stoppages. Beginning in June 1944, five Luxembourgers successfully deserted and two others were killed trying to go over to the Russians.[39] Crucially, neither account mentioned even the presence of Jews, much less the battalion's participation in their mass murder. Faced with these two accounts, I suggested two arguments from silence, i.e. drawing inferences from what was not said. First, Vietor and Heinen had detailed various aspects of dissident behavior to portray themselves as victims, not collaborators, of the Germans; if they had been among the non-shooters, would they not have claimed this to their credit in postwar accounts as well? If many German witnesses could remember the non-shooters in the battalion twenty years later but made no comment about the Luxembourgers in this regard, was it because they had behaved like most of their German comrades in 1942? Arguments from silence are suggestive, not definitive. They constitute circumstantial evidence concerning probability, not proof. Thus the role of the Luxembourgers in RPB 101 remained intriguing but unresolved.

When my comments about the Luxembourgers in RPB 101 were published in Germany in 1998,[40] they received coverage in several Luxembourg newspapers. This in turn led to a vigorous response from Jean Heinen in the *Luxemburger Wort*.[41] He admitted that first company of RPB 101 had shot Jews, but he "had not seen whether a Luxembourger had shot." He had not made any mention of his unit's involvement in killing Jews because he was "no historian" and because "he concerned himself with the fate of the Luxembourg group and not the unfortunate fate of the Jews."

Heinen admitted that he had been involved in two deportation actions, escorting Jews from the ghetto to the train station, but he made no mention of the routine brutality and shooting that accompanied such ghetto-clearing actions. On one occasion he accompanied the train, to where he did not know, but "the destination could have been Treblinka." As first company was involved in six deportations to Treblinka and two large relocations from Radzyń to Międzyrzec and from Kock to Łuków, it seems likely that Heinen was involved in more than two deportation actions.

Heinen admitted that he was present at two mass shootings in November 1943, and his descriptions of the *Erntefest* massacre at Majdanek and Poniatowa coincide with other testimony. He admitted that on the second day he left his cordon post briefly to observe firsthand the shooting at the mass grave and the piles of corpses. "The horror that I saw there, I cannot describe, because the appropriate words fail me," he wrote. But he denied being present at any other shooting actions, though first company carried out shootings at Serakomla, Talcyn and Kock, and Łuków. He admitted involvement in a Parczew forest sweep in late 1942, in which hundreds of Jews who had fled the ghettos were killed, but claimed it and other patrols were only anti-partisan actions, not "Jew hunts."

In short, like many German witnesses, Heinen admitted to some involvement by his unit in killing Jews but denied any personal involvement in killing by himself or his Luxembourg comrades on the one hand and most likely minimized and sanitized the extent of his unit's involvement on the other. His letter to the editor admitted far more than either he or any other Luxumbourger had done previously, but nonetheless he asserted that I had made "a fool of myself" in suggesting that there had previously been any conspiracy of silence. What has subsequent research added to our knowledge of the Luxembourgers in RPB 101 and their previous silence?

Paul Dostert discovered that following the verdict in the Hamburg trial of Wohlauf, Hoffmann, and others, the investigation of several other members of the battalion continued, including Sergeant Hans Keller of first company. In a lengthy interrogation in July 1964, he denied any memory of events before August 1942 (such as Józefów) but admitted that his unit took part in the ghetto clearings of Parczew and Międzyrzec, and that many hundreds of Jews had been shot in the course of the latter. He was stationed for cordon duty during the Serakomla and Talcyn-Kock killings and described the former in great detail. He admitted that the first two sweeps of the Parczew Forest in late 1942 were aimed at escaped Jews, and only in the spring of 1943 did patrols there target non-Jewish partisans. He participated in three other "Jew hunts," operating under an explicit "shooting order" for all Jews discovered.[42] Subsequently he denied everything he had admitted.

In February 1973, Keller traveled to Luxembourg and prevailed upon three former Luxembourgers in his unit to sign a statement that he had carefully drafted to exonerate himself (and thereby also the Luxembourgers in his unit) of participating in atrocities in Poland. During the first weeks in Poland, they were guarding a sawmill and knew nothing of Józefów. Again sent on distant guard duty, they heard of a great deportation action (possibly Parczew), and likewise were not present at Talcyn or Serakomla because they had been sent on patrol. They knew of no deportations from Kock (though they were stationed there). The Parczew sweep was a fruitless search for partisans.[43]

Interviewed by German judicial authorities the following December, all three repeated their denials of having been involved in any shootings or deportation actions. Two admitted that they had been sent to Międzyrzec but had been detached to guard a leather factory producing for the Wehrmacht, where they helped the Jewish manager to rescue his Jewish workers from the roundup and in gratitude had been rewarded each with pieces of leather. As one Luxembourger testified: "We never had anything to do with Jews. We never rounded them up or took them from one place to another. We were only always underway with our bicycles in the fields and forests in search of partisans. . . . During our patrols we never encountered Jews."[44] The German investigators reinterviewed five German witnesses from the same unit as the Luxembourgers. Their verdict was unanimous, that the Luxembourgers had never been exempted from any tasks, including anti-Jewish actions.[45] More specially, one witness recalled that Keller had badgered him so relentlessly to change his testimony that finally he had refused to let him in the door.[46] Another noted that one officer in the company was a "special friend" of the Luxembourgers, and for entertainment they would go into Kock after the nightly blackout and shoot out lights that were still on inside houses.[47] And a third claimed that on platoon commander Brand's order a Luxembourger had shot a pregnant women who had been caught sheltering Jews.[48]

If three men concerting together to give transparently false testimony, followed by failure of the written accounts of Wietor and Heinen to mention Jews at all, does not constitute a tacit "conspiracy of silence" among the Luxembourgers, then the term has no meaning whatsoever. Clearly the Luxembourgers as a group were involved in the battalion's activities, including anti-Jewish actions as Heinen later admitted, even if there is no evidence concerning any identifiable individual's personal complicity. Dostert's investigation into the historical background of the Luxembourgers' incorporation into the

German police does indicate, however, that the path these men took to RPB 101 was so different from that of their German counterparts that it renders any comparison problematic.[49]

The Freiwellegekompanie, comprised of 455 men, was tiny Luxembourg's military force prior to its conquest by Nazi Germany in May 1940. Many more men applied to the Freiwellegekompanie than space allowed, because a three-year term of service made them eligible for a subsequent career in the police. Thus the acceptance of many suitable applicants was often deferred. In September 1940, Heinrich Himmler visited Luxembourg, inspected the Freiwellegekompanie, and decided that those deemed suitable should be incorporated into either the SS or German Order Police. A significant number of these Luxembourgers must have been excluded in the vetting process (which examined both racial background and political reliability), since many previously deferred applicants were now asked if they were still interested and invited to join.

The personnel files of eleven of the fourteen Luxembourgers in RPB 101 survived in the Hamburg Staatsarchiv, but one is incomplete.[50] From the other ten, it can be seen that five were members of the Freiwellegekompanie before the German occupation, but the other five were deferred candidates invited to join in September 1940. In short, they were not transferred automatically or against their will into German service. They decided to join what they now knew to be an auxiliary police force of the German occupier, taking advantage of an employment opportunity that that occupation created.

Clearly the attitudes and reactions of the Luxembourgers varied widely. While some actively chose to join in September 1940, attrition among the former members of the Freiwellegekompanie was high, as was the cost of refusing to serve. Of the original 455 members, Dostert calculates that 264 ended up in German prisons or concentration camps, where 48 died before the end of the war. From December 1940 to May 1941, the Luxembourgers then in the unit were taken to Germany for training and National Socialist indoctrination. Despite promises that they would return to serve in Luxembourg, only 55 were reassigned there. One group of 116 (including the future RPB 101 contingent) was sent to Cologne and then to anti-partisan duty in Slovenia. Many requested release from police service but were refused. When this large unit of Luxembourgers proved unreliable in the anti-partisan war, however, they were withdrawn from Slovenia and dispersed in small groups to other German units. This is how 14 came to RPB 101 in June 1942. However, 44 refused either to accept reassignment or to take an additional oath to the Führer and were sent to concentration camps in Buchenwald, Sachsenhausen, Neuengamme, and Dachau. Of the 14 in RPB 101, 5 were killed in the last two years of the war, 3 deserted in 1944 by not returning from leave and going underground in Luxembourg, and one ended his service through a self-inflicted wound in January 1945. Like other populations occupied by Nazi Germany, different Luxembourgers made different choices at different times and paid different costs. But unlike the German rank and file in RPB 101, the 14 Luxembourgers were not random, middle-aged conscripts called up to serve their country in the middle of the war.

THE PHOTOGRAPHIC EVIDENCE: INSIGHTS AND LIMITATIONS

When I was researching and writing *Ordinary Men* in the late 1980s and early 1990s, I asked several archives about relevant photographs. Yad Vashem in Jerusalem, YIVO in New York, and the Jewish Historical Institute in Warsaw all kindly made available the small number of photographs (sometimes duplicate copies) that they had, and these photos were included in the first edition with my brief captions but no further comment or analysis. In part, this was because the archives themselves had provided so little information about these photographs.

Twenty-five years later the situation has changed significantly in three ways. Photo archivists have researched their collections with greater care and corrected some of the erroneous captions they previously offered. The United States Holocaust Memorial Museum photo archive has obtained a collection of private family albums, one compiled by a member of RPB 101 during its second tour of duty in Poland in 1940–1941. And photographs collected by the Hamburg prosecutors in the RPB 101 case, authenticated according to legal standards of evidence, have now become available. As a result, a number of photos have been added for this edition, additional commentary has been provided for some of the earlier photos, and one major error has been corrected.

Sadly, iconic photos are often the most carelessly used.[51] A prime example is provided by the photograph I chose for the cover of *Ordinary Men* from a sequence of three photographs held in multiple copies and vaguely identified by site—namely Łuków in Poland—in three different archives: the Jewish Historical Institute in Warsaw, Yad Vashem in Jerusalem, and YIVO in New York. (Copies are now also in the photo archive of the USHMM, which had not yet opened at that time.) The photos were undated, and none of the Germans were identified. According to YIVO, the first photo in the sequence was donated in the late 1940s by someone from the Bronx who claimed that the man standing center-left with the white beard was a family relative, Motl Hershberg of Łuków. According to Yad Vashem, the kneeling Jew of the third photo was identified as Rabbi Izek Verobel of Łuków, and that this photo was found in Łuków after the war and given to returning Jews. However, the photo archive in Yad Vashem also now notes that there is an equally valid, rival claim that these photos are from Tarnow, and that it has insufficient evidence to determine the site of the photos either way.[52]

In the illustration section of *Ordinary Men,* two photos of this sequence were cautiously labeled: "Łuków, probably in the fall of 1942." But the sequence of the three photos was not further analyzed, as ought to have been done.[53] The photos were not used as evidence in the Hamburg court case against RPB 101. No one from the battalion was identified in the pictures. Let us examine the photos as a sequence. The first photo[54] is especially interesting because, in addition to the men in great coats, there are two men clearly in Wehrmacht uniforms (far right and third from left). Several of the men are not yet looking at the camera or smiling, and one German seems to be pointing his hand—as if he were holding a pistol—at one of the kneeling Jews and feigning a mock execution. In the second photo[55] the two obvious Wehrmacht men have disappeared, and only the men in great coats remain in the picture. Clearly the photographer has alerted the men that he is about to take the picture, since they are all looking directly at the camera and one is smiling. It is the obscenely wide grin on the face of the German on the left that riveted my attention and caused me to select this particular photo for the book cover. Whether this was a smile of schadenfreude, of expressing ghoulish pleasure at the humiliation of the Jews, or simply a reflex action of smiling at the camera, I do not know, though at the time of my selecting the photo for the cover I incautiously assumed the former. The third photograph[56] was taken as the staged scene was breaking up. Most of the Jews and several of the Germans are turning away, only one Jew in his finery remains kneeling, and only one German is still looking at the cameraman. We do not know what happened between the second and third photos, other than that the kneeling Jew is no longer wearing his head cover, suggesting that he may have been physically roughed up. Six different copies of this photo were donated to Yad Vashem, and YIVO holds multiple copies as well. Most macabre, one of YIVO's copies is a postcard, with a place for address, stamp, and writing on the back. Clearly the third photo had "iconic" status and was in open circulation in Poland after the war.

The rival claim of Tarnow is only one possible reason why no one in these photos was identified as an Order Policeman from RPB 101. Studying with enhanced technology the emblems on the berets of the men in great coats, previously assumed to be members of the Order Police, the archivists at Yad Vashem have now concluded that they were members of the Wehrmacht instead.[57] In short, possibly by time (unspecified), place (Tarnow rather than Łuków), and unit involved (Wehrmacht, not Order Police), these pictures have nothing to do with Reserve Police Battalion 101 at all. These photos illustrate what we already know, namely that the Germans in Poland often conducted rituals of humiliation and staged trophy photos of their exploits. But they do not provide evidence of individual participation much less the world view and anti-Semitic convictions of members of RPB 101. They also provide a salutary lesson on the careless and casual mistakes that frequently characterized the archival filing and historians' use of photographic evidence a quarter-century ago.

Let us know turn to the three photo albums acquired by the USHMM that were compiled by the Hamburg family of Bernhardt Colberg, born in 1900 and a member of PB 101 during its second tour of duty in Poland in 1940–1941. Family scenes dominate the first two albums, but many photos in the third volume were taken by Bernhardt during this tour of duty in Poland and suggest that he was an enthusiastic photographer.[58] A few photos of the pre-1933 period show demonstrations of the Reichsbanner, a SPD affiliate supportive of the Weimar Republic. By the mid-1930s, his son is in the Deutschen Jungvolk (the Hitler Youth level for ten- to fourteen-year-olds). This suggests that members of the Colberg family, like many other Germans, may well have made the transition from social democratic affiliation to accommodation with the Nazi regime

Colberg was sent to serve in PB 101 in Poland from October 1, 1940, to April 7, 1941. In many posed photographs, he proudly displayed himself in uniform.[59]

On one occasion only he recorded German repressive measures, in this case one photo of a public hanging in progress with many spectators, followed by another of the bodies left hanging after all the spectators have departed—a not uncommon sight in Nazi-occupied Europe.[60]

He seemed fascinated with pictures of war-damaged buildings, which seemed incidentally to show, at a distance, Jewish workers involved in cleanup work.[61]

The few close-up pictures of Jews did not negatively portray them as the stereotypical Ostjuden of Nazi propaganda. One portrays a strong, handsome Jewish worker; another a Jewish family in repose by the roadside.[62]

Most interesting, perhaps, are Colberg's photos of the Łódź ghetto, where PB 101 members served external guard duty. Rather than examples of "ghetto tourism" recording unattractive Jews living in filth and hunger that confirmed Nazi stereotypes, Colberg deliberately photographed a ghetto without Jews. He was interested in using the night lighting and ghetto fencing for photographic effect and composition, not in recording ghetto life.[63]

In one case where Jews appear in his photographs of ghetto fencing, it does seem to be the rare case of a staged scene, in which uniformed Jewish ghetto police are kneeling in the snow across the fence from German police.[64]

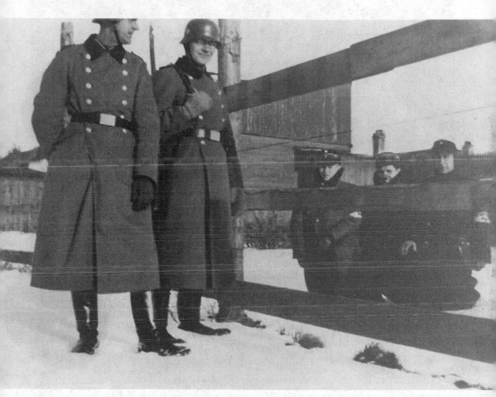

Ironically, the last photo in the Colberg album is of himself once again in uniform, serving as a policeman in the postwar British occupation of northern Germany. The man who accommodated himself to the Nazis after 1933 did likewise for the Allied occupation after 1945.

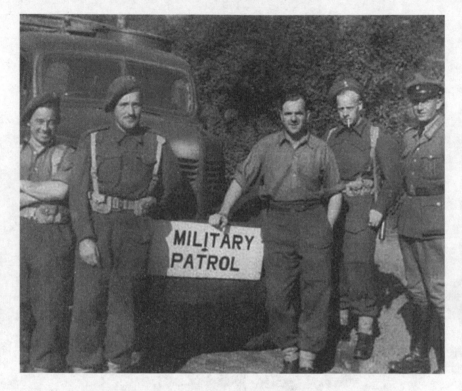

Let us turn now to the photographs from the photo collection or *Lichtbildmappe* in the prosecuting attorney's files for the trial of RPB 101 in Hamburg. Some of these photographs were provided by battalion members summoned for interrogation. Others were obtained from photo archives, particularly in Poland, and authenticated during interrogation. These photos can be divided into four categories: (1) official head shots of the officers and noncommissioned officers; (2) informal "buddy" pictures of groups of men from the battalion; (3) informal snapshots recording various seemingly innocent, "normal" activities of the battalion; and (4) snapshots—both single and in sequence—documenting aspects of the battalion's participation in its destructive mission against the Jews.

Both typical and most important of the thirty-two official head shots are three senior officers of the battalion: Major Wilhelm Trapp, Captain Julius Wohlauf, and Lieutenant Hartwig Gnade.[65]

Among the various group "buddy" pictures, there is an extensive collection of seven of Gruppe Bekemeier from Lieutenant Gnade's Second Company stationed in Łomazy in August 1942.[66] Of the two examples here, the second is rare in showing fraternization with the local population. Two of the four men are holding two children, with a couple who are presumably the parents—one of whom is identified in another picture as the Polish cook for the unit—standing behind. This is on the site where the battalion either was going to carry out or had already carried out one of its most ferocious massacres of local Jews on August 18, 1942. The *Lichtbildmappe* does not identify the photographer of this Gruppe Bekemeier sequence, though a number of the men in the pictures are identified.

Among other group pictures is a more formally composed collective portrait of Major Trapp and his staff at Radzyń.[67]

Of the "normal activity" pictures of the battalion, the single most striking one is an outdoor officers' dinner that includes the wives of Captain Wohlauf and Lieutenant Brand, Vera and Lucia.[68] In the rear area of the Lublin District, wives of officers were able to visit their husbands. The presence of Vera Wohlauf at the marketplace during the first massive and deadly ghetto-clearing of Międzyrzec Podlaski (during which close to a thousand Jews were killed on the spot and some ten thousand were dispatched to Treblinka), on August 25–26, 1942, disturbed many of the men.[69] And Lucia Brand provided one of the more revealing testimonies concerning the brutal mentality that had developed within the battalion by the time she visited her husband.[70]

Also among the "normal activity" photos are a sequence of four pictures (two shown here) of men assembled for an outdoor concert that is being given by musicians in uniform using the flat roof of a low building as their stage. The odd assortment of instruments—including two accordions, one base, one violin, and one guitar—would suggest that this was a performance given by an improvised group of battalion members and not some more professional traveling entertainment unit.[71] Neither date nor location is given. In yet another single photo, the battalion's truck drivers are led in singing.[72] For historical purposes these photos attest to the attempt to create a certain "normalcy" for men who we know from other evidence were engaged in anything but "normal" behavior. In Himmler's extraordinary memorandum of December 12, 1941, the Reichsführer-SS himself explicitly recommended quiet evenings of cultural activity as a soothing antidote to the stresses of mass killing and the preferred alternative to heavy drinking. It was a "sacred duty" (*heilige Pflicht*) of the officers, Himmler wrote, to ensure that none of those "who had to fulfill this difficult task were ever brutalized or suffered damage to their soul and character" (*die diese schwere Pflicht zu erfüllen haben, jemals verroht oder an Gemüt und Charakter erleidet*). For this purpose "comradely get-togethers" (*kameradschaftliches Beisammensein*) were to be held on the evenings of such difficult tasks, which were never to involve "alcohol abuse" but rather were to be devoted to music and presentations that would lead the men back to "the beautiful realm of German spiritual and inner life" (*die schönen Gebiete deutschen Geistes-und Gemütslebens*).[73] These photos indicate that Himmler's exhortation was taken to heart and acted upon in RPB 101.

That did not, of course, preclude the more normal forms of rau-
cous evening entertainment that included the heavy use of alcohol,
the Reichsführer's wishes to the contrary notwithstanding. Such an
evening is captured in the photo of members of First Platoon, Third
Company, in Czemierniki.[74]

Of greatest interest for both prosecutors and historians are the
photos of the battalion in action, carrying out its lethal task. The
most striking set of photos in this regard are a sequence of five of the
Łomazy *Aktion* on August 18, 1942, in which seventeen hundred
Jews were collected on the sports field in town, marched to the forest,
and murdered in a mass grave.[75]

Of the five photos, the first two provide distant and close-up pictures of Jews sitting on the ground in the sports field. The third shows additional seated Jews assembled in a field partially shaded by trees. The fourth shows nine shirtless, strong young men digging a large rectangular pit. The fifth shows seventeen women, still fully clothed, being rushed forward toward the cameraman, with the capped face of a German policeman just visible behind the group. An armband with the Star of David is fully visible on the lead woman. The strained expressions on the women's faces indicate the frenetic pace of the forced march from the sports field to the killing pit. In all the photos, the focus is clearly on the victims and the *Aktion*, with individual Germans included only incidentally and distantly in the first, third, and fifth photos.[76]

If the Łomazy photos depict events leading up to the mass shooting, one single photo from Międzyrzec Podlaski—a "collection ghetto" that was repeatedly cleared and refilled—confirms the description of a mass shooting that took place there on October 6, 1942.[77] On this day thousands of Jews were deported to Treblinka. Despite their utmost efforts, the Germans could not cram all of the intended victims into the inadequate number of available train cars, and Lieutenant Gnade ordered the remaining 150 Jews—mostly women and children—to be taken to the nearby cemetery and shot by the cemetery wall.[78] This photo—the only one in the entire collection that actually shows the bodies of murdered victims of the battalion—provides gruesome confirmation of an improvised execution, in which no preparations had been made beforehand to either dig a mass grave or collect the clothing of the victims.

Following the ghetto clearing operations in the northern Lublin District in the fall of 1942, members of RPB 101 engaged in
repeated "Jew hunts" for escaped and hiding Jews.[79] Once again it is
Lieutenant Gnade and men of the Second Company for whom two
photos have survived that record them on patrol in the forest and
fields outside Międzyrzec.[80]

Following a long pause over the winter of 1942–1943, the ghetto of Międzyrzec Podlaski was subjected to the "fifth" and "sixth actions" of May 1 and 26, 1943. In the "sixth action" some one thousand Jews were sent to the concentration camp at Majdanek on the outskirts of Lublin rather than to Treblinka. By this time Gnade had constructed an undressing barracks outside the city, where the deportees were deprived of their valuables and most of their clothing before being loaded into the waiting train cars.[81] Numerous photos capture four distinct stages of the deportation *Aktion* from Międzyrzec: collection on the town square, the march from town, the strip search at Gnade's undressing barrack, and loading the train. Two sequences—whether from one or two different photographers is uncertain—can be dated to the "sixth action" of May 26. They were not recovered from the private possession of members of the battalion but rather sent to the prosecution by the Jewish Historical Institute in Poland and verified during subsequent interrogations. Some of the other photos may also date to this action, but some of them also appear to have been taken at an entirely different time.

A single sequence of four photographs was taken on the town square in Międzyrzec, as the Jews are collected and marched off on May 26, 1943.[82]

An additional photograph, seemingly taken with long shadows early in the morning, shows heavily clothed Jewish women sitting in the town square without any Germans in the picture and may well date to the previous fall.[83]

Four additional photographs document the march out of town. Two seem to be taken by the same photographer.[84] A third, in which the Germans are dressed in a similar manner, was probably taken on the same day.[85] In a fourth, showing some Jews being taken out of town on peasant wagons, the sole German guard is dressed in heavier clothing, suggesting a deportation action the previous fall.[86]

An extensive set of six photographs captures scenes at Gnade's undressing barracks. It seems very likely that all six were taken by the same photographer at the same time, namely during one of the May 1943 actions. Five of these photos portray the most direct and intimate interaction between German policemen and their Jewish victims.[87] Clearly the photographer's focus is on Jewish women, not men, including: (1) one of a fully-clothed woman facing three Germans in front of the barracks; (2) two of a women clad only in a white undergarment that she holds to her body while talking directly to German officers (identified as Gnade and a Bavarian gendarmerie officer); and (3) one of a solitary, short, and somewhat hunchbacked Jewish woman surrounded by German policemen (Gnade in profile; the Bavarian facing the camera) who tower above her, to the side of the barracks. The photographer seemed to have no interest at all in taking pictures of Jewish men.[88]

The final stage of the deportation process was the loading of the train cars. There are three surviving photographs that were not included in the prosecutor's collection for the Hamburg trial of RPB 101 but which were sent to the USHMM from the Main Commission for the Investigation of Nazi Crimes in Poland at a later date. The archival caption at the USHMM states that it is "likely" that these are photos of the "sixth action" in Międzyrzec Podlaski on May 26, 1943.[89] I find this dating quite dubious. The Jews are mostly women and some children, while the other photos show many men and no children at this late date. And the Jews are wearing far heavier clothing than seems likely for a late May deportation following a strip search at Gnade's undressing barracks. Moreover, none of these photos was used in evidence in the Hamburg trial, which suggests that none of the German personnel was identified as definitely from RPB 101.

The lack of framing of these pictures, the shaky focus of the first, and the fact that no one is looking at the photographer suggests the possibility that this series of three was most likely taken surreptitiously, perhaps by a Polish railway worker or some other non-German observer. As with the Łuków photos, therefore, we are left with photographs for which the precise time, place, and circumstances of the events depicted—to say nothing of the identity of the photographer—are difficult to corroborate.

The last major killing action in which RPB 101 was involved was the great *Erntefest* massacre of the Lublin labor camps in November 1943. RPB 101 participated in the liquidation of the Jewish prisoners of Majdanek on November 3 and of Poniatowa on November 4. There is a sequence of ten photos from Poniatowa that shows no Germans and no killing, but once again ominously documents the preparatory stages.[90] They show in succession the factory where the Jews worked, Jews standing outside wooden barracks where they were lodged, a column of Jews carrying their bundles and marching down a road with high fences on each side and a watchtower in the background, and finally Jews sitting and standing in an open compound surrounded by a high wire fence and overlooked by a watchtower. The sequence seems to have been taken by someone who was free to move about and openly photograph the people whom he was guarding. The Jews are in civilian clothing, not concentration camp garb since Poniatowa was a "forced labor camp" (*Zwangsarbeitslager*), not an official concentration camp (*Konzentrationslager*), and only the last three photos—with wire and watchtower—make clear that the photos were taken inside a camp. The sequence tells an ominous story only because we know the context and outcome from other sources.

Dan Porat argues that "in order to understand a historical event as presented in a photograph, narration is essential."[91] One very positive benefit of photos collected for judicial proceedings is that they join together the photographic image, the narrative historical background, and verification of specifics by witnesses. Concerning historical photographs, Judith Levin and Daniel Uziel have suggested that, in addition to the time and place they were taken, it is desirable to know the photographer, the people in the photograph, the provenance of the photograph, and whether it is a single shot or part of a collection or album.[92] Few photographs from the Holocaust are so amply documented, but at least in this collection some of these questions can be answered some of the time. In the judicial process, history illuminates the photos, and the photos illuminate history in a reciprocal and reinforcing manner. Historians almost invariably work with imperfect and problematic evidence, and photographic evidence is no exception.

Levin and Uziel also write, "We would expect a German photographer imbued with Nazi ideology to focus his lens differently than an 'ordinary' German would. . . ." But even concerning "ordinary Germans" taking pictures in the occupied east, Levin and Uziel "assumed as a point of departure that the anti-Semitic climate and propaganda had an immense impact on the entire population," and hence that "the shutters were pressed by people whose ideological consciousness manifested itself in the photographs they took or collected."[93] Taken as a whole, do the photos in the Colberg album and this judicial collection broadly reflect the impact of a pervasive anti-Semitic climate and even an unconscious Nazi ideological framing on the part of the perpetrators?

Unquestionably there are numerous photographs, especially ones like the staged ritual humiliation at Łuków or Tarnow with which we began the discussion in this section, that reflect the anti-Semitic attitudes and sense of racial superiority of those having themselves photographed. But such staged photographs explicitly reflecting a Nazi outlook are not found in the collection of photos that can be clearly identified as pertaining to RRB 101.[94] Indeed, it is possible that some of these photographs were taken by Poles as evidence of Nazi crimes in Poland, not by Germans as trophies of Nazi accomplishments. I suspect that the photo of the dead Jewish women by the cemetery wall in Międzyrzec, with no Germans visible in the picture, was taken after the German killers had departed. I suspect the loading of the train at Międzyrzec was also taken surreptitiously by a Polish photographer. And some of the other photos reflect a seeming "normalcy" of military life that we know not to be normal only because of additional knowledge that we as viewers bring to our viewing of them.

But what of the Łomazy and Międzyrzec photos? In the remarkable Łomazy sequence, the Jewish victims, not the German killers, are at the center. These are quick snapshots, not staged scenes, and the one caption simply identifies the subjects factually as "condemned Jews" but without further derogatory comment. The assembly of Jews on the Międzyrzec town square and the march out of town shows many Germans, but again these photos are quick snapshots that record the scene. They are neither staged nor captioned, nor are they particularly triumphalist, celebratory, or ideological in their framing. The ease with which the photographer could move about and take these pictures seems to indicate he was a German. These photos portray men not in staged celebration but simply at work. It is the matter-of-factness of the photographer's recorded preparations for the mass shooting at Łomazy and the deportation from Międzyrzec that is perhaps most disturbing.

The sequence taken at Gnade's undressing barracks again is stunning in that several of them capture groups of German officers and individual Jewish women in unusual proximity and interaction. The photos certainly capture the asymmetry of power between Germans and Jews. There is also a clear gendered dimension, with individual, small Jewish women being confronted by groups of big, bullying men. These photos are very revealing of how the Germans treated the Jewish women of Międzyrzec. That someone took these photos to preserve a suitable record of the battalion's activities demonstrates a severely stunted sensibility.

One of the controversies surrounding RPB 101 has been whether the eager, ideologically driven, anti-Semitic killers within the battalion constituted a zealous minority or the vast majority of its members. And Levin and Uziel have argued that the photographs even of "ordinary" Germans would reflect the pervasive anti-Semitism and propaganda of the regime. We do not know, of course, how many highly incriminating photos were taken that have been kept secret or were destroyed. But what does this collection of recovered photos of the battalion indicate? The photos of the Colberg album from 1940 to 1941 are remarkable for their general lack of reflecting a nazified outlook. The pictures that record the destructive work of the battalion on its third tour of duty in Poland seem devoid of the explicit ideological or propagandistic framing that can be seen in the staged and celebratory Wehrmacht photos from Łuków. But they do reflect a moral numbness, a routinization of destruction as everyday work that speaks less to the motivation of the policeman than to the impact of their actions on themselves.

APPENDIX

TABLE 1
NUMBER OF JEWS SHOT BY RESERVE POLICE BATTALION 101

Location	Mo./yr.	Est. # Jews shot (minimum)
Józefów	7/42	1,500
Łomazy	8/42	1,700
Międzyrzec	8/42	960
Serokomla	9/42	200
Kock	9/42	200
Parczew	10/42	100
Końskowola	10/42	1,100
Międzyrzec	10/42	150
Łuków	11/42	290
Lublin district (misc. roundups)	from 7/42	300
Lublin district ("Jew hunts")	from 10/42	1,000
Majdanek	11/43	16,500
Poniatowa	11/43	14,000
TOTAL		38,000

TABLE 2
NUMBER OF JEWS DEPORTED TO TREBLINKA BY RESERVE POLICE BATTALION 101

Location	Mo./yr.	Est. # Jews deported (minimum)
Parczew	8/42	5,000
Międzyrzec	8/42	10,000
Radzyń	10/42	2,000
Łuków	10/42	7,000
Międzyrzec	10/42–11/42	
Biała		4,800
Biała Podlaska county		6,000
Komarówka		600
Wohyn		800
Czemierniki		1,000
Radzyń		2,000
Łuków	11/42	3,000
Międzyrzec	5/43	3,000
TOTAL		45,200

NOTES

ABBREVIATIONS

BA   Bundesarchiv, Koblenz

BDC   Berlin Document Center

BZIH   *Biuletyn Żdyowskiego Instytutu Historycznego* (Bulletin of the Jewish Historical Institute)

G   Investigation of G. and others, Office of the State Prosecutor, Hamburg, 141 Js 128/65

HW   Investigation and trial of Hoffmann, Wohlauf, and others, Office of the State Prosecutor, Hamburg, 141 Js 1957/62

IMT   *Trials of the Major War Criminals before the International Military Tribunal*, 42 vols.

JNSV   *Justiz und NS-Verbrechen. Sammlung Strafurteile wegen Nationalsozialistische Tötungsverbrechen 1945–1966*, 20 vols.

NO   Nürnberg document relating to party organizations

NOKW   Nürnberg document relating to the military

YVA   Yad Vashem Archives, Jerusalem

ZStL   Zentrale Stelle der Landesjustizverwaltungen, Ludwigsburg

PREFACE

1. Raul Hilberg estimates that more than 25 percent of the victims of the Holocaust died in shootings. More than 50 percent perished in the six major death camps equipped with gassing facilities, and the remainder under the terrible conditions of ghettos, labor and concentration camps, death marches, etc. *The Destruction of the European Jews* (New York, 1985), 1219.

2. The only other major study of an individual killing unit is Hans-Heinrich Wilhelm, "Die Einsatzgruppe A der Sicherheitspolizei und des SD 1941–42: Eine exemplarische Studie," part 2 of *Die Truppe des Weltanschauungskrieges: Die Einsatzgruppen der Sicherheitspolizei und des SD 1938–1942*, by Helmut Krausnick and Hans-Heinrich Wilhelm (Stuttgart, 1981). Wilhelm's study is based on much more plentiful contemporary documentation than exists for Reserve Police Battalion 101. However, Wilhelm did not have available a roster of this unit. His study of personnel is thus limited to the officers.

3. Marc Bloch, *The Historian's Craft* (New York, 1964), 143.

4. Raul Hilberg, "The Bureaucracy of Annihilation," in *Unanswered Questions: Nazi Germany and the Genocide of the Jews*, ed. François Furet (New York, 1989), 124–26.

1. ONE MORNING IN JÓZEFÓW

1. Adolf B., HW 440.

2. Erwin G., HW 2502–3; Johannes R., HW 1808; Karl F., HW 1868.

3. On Trapp's behavior during the speech: Georg A., HW 421; Alfred L., HW 1351; Bruno P., HW 1915; Walter N., HW 3927; Heinz B., HW 4415; August Z., G 275. On the contents of the speech: Georg A., HW 421; Adolf B., HW 439; Martin D., HW 1596; Walter N., HW 1685; Bruno D., HW 1874; Otto-Julius S., HW 1952; Bruno G., HW 2019; August W., HW 2039–40; Wilhelm Gb., HW 2146; Franz K., HW 2482; Anton B., HW 2655, 4346; Ernst Hn., G 505. For the extraordinary offer; Otto-Julius S., HW 1953, 4577; August W., HW 2041–42, 3298, 4589.

2. THE ORDER POLICE

1. The only institutional history of the Order Police is *Zur Geschichte der Ordnungspolizei 1936–1945* (Koblenz, 1957): part 1, Hans-Joachim Neufeldt, "Entstehung und Organisation des Hauptamtes Ordnungspolizei," and part 2, Georg Tessin, "Die Stäbe und Truppeneinheiten der Ordnungs-

polizei." Heiner Lichtenstein's *Himmlers grüne Helfer: Die Schutzpolizei und Ordnungspolizei in "Dritten Reich"* (Köln, 1990) appeared too late to be consulted.

2. Tessin, 7–8.
3. Tessin, 13–15, 24, 27, 49.
4. Tessin, 32–34.
5. Tessin, 15, 34.
6. NO-2861 (Daluege's annual report for 1942, presented to high-ranking Order Police officers in January 1943). Slightly different figures are given in *Das Diensttagebuch des deutschen Generalgouverneurs in Polen 1939–1945*, ed. Werner Präg and Wolfgang Jacobmeyer (Stuttgart, 1975), 574. On November 21, 1942, the commander of the Order Police in the General Government reported a force of 12,000 German police, 12,000 Polish police, and 1,500 to 1,800 Ukrainian police (presumably in Galicia). The commander of the Security Police reported a force of 2,000 Germans and 3,000 Polish employees.

3. THE ORDER POLICE AND THE FINAL SOLUTION: RUSSIA 1941

1. Krausnick and Wilhelm, 146; Tessin, 96.
2. *IMT* 38:86–94 (221-L: Hitler conference of July 16, 1941, with Göring, Lammers, Rosenberg, and Keitel).
3. Yehoshua Büchler, "Kommandostab Reichsführer-SS: Himmler's Personal Murder Brigades in 1941," *Holocaust and Genocide Studies* 1, no. 1 (1986):13–17.
4. For example, the direct subordination of Police Battalion 322 to HSSPF von dem Bach-Zelewski "for the imminent tasks of the battalion" took place on July 23, 1941. YVA, 0-53/127/53 (war diary of PB 322, entry of July 23, 1941; hereafter war diary).
5. NOKW-1076 (*Kommissarbefehl*, June 6, 1941).
6. *Gerichtsbarkeiterlass Barbarossa*, signed by Keitel, May 13, 1941, in Hans-Adolf Jacobsen, "Kommissarbefehl und Massenexekutionen sowjetischer Kriegsgefangener," *Anatomie des SS-States* (Freiburg, 1965), 2:216–18 (doc. 8).
7. YVA, TR-10/823 (Landgericht Wuppertal, judgment 12 Ks 1/67):29–30.
8. YVA, TR-10/823 (Landgericht Wuppertal, judgment 12 Ks 1/67):40–65.
9. War diary, 15, entry of June 10, 1941.
10. War diary, 28, entry of July 2, 1941.
11. War diary, 35–41, entries of July 5, 7, and 8, 1941.

12. War diary, 40–42, entries of July 8 and 9, 1941.
13. YVA, 0-53/128/219 (confidential order of Colonel Montua, July 11, 1941).
14. For Police Battalion 322, see *JNSV* 19, no. 555 (Landgericht Freiburg, judgment 1 AK 1/63):437–8. For Police Battalion 316, see YVA, TR-10/721 (Landgericht Bochum, judgment 15 Ks 1/66):142–77.
15. War diary, 53, entry of July 23, 1941.
16. War diary, 64, entry of August 2, 1941.
17. YVA, 0-53/128/80 (Riebel, 3d Company, to PB 322, August 10, 1941).
18. YVA, 0-53/128/81 (Riebel, 3d Company, to PB 322, August 15, 1941).
19. War diary, 79, entry of August 29, 1941.
20. War diary, 82, entry of August 30, 1941.
21. War diary, 83–85, entries of August 31 and September 1, 1941.
22. YVA, 0-53/128/87 (Riebel, 9th Company, to 3rd Pol. Batl. Reg. "Mitte," September 1, 1941).
23. War diary, 116, 118, entries of October 2 and 3, 1941. Riebel's report in fact claims 555 for his Ninth Company. YVA, 0-53/86/150 (Riebel, "Report on the Jewish action of October 2–3, 1941," to 3d Pol. Batl. Reg. "Mitte").
24. YVA, 0-53/128/242–75, 0-53/86/14–62 (incomplete collection of daily reports of HSSPF South, Friedrich Jeckeln, to RF-SS Himmler, August 19–October 5, 1941).
25. ZStL, II 204 AR-Z 1251-65 (Landgericht Regensburg, judgment Ks 6/70):9–35; and 204 AR-Z 1251/65, 2:370–77 (report of Bavarian State Criminal Office, Munich, September 10, 1968).
26. ZStL, 204 AR-Z 1251/65, 1:53–54, 58–60, 94–96 (interrogations of Johann L., Franz P., and Karl G.); 3:591–95 (notes from Balek diary).
27. For a highly flawed legal judgment containing useful background on the activities of Police Battalion 11, see *JNSV* 18, no. 546a (Landgericht Kassel, judgment 3a Ks 1/61):786–835.
28. *IMT* 27:4–8 (1104-PS: Gebietskommissar Carl in Slutsk to Generalkommissar Kube in Minsk, October 30, 1941).
29. *JNSV* 18, no. 546a (Landgericht Kassel, judgment 3a Ks 1/61):786–87, 835.
30. The only document I have found on Order Police participation in the execution of Russian Jews in 1942 is an Order Police company report on the role of two battalions in the final liquidation of 15,000 Jews in the Pinsk ghetto between October 29 and November 1 (YVA, 0-53/129/257–58, USSR 199A). The German judicial investigation stemming from this document uncovered a wider pattern of executions. Police Battalion 306, along with one company each from Police Battalions 310 and 320 and a squadron of

mounted policemen, was involved in Pinsk. Throughout September 1942, units of Police Battalions 69 and 306, as well as the mounted police squadron, had also participated in liquidating the ghettos in Lachwa (200–500), Luninets (1,000–1,500), Stolin (5,000), Janow (2,000), and Drohotschin (1,500). See Staatsanwaltschaft Frankfurt, 4 Js 90/62, indictment of Kuhr, Petsch, et al., 66–107.

31. NO-2861 (Daluege report for Order Police activities in 1942).

32. NO-600 (Grawitz to Himmler, March 4, 1942).

4. THE ORDER POLICE AND THE FINAL SOLUTION: DEPORTATION

1. For the most recent analysis of the deportations from Germany, see Henry Friedlander, "The Deportations of the German Jews: Post-War Trials of Nazi Criminals," *Leo Baeck Institute Yearbook* (1984): 201–26.

2. *IMT* 22:534–36 (3921-PS; Daluege to inspectors of the Order Police, October 27, 1941); YVA, 0-51/63/4, 6 (Butenop, KdSchupo Wien, October 24, 1941, to local Orpo units; Bomhard memorandum on the evacuation of the Jews, October 4, 1941).

3. This figure does not include smaller transports of less than 100 Jews at a time, of which there were many. A comprehensive list of the deportation trains from the Reich has not yet been compiled.

4. YVA, TR-10/835 (Staatsanwaltschaft Düsseldorf, 8 Js 430/67, indictment of Ganzenmüller):177–78. For the takeover of transports from Bulgaria to Treblinka by the Order Police in Vienna, see YVA, 0-51/63/109 (note by Butenop, KdSchupo, March 26, 1943). This file contains the correspondence of the Order Police in Vienna concerning the guarding of Jewish transports to various places in Poland, Minsk (Maly-Trostinez), and Theresienstadt from the spring of 1942 to the summer of 1943.

5. Gertrude Schneider, *Journey into Terror: Story of the Riga Ghetto* (New York, 1979), 195–211; Krausnick and Wilhelm, 591–95.

6. YVA, 0-51/63/42–43 (Fischmann report, June 20, 1942).

7. This document has been published in German in Adalbert Rückerl, *NS-Vernichtungslager im Spiegel deutscher Strafprozesse* (Munich, 1977), 56–60. A copy of the report, from Soviet archives, is found in ZStL, USSR Ord. No. 116, Bild 508–10.

5. RESERVE POLICE BATTALION 101

1. ZStL, 3 AR-Z 52/61, in HW 1–6; Kurt A., HW 11; Ernst Hr., HW 2712.
2. BA, R 20/51/3–7 (activity report of Reserve Police Battalion 101, May 5, 1940–April 7, 1941).
3. Bruno P., HW 1912–13.
4. Alfred H., HW 43–44; Georg L., HW 1425; Heinrich S., HW 1561; Walter Z., HW 2683; Ernst Hr., HW 2712; Ernst R., G 607.
5. Paul H., HW 1647.
6. BA, R 20/51/3–7 (battalion activity report).
7. Bruno G., HW 2017.
8. YVA, TR-10/462 (Landgericht Dortmund, judgment 10 Ks 1/53):3–4.
9. Bruno P., HW 1913–14.
10. Hans K., HW 2246; Ernst Hr., HW 2713.
11. Anton B., HW 2684; Wolfgang Hoffmann, HW 4319.
12. YVA, 0-53/141/4378–86 (Jäger report of EK 3, Kovno, December 1, 1941); Schneider, 23–30.
13. See YVA, BD 23/4 (International Tracing Service Lists), and *Dokumenty i Materiały Do Dziejów Okupacji W Polsce,* vol. 3, *Ghetto Łódzkie* (Warsaw, 1946): 203–5 (*Erfahrungsbericht,* November 13, 1941), for the Łódź transports; *JSNV* 19, no. 552 (Landgericht Koblenz, judgment 9 Ks 2/61):190, for the transports to Minsk; and Schneider, 155, for the transport to Riga.
14. Heinrich Ht., HW 1173; Wilhelm J., HW 1320; Hans K., HW 2246; Franz K., HW 2475; Anton B., HW 2689.
15. Otto G., HW 955.
16. For Łódź, Arthur K., HW 1180; for Minsk, Bruno P., HW 1930–32; for Riga, Hans K., HW 2246, and Max F., HW 1529.
17. Hans K., HW 2246.
18. Bruno P., HW 1930–31.
19. Salitter report, December 26, 1941, cited in Krausnick and Wilhelm, 594.
20. Staatsanwaltschaft Hamburg, 141 Js 1957/62 (indictment of Hoffman and Wohlauf):206 (hereafter Hoffman/Wohlauf indictment).
21. Ernst G., HW 1835.
22. BDC, Wilhelm Trapp party card. Julius Wohlauf, HW 2882, 4326; Wolfgang Hoffmann, HW 2930, 4318–19, 4322.
23. Hoffmann/Wohlauf indictment, 47–49.
24. Hoffmann/Wohlauf indictment, 49–51.

25. Staatsanwaltschaft Hamburg, 141 Js 1457/62, Sonderband: DC-Unterlagen.

26. This statistical breakdown of Reserve Police Battalion 101 is based upon information from 210 interrogations conducted by the Hamburg prosecuting attorney in the 1960s. Not including the officers, administrative officials, and noncommissioned officers, the interrogations provided a sample base of 174 men from the ranks. While all interrogations included data on age, not all included full information on employment. Some men gave only postwar employment status, and many of those—given the age group—were listed merely as pensioners. Thus the employment sample consists of only 155 men.

27. These Party membership statistics are based on Party membership cards held in the BDC.

6.   ARRIVAL IN POLAND

1. Experimental gassing with Zyklon-B began in the Auschwitz main camp (Stammlager, or Auschwitz I) in September and October 1941. The systematic use of the new gas chamber (a converted farmhouse) at nearby Birkenau (Auschwitz II) began on February 15, 1942. Danuta Czech, *Kalendarium der Ereignisse im Konzentrationslager Auschwitz-Birkenau 1939–1945* (Reinbeck bei Hamburg, 1989), 116, 174–75.

2. There was a total of 3,000 men in the Sonderdienst for the entire General Government. That many were apparently Polish collaborators with only a specious claim to ethnic German status can be seen from the fact that only 25 percent of them spoke German. *Diensttagebuch*, 574.

3. For the dates and numbers of Jews killed in the Lublin district, I have relied upon Yitzhak Arad, *Bełżec, Sobibór, Treblinka: The Operation Reinhard Death Camps* (Bloomington, Ind., 1987), 383–87, 390–91; Tatiana Brustin-Berenstein, "Martyrologia, Opór I Zagłada Ludności Żydowskiej W Distrykcie Lubelskim," *BZIH* 21 (1957): 56–83; and various German court cases.

4. *Diensttagebuch*, 511 (Polizeisitzung, June 16, 1942).

5. Hoffmann/Wohlauf indictment, 205–6.

6. Johannes R., HW 1807.

7. For the stationing of the various units of Reserve Police Battalion 101 throughout 1942, see Hoffmann/Wohlauf indictment, 208–12.

8. Alfred S., HW 294–95; Albert D., HW 471; Arthur S., HW 1161; Friedrich B., HW 1581–82; Martin D., HW 1598–99; Wilhelm K., HW 1770; Herbert R., HW 2109; Heinrich E., HW 2169; Walter Z., HW 2622; Bruno G., HW 3300; Ernst N., HW 1648; August W., HW 2039.

7. INITIATION TO MASS MURDER: THE JÓZEFÓW MASSACRE

1. As neither Trapp, his adjutant Hagen, nor Lieutenant Gnade survived to be interrogated in the 1960s, the only direct witness to this meeting was Captain Wohlauf. His versions were so numerous and self-serving, and crucial aspects of the rest of his testimony so overwhelmingly contradicted by other witnesses, that he simply cannot be relied on.
2. Heinz B., HW 819–20, 2437, 3355, 4414.
3. Julius Wohlauf, HW 4329–30.
4. Friedrich Bm., HW 2091.
5. Hans S., G 328.
6. Bruno D., HW 1874
7. Alfred B., HW 440.
8. Rudolf B., HW 3692.
9. Otto-Julius S., 1953–54, 4576–79; August W., HW 2041–42, 3298, 4589. S. and W. were the only two witnesses who recalled Trapp's offer in precisely this way. Several others initially remembered a call for volunteers for the firing squad instead (Alfred B., HW 439–40; Franz G., HW 1189–90; Bruno G., HW 2020). Others, when questioned about the incident, either conceded the "possibility" that Trapp had made the offer (Anton B., HW 2693; Heinz B., HW 3356–57, 4415) or at least said they would not contest or deny it had happened. Trapp's stipulation about "older" men appears in S.'s testimony (HW 1953, 4578). W., who most explicitly confirmed S.'s testimony in other respects, did not mention this qualification and claimed that younger men stepped out as well. However, he does seem to have understood that Trapp made his offer to the older reservists. When asked to explain why he himself did not step out, he indicated that he was a relatively young volunteer, an "active" policeman—i.e., not a conscripted reservist (HW 2041–42, 4592). The greater precision and vivid detail of the S. and W. testimony and the subsequent behavior of the officers and noncoms of the battalion in accordance with Trapp's offer (i.e., those who belatedly asked out were released from firing squad duty—something the officers and noncoms could never have done so consistently without the prior sanction of the commanding officer) have persuaded me that a much greater probability rests with their version than with any other.
10. It may well be that First and Second Platoons of Third Company had already been stationed in a cordon surrounding the village *before* Trapp's speech. None of the men from these two platoons remembered the speech, and one witness (Bruno G., HW 2020) testified that the two platoons were not present.

11. Heinrich S., HW 1563; Martin D., HW 1596; Paul H., HW 1648; Ernst N., HW 1685; Wilhelm K., HW 1767, 2300; Bruno G., HW 2019; August W., HW 2039; Wilhelm Gb., HW 2147; Heinrich B., HW 2596; Walter Z., HW 2618; Anton B., HW 2656; Ernst Hr., HW 2716; Joseph P., HW 2742; Kurt D., HW 2888; Otto I., HW 3521; Wolfgang H., HW 3565; August Z., G 275; Eduard S., G 639; Hellmut S., G 646; Karl S., G 657.

12. Georg G., HW 2182.

13. Hellmut S., G 647.

14. Friedrich E., HW 1356.

15. Bruno R., HW 1852.

16. Harry L., G 223.

17. Ernst G., G 383.

18. Hans Kl., G 363.

19. Oskar P., HW 1743.

20. Erwin G., HW 2503.

21. Georg K., HW 2633; Karl S., G 657.

22. Wilhelm K., HW 1769; Friedrich Bm., HW 2091; Ernst Hn., G 506. For other accounts of the search, see Max D., HW 1345–46; Alfred L., HW 1351; Friederick V., HW 1539; Friedrich B., HW 1579; Bruno D., HW 1875; Hermann W., HW 1947–48; Otto-Julius S., HW 1954; Bruno G., HW 2019; August W., HW 2040; Bruno R., HW 2084; Hans Kl., HW 2270; Walter Z., HW 2168–69; Anton B., HW 2687; Ernst Hr., HW 2716; Joseph P., HW 2742; August Z., G 275; Karl Z., G 318; Eduard S., G 640.

23. Friedrich B., HW 1579; Bruno G., HW 2019; August W., HW 2041.

24. Ernst Hr., HW 2716–17.

25. Walter Z., HW 2618. For confirming testimony, see Anton B., HW 2688; Joseph P., HW 2742.

26. Hermann W., HW 1948.

27. Ernst Hn., G 507. Two witnesses (Eduard S., G 642; Hellmut S., G 647) remembered the first sergeant but not the doctor.

28. August W., HW 2042.

29. Martin D., HW 1597.

30. Anton B., HW 2658–59.

31. Heinz B., HW 821–22. Not a single policeman interrogated in Hamburg had been part of the escort, so Buchmann's account is the only version of the fate of the work Jews. On the Luxembourgers making up the escort, see Heinrich E., HW 2167. For other accounts of the sorting of the workers and their being marched out of Józefów by Buchmann, see Wilhelm K., HW 1768; Hermann W., HW 1948; Friedrich Bm., HW 2092–93; Ernst Hn., G 507.

32. For the testimony of First Company shooters, see especially Friedrich

B., HW 1580–81; Friedrich Bm., HW 2091–93; Ernst Hn., G 507–8; Heinrich R., G 623; Hellmut S., G 646–47; Karl S., G 658–59.
33. Paul H., HW 1648–49.
34. Heinrich H., G 453.
35. Wilhelm I., HW 2237.
36. Friedrich Bm., HW 2092.
37. Hellmut S., G 647.
38. Heinrich Bl, HW 462.
39. Hermann W., HW 1948.
40. Alfred L., HW 1351.
41. Bruno R., HW 1852.
42. Erwin N., HW 1686.
43. Bruno D., HW 1870; Anton B., HW 4347; Wilhelm Gb., HW 4363; Paul M., G 202.
44. Ernst Hr., HW 2717.
45. Erwin G., HW 1640, 2505.
46. Friedrich Bm., HW 2092.
47. Wilhelm G., HW 2149.
48. Ernst Hr., HW 2718.
49. Wilhelm Gb., HW 2538.
50. Ernst Hr., HW 2719.
51. Ernst Hr., HW 2720.
52. Wilhelm Gb., HW 2539, 2149.
53. Erwin G., HW 1639–40, 2504; Alfred B., HW 2518.
54. Anton B., HW 4348. See also Max D., HW 2536.
55. Walter Z., HW 2619–20; Erwin G., HW 4345.
56. Heinrich S., HW 1567, 4364; Georg K., HW 2634.
57. Joseph P., HW 2743–45.
58. Paul M., G 206–7.
59. Gustav M., G 168.
60. Hans D., HW 1336, 3542.
61. Walter N., HW 3926, G 230.
62. August Z., G 277.
63. Georg K., HW 2634.
64. Otto-Julius S., HW 4579; Friederick V., HW 1540.
65. Rudolf B., HW 2434, 2951, 4357.
66. Franz K., HW 2483–86.
67. In addition to the above cases, another policeman who asked to be released when his nerves were finished after a few rounds was Bruno D., HW 1876, 2535, 4361.
68. Erwin G., HW 2505; confirmed by Rudolf K., HW 2646–47.

69. Anton B., HW 2691–93, 4348.
70. Willy R., HW 2085.
71. Alfred B., HW 440; Walter Z., HW 2621; Georg K., HW 2635; August Z., G 278.
72. Friedrich B., HW 1581.
73. Julius Wohlauf, HW 758.
74. Heinrich B., HW 2984.
75. Alfred B., HW 441.
76. August W., HW 2042.
77. Otto-Julius S., HW 1955.
78. Witness after witness used the terms *erschüttert, deprimiert, verbittert, niedergeschlagen, bedrückt, verstört, empört,* and *belastet* to describe the men's feelings that evening.
79. Friedrich Bm., HW 2093; Hellmut S., G 647.
80. Heinrich Br , HW 3050.
81. Wilhelm J., HW 1322.
82. Willy S., HW 2053. See also Wolfgang Hoffmann, HW 774–75; Johannes R., HW 1809; Bruno R., HW 2086.
83. Karl M., HW 2546, 2657.
84. Friedrich Bm., HW 2093–94. See also Karl G., HW 2194.

8.   REFLECTIONS ON A MASSACRE

1. Heinz B., HW 4413; Kurt D., HW 4339.
2. In her analysis of Polish rescuers, Nechama Tec also notes that the initial decision to help Jews was impulsive and instinctive, not the result of prolonged reflection and calculation. *When Light Pierced the Darkness: Christian Rescue of Jews in Nazi-Occupied Poland* (New York, 1986), 188.
3. Anton B., HW 2693.
4. Bruno D., HW 2535, 2992.
5. August W., HW 4592.
6. Erwin G., HW 1640, 2505, 4344.
7. Friedrich M., HW 1708.
8. *IMT* 29:151 (1919-PS).
9. Karl G., HW 2194.
10. Hans Pz., HW 3938.
11. Hero B., HW 890.
12. Arthur S., HW 1165.
13. Hermann W., HW 1947.
14. Gustav M., G 169–70.
15. Heinz B., HW 2439–40.

16. Heinrich Br., HW 3050.
17. Heinrich R., G 624; August W., HW 3303.
18. Heinz B., HW 647, 822, 2438, 3940–41.

9. ŁOMAZY: THE DESCENT OF SECOND COMPANY

1. YVA, 0-53/121/27–31 (order of Kintrupp, KdO Lublin, July 9, 1942).
2. Brustin-Berenstein, table 2.
3. Kurt D., HW 1230, 4368; Anton B., HW 4371.
4. Heinrich B., HW 2600, 2985.
5. Kurt D., HW 1230, 1232, 2892, 4368; Ernst Hr., HW 2732.
6. Paul M., G 207.
7. Max F., HW 1387; Ernst Hr., HW 2722; Walter L., G 184; Fritz S., G 303.
8. Anton B., HW 2698–99, 4371; Ernst Hr., HW 2722; Wolfgang H., HW 2211; Kurt D., HW 4368; August Z., G 273.
9. Fritz S., G 303–4. See also Bernhard S., HW 1717; Ernst Hr., HW 2723; Heinrich B., HW 2985; Friedrich P., G 240.
10. Ernst Hr., HW 2723; Joseph P., HW 2749–50; Walter L., G 185; Paul M., G 208.
11. Gustav M., HW 1709.
12. For the phrase, Max F., HW 1386; for the distance, Heinrich B., HW 2601; Walter L., G 185.
13. Max F., HW 1386; Paul M., G 207.
14. Walter Z., HW 2624; Georg K., HW 2638; Anton B., HW 4372.
15. Anton B., HW 2700–2701.
16. Wilhelm Gb., HW 2150; Karl G., HW 2197; Heinrich B., HW 2600; Georg K., HW 2638; Joseph P., HW 2750; Hermann Bg., G 98; Walter L., G 185; Paul M., G 207; August Z., G 282; Fritz S., G 313.
17. Kurt D., HW 4335, 4368–70; Anton B., HW 2703, 3960, 4348; Joseph P., HW 2750; Henry D., HW 3071; Walter N., HW 3927; Ernst Hr., HW 3928; Heinz B., HW 3943; Walter Z., HW 3954. The only contrary testimony about Gnade is Ernst Hr., HW 3929; Walter Z., HW 3954; and Wolfgang Hoffmann, HW 4318.
18. Wilhelm I., HW 2239.
19. Friedrich P., G 241–42. This account is fully confirmed by August Z., HW 3519.
20. Hermann Bg., G 98; Joseph P., HW 2750.
21. Walter Z., HW 2625; Georg K., HW 2638.
22. Friedrich P., G 241–42.
23. Ernst H., HW 2725.

24. Johannes R., HW 1810; Rudolf K., HW 2650; Joseph P., HW 2750–51; Kurt D., HW 4368; Paul M., G 209.
25. Ernst Hr., HW 2725–26.
26. Ernst Hr., HW 2256.
27. Ernst Hr., HW 2256–57; Kurt D., HW 4368; August Z., G 282; Joseph P., HW 2750–51; Walter L., G 186–87; Max F., HW 1388.
28. Bernhard S., HW 1717.
29. Rudolf B., HW 405; Bruno D., HW 2535; Heinrich B., HW 2613–14; August Z., HW 3365–66, G 284.
30. Fritz S., G 303–4; Paul M., G 209; Bernhard S., HW 1717.
31. Anton B., HW 4374.
32. August Z., G 282.
33. Ernst Hr., HW 2727–28; August Z., G 284.
34. Ernst Hr., HW 2727.
35. Georg K., HW 2638.
36. Paul M., G 200, 209.
37. Adolf B., HW 441.
38. Anton B., HW 2703–4.

10. THE AUGUST DEPORTATIONS TO TREBLINKA

1. Heinrich S., HW 1569.
2. Georg K., HW 2637; Joseph P. HW 2747.
3. Erwin G., HW 1642, 2507.
4. Hans K., HW 2251; Georg K., HW 2636.
5. On First Company's role as the "search troops," see Paul H., HW 1652; Hans K., HW 2251.
6. For the Parczew deportations in general, see Heinrich S., HW 1569–73, 4383; Erwin G., HW 1641–42, 2507; Paul H., HW 1652; Bruno D., HW 1876–77; Heinrich E., HW 2170; Otto H., HW 2220; Hans K., HW 2251–52; Max D., HW 2536; Heinrich B., HW 2608; Georg K., HW 2636; August Z., HW 3366, G 278–79; Alfred K., G 575–76.
7. Heinrich S., HW 1572. Steinmetz's admission was the exception. It was far more common, of course, for the policemen to deny under interrogation that they had any notion about the impending fate of the deported Jews.
8. Heinrich B., HW 2608; August Z., G 279.
9. In the memories of almost all the policemen, the August deportation from Międzyrzec was telescoped into a single day. However, one policeman (Heinrich R., G 626) and all the Jewish witnesses (Tauba T., HW 1066–67; Berl C., HW 1092; Rywka G., HW 1112; ZStL, 8 AR-Z 236/60 [investigation of KdS Aussenstelle Radzyń], 1:3–4 [excerpt from Feigenbaum]) remember

two-day action. Given the number of Jews deported, two days were almost certainly needed.

10. YVA, TR-10/710 (Landgericht Dortmund 8 Ks 1/70 judgment against Josef Bürger), 16.

11. Policemen from both First and Third Companies testified that Second Company also took part. However, outside of Third Platoon, not a single member of Second Company—even those who testified quite frankly about Lomazy and Józefów—remembered the August Międzyrzec deportation. I consider it most likely, therefore, that First and Second Platoons of Second Company were not present on this occasion.

12. Ernst Hn., G 512; Heinrich R., G 625.

13. Hei...ich H., HW 976, 3219. See also Friedrich B., HW 1582, 3529; Hans K., 2252, 3220.

14. H. evaluations of December 6, 1940, and March 31, 1941, in HW 565–67.

15. R. evaluation of April 10, 1941, in HW 569.

16. Trapp evaluation of July 21, 1941, in HW 574–80.

17. Hans Pg., HW 1945; Ernst Hr., HW 2713.

18. Heinrich E., HW 3351, 3354.

19. Heinz B., HW 4414.

20. Julius Wohlauf, HW 750–51, 760.

21. Friedrich B., HW 1582; Friedrich Bm., HW 2099; Heinz B. and Arthur K., HW 3357; Ernst R., G 610; Heinrich R., G 627.

22. The most detailed accounts of the Międzyrzec deportation are Heinrich H., HW 976–78; Friedrich B., HW 1582–83; Hans K., HW 2253–54; Ernst Hn., G 512–13; Ernst R., G 610–12; Karl S., G 659–60.

23. Hans K., HW 2253.

24. Karl S., G 659.

25. Heinrich R., G 610.

26. Friedrich B., HW 3529.

27. Friedrich B., HW 1583; Ernst Hn., G 512.

28. Heinrich H., HW 978, 3219; Hans K., HW 3220; Ernst R., G 611.

29. Heinrich H., HW 977; Friedrich B., HW 1584; Hans K., HW 2254; Ernst Hn., G 513; Ernst R., G 612.

30. Heinrich H., HW 977–78.

31. Ilse de L., HW 1293.

32. Heinrich H., HW 978; Hans K., HW 2254.

33. Berl C., HW 1091.

34. YVA 0-53/105/III (reports of the Warsaw Judenrat).

35. ZStL, 8 AR-Z 236/60 (investigation of KdS Aussenstelle Radzyń) 3:464 (Ostbahn travel plan of August 25, 1942). For more on the breakdown at

Treblinka, see Gitta Sereny, *Into That Darkness* (London, 1974), 156–64;
Arad, 89–96, 119–23.

11.   LATE-SEPTEMBER SHOOTINGS

1. Ferdinand H., HW 3257–58.
2. Hans K., HW 2256.
3. The most important testimony for the Serokomla shootings is Friedrich
B., HW 1586–89, 3534; Hans K., HW 2256–60; Ernst R., G 612a–b; Karl
S., G 661–62.
4. Friedrich P., HW 3534.
5. Hans K., HW 2258.
6. Albert D., HW 3539; Arthur S., HW 3540.
7. Heinrich Bl., HW 464; Hans K., HW 2255; Friedrich Bm., HW 2096.
8. Heinrich E., HW 2173.
9. Hans K., HW 2256.
10. Ernst Hn., G 509.
11. Ernst Hn., G 509; Friedrich B., HW 1590.
12. Heinz B., HW 826.
13. Georg W., HW 1733.
14. Gerhard H., G 541.
15. Hans K., HW 2255; Friedrich Bm., HW 2097; Hellmut S., G 648.
16. Alfred H., HW 286.
17. Heinrich Bl., HW 464–65.
18. Friedrich Bm., HW 2097–98; Hans K., HW 2255–56; Hellmut S., G
648–49; Karl S., G 662.
19. Trapp report to Police Regiment 25, September 26, 1942, HW
2548–50.
20. Heinz B., HW 648, 822, 824, 2438, 2440–41, 3941, 4415.
21. Heinrich E., HW 2172.
22. Hans K., HW 2242; Kurt D., HW 2678; Arthur S., HW 3539; Alfred
K., G 582; Ernst R., G 612d.
23. Heinrich E., HW 2174.
24. Heinz B., HW 648, 2438.
25. Heinz B., HW 2441.
26. Heinrich E., HW 2174.

12.   THE DEPORTATIONS RESUME

1. Brustin-Berenstein, 21–92.
2. YVA, 0-53/121 W I/124–25 (order of Kintrupp, August 27, 1942,
effective September 2, 1942).

3. Testimony of survivors Jozef B., HW 1122, and Sara K., HW 3250. According to Brustin-Berenstein, table 2, some 6,000 Jews from the smaller villages of Biała Podlaska county were deported to Międzyrzec on September 23–24. She lists the deportations from the town of Biała Podlaska itself (4,800 Jews) on September 26 and October 6 as going directly to Treblinka, but survivor testimony indicates that at least the September deportation from Biała went first to Międzyrzec.

4. Brustin-Berenstein, table 1, gives the figure of 610 Jews from Komarówka, 800 from Wohyn, and 1,019 from Czemierniki.

5. Johannes R., HW 1810–11; Kurt D., HW 1621; Anton B., HW 2705–6.

6. Paul M., HW 2659.

7. According to Brustin-Berenstein, table 10: 1,724 from Adamów, 460 from Stanin gmina, 446 from Ulan gmina, and 213 from Wojcieszków.

8. YVA, TR-10/710 (Landgericht Dortmund, 8 Ks 1/70, judgment against Josef Bürger):10, 16 (hereafter Bürger judgment).

9. For estimates of Security Police and Gendarmerie manpower in Radzyń county, see ZStL, 8 AR-Z 236/60 (investigation of KdS Aussenstelle Radzyń), 1:28 (Braumüller), 113 (Bürger), 120 (Käser); 2:176–79 (Reimer), 209–10 (Brämer), 408 (Behrens), 420 (Kambach); 4:550 (Schmeer), 715 (Avriham); and Sonderband (testimony of Rumminger, Schoeja, and Waldner), no pagination.

10. Brustin-Berenstein, table 10.

11. Helmuth H., HW 317–20, 991; Heinz B., HW 823; Heinrich E., HW 2176; Richard G., G 389.

12. Heinrich S., HW 1573–74; Max D., HW 2536.

13. Alfred H., HW 45, 279–80.

14. Kurt D., HW 1266, 2966–67, 4391; Paul M., HW 2663.

15. Alfred H., HW 45, 280–82.

16. Peter Ö., HW 1790; Walter L., G 189–90; Friedrich P., G 244.

17. Kurt D., HW 1268, 2968, 4390.

18. Friedrich P., G 244.

19. August Z., HW 3367–68, G 288.

20. Alfred H. (HW 45, 282) initially testified to the deportation of 6,000 to 10,000 but later lowered his estimate to 1,000. Kurt D. (HW 1621) likewise gave a figure of 1,000. However, all witnesses agree that a Hiwi unit was sent to assist the Order Police in carrying out the early October action. It is very unlikely that a sizable contingent of Hiwis would have been sent for so small an action, given the availability of an entire company of Order Police. Such a small number of deportees is also unlikely in view of the many thousands of Jews who had been concentrated in Międzyrzec in the previous weeks.

21. Helmuth H., HW 991; Stephan J., HW 1041–43; Tauba T., HW 1069; Friedrich B., HW 1585.

22. Kurt D., HW 1270–71, 2790, 4391; Max F., HW 1389–90; Johannes R., HW 1012; Franz K., HW 2479.

23. Lucia B., G 595–96; Hoffmann letter of May 5, 1943, HW 512.

24. Julius Wohlauf, HW 752, 762–64.

25. Heinrich H., HW 972; Rudolf B., HW 406–7; Max D., HW 1347.

26. August Z., G 286; Konrad H., G 404–5; Wilhelm K., G 568.

27. Wilhelm Gs., HW 2466.

28. Bürger judgment, 18.

29. Alfred K., G 579.

30. Bürger judgment, 20; Aviram J., HW 1059–60; Gedali G., HW 1080; Friedrich Bm., HW 2100; Hans K., HW 2262–63. According to Hans K., Jurich shot the head of the Jewish council in a dispute over a sewing machine.

31. Bürger judgment, 20.

32. Georg W., HW 1731–32.

33. Brustin-Berenstein, table 10, lists only one November shooting in Łuków, of 200 Jews. The testimony of the policemen indicates that there were two. The Bürger judgment, 20–21, confirms two Łuków shootings, on November 11 and 14, each with 500 victims—a rare case in which a German court estimates casualties higher than do other sources.

34. The one key exception was Buchmann, who claimed in the 1960s (Heinz B., HW 822, 824, 3942, 4417) that no unit under his command shot Jews, that after Józefów he had witnessed no other Jewish action except the ghetto clearing in Radzyń, where he was stationed but given no duties, and indeed that he had returned to Hamburg on November 4, one week before the first Łuków shooting. In view of the very clear memory and testimony of various staff members, some of whom had been with him in Radzyń and Łuków for some time and knew him well, it seems that Buchmann either unconsciously repressed the incident or intentionally concealed it from the interrogators.

35. Heinrich H., G 456.

36. Heinrich H., G 455–56; Hans Pz., HW 3525.

37. Hans S., G 328; Ernst S., G 330; Paul F., HW 2242.

38. Heinrich H., G 456–57; Hans Pz., HW 3525; Henry J., G 411–12.

39. Hans S., G 330; Ernst S., G 334–335; Paul F., HW 2243.

40. Henry J., G 413–14.

41. Heinz B., HW 648, 824–25, 2438, 2441, 4417.

13. THE STRANGE HEALTH OF CAPTAIN HOFFMANN

1. Hoffmann's "complaint" of May 3, 1943, HW 509.
2. Bruno G., HW 2026.
3. Erwin H., HW 1168; Martin D., HW 1602; August W., HW 2043.
4. Alfred S., HW 298; Erwin H., HW 1169; Martin D., HW 1602; Peter C., HW 1865; August W., HW 2043–44.
5. Martin D., HW 1602; August W., HW 2043–44.
6. August W., HW 2045.
7. Erwin H., HW 1169; Wilhelm J., HW 1323; Georg L., HW 1427; Friederick V., HW 1542; Martin D., HW 1603; Peter C., HW 1865; Bruno G., HW 2025; August W., HW 2044-45.
8. Martin D., HW 1605.
9. Friederick V., HW 1542.
10. Martin D., HW 1605–6.
11. Alfred S., HW 299; Georg L., HW 1428; Martin D., HW 1603; Bruno G., HW 2025–26; August W., HW 2045, 3305–6.
12. Amandus M., HW 1631–32.
13. Friederick V., HW 1592.
14. August W., HW 2045.
15. Hoffmann's "complaint" of May 3, 1943, HW 513: Wolfgang Hoffmann, HW 2304, 2925.
16. Friederick V., HW 1541; Martin D., HW 1605–6, 3212–13, 3319; Erwin N., HW 1693–94, 3319–20; Wilhelm K., HW 1776, 3345–49; Bruno G., HW 2030–31, 3301, 3347; Bruno R., HW 2086; Erwin H., HW 1167.
17. Hoffmann letter of January 30, 1943, HW 523–24.
18. Trapp letter of February 23, 1943, HW 509–10.
19. Hoffmann "complaint" of May 3, 1943, HW 509–15.
20. Rheindorf to police president of Hamburg, July 2, 1943, HW 538–39.
21. Wolfgang Hoffmann, HW 788–89.

14. THE "JEW HUNT"

1. YVA, TR-10/970 (Staatsanwaltschaft Hamburg, 147 Js 8/75, indictment of Arpad Wigand):81–92. See also Christopher R. Browning, "Genocide and Public Health: German Doctors and Polish Jews, 1939–41," *Holocaust and Genocide Studies* 3, no. 1 (1988): 21–36.
2. YVA, TR-10/970 (Staatsanwaltschaft Hamburg 147 Js 8/75, indictment of Arpad Wigand):92–99; Ferdinand H., HW 3257–58; *Diensttagebuch*, 456.
3. YVA, TR-10/542 (Staatsanwaltschaft Augsburg, 7 Js 653/53, indictment of Günther Waltz).

4. Heinrich S., HW 1573.
5. Kurt D., HW 1623.
6. Arthur S., HW 1164.
7. Georg L., HW 1429; Friedrich B., HW 1552; Paul H., HW 1653; Johannes R., HW 1812; Bruno G., HW 2030; August W., HW 2048; Heinrich E., HW 2177; Heinrich B., HW 2206; Hans K., HW 2261–62; Wilhelm K., HW 2379; Anton B., HW 2708; Ernst Hr., HW 2731; Martin D., HW 3213; Walter L., G 192; Friedrich P., G 247; Hugo S., G 474; Alfred K., G 580.
8. Erwin G., HW 4400.
9. Paul H., HW 1653.
10. Georg L., HW 1428–30.
11. Peter Ö., HW 1794; Otto H., HW 2227; Hans K., HW 2261.
12. Alfred S., HW 302.
13. Heinrich H., HW 975–76; Rudolf B., HW 408; Heinrich E., HW 2178; Hans K., HW 2261; Karl S., G 664.
14. Rudolf B., HW 403; Franz G., HW 1192.
15. Wilhelm K., HW 1774, 2379; Bruno G., HW 2033–34.
16. Alfred S., HW 300–301.
17. Martin D., HW 1600; Erwin N., HW 3321–22.
18. Friedrich Bm., HW 2101; Hans K., HW 2263–64.
19. Friedrich Bm., HW 2102.
20. For First Company, see Arthur S., HW 1164; Max F., HW 1531; Friedrich Bm., HW 2101; Heinrich E., HW 2175; Hans K., HW 2262–66; Hans Pz., HW 3256; Friedrich B., HW 3531; Alfred K., G 580; Ernst R., G 612; Karl S., G 663. For Second Company, see Rudolf B., HW 403, 407–8; Adolf B., HW 442–43; Max D., HW 1346; Heinrich S., HW 1573; Erwin G., HW 1641–42; Peter Ö., HW 1743–44; Wilhelm G., HW 2153–56; Helmuth H., HW 2207; Otto H., HW 2206–7; Walter Z., HW 2267–68; Georg K., HW 2639–40, 3344–45; Anton B., HW 2708–11; Ernst Hr., HW 2731; August Z., HW 3066–67, G 286; Richard Gm., HW 3545; Walter N., HW 3553; Wolfgang H., HW 3563–64; Paul M., HW 3935; Hermann Bg., G 100–111; Gustav M., G 169; Walter L., G 192; Friedrich P., G 248. For Third Company, see Karl E., HW 897; Walter F., HW 903; Martin D., HW 1600–1601, 1609, 3321; Erwin N., HW 1689, 1693–95; Richard M., HW 1890; Bruno P., HW 1916, 1924–25; Arthur R., HW 1938–39; Bruno G., HW 2030–34; August W., HW 2046–48, 3304; Alfred S., HW 2067; Friedrich S., HW 2072–73; Herbert R., HW 2111–12.
21. Erwin N., HW 1693.
22. Bruno P., HW 1917.
23. Hans Kl., HW 3565.

24. Wolfgang H., HW 3564.
25. Lucia B., G 598.
26. Ernst Hn., G 511.
27. Adolf B., HW 2532.
28. Heinrich B., HW 3615.
29. Walter Z., HW 2629.
30. Otto-Julius S., HW 4577–78.
31. Adolf B., HW 442–43.
32. Gustav M., G 169. Another policeman (Hero B., HW 890) also ascribed his being picked only once for a Jewish action to his reputation as politically unreliable and quarrelsome.
33. Heinrich F., G 445–46.
34. Hugo S., G 474.
35. Bruno P., HW 1925.
36. Arthur R., HW 1938–39.
37. Martin D., HW 3213.
38. Henry J., G 415.
39. Friedrich P., G 248.
40. YVA, 0-53/121 II w (May 1943); 0-53/122 X I (June 1943); 0-53/122 X II (July and August 1943); 0-53/123 Y I (September and October 1943).
41. YVA, 0-53/115/2–170, 673–725. See also YVA, TR-10/970 (Staatsanwaltschaft Hamburg, 147 Js 8/75, indictment of Arpad Wigand):103–7.
42. ZStL, Ord. 410, 994–96, 498, 500–501 (weekly reports of Fifth Company Reserve Police Battalion 133, Police Regiment 24, November 7–December 12, 1942).

15. THE LAST MASSACRES: "HARVEST FESTIVAL"

1. Krüger decree of October 28, 1942, in *Faschismus—Ghetto—Massenmord* (Berlin, 1960), 342–44.
2. Karl E., HW 896.
3. Jakob A., HW 1064.
4. Excerpts from memoirs of Feiga Cytryn and J. Stein, in ZStL, 8 AR-Z 236/60 (hereafter KdS Radzyń case), 1:6–7.
5. Testimony of Lea Charuzi, KdS Radzyń case, volume of miscellaneous testimony, 30.
6. Johannes R., HW 1811; Karl M., HW 2660; Wilhelm K., G 106–8.
7. Testimony of Rywka Katz, KdS Radzyń case, volume of miscellaneous testimony, 18.
8. For further German accounts, see Herbert F., HW 1389; August Z., G 287–89. For Jewish accounts, see Berl C., HW 1094; Rywka G., HW

1113–14; and KdS Radzyń case, Moshe Feigenbaum, 1:4–5; Liowa Friedmann, 1:10; volume of miscellaneous testimony, Feigenbaum, 6: Rywka G., 24; Moshe Brezniak, 18; Mortka Lazar, 28. For the participation of Trawniki personnel, see ZStL, II 208 AR 643/71 (Staatsanwaltschaft Hamburg, 147 Js 43/69, indictment of Karl Streibel; hereafter Trawniki indictment):104.

9. There is confusion in the testimony as to the destinations of the early and late May deportations. I have followed Brustin-Berenstein, table 10.

10. Trawniki indictment, 104; Jakob A., HW 1063.

11. Memo of May 21, 1963, HW 1348; Arthur S., HW 1165; Otto-Julius S., HW 1955; Friedrich Bm., HW 2105; Heinrich E., HW 2161; Joseph P., HW 2756; Otto I., HW 3522; Ernst Hn., G 505.

12. Herbert R., HW 2112; Karl G., HW 2201; Ernst Hr., HW 2715.

13. Georg L., HW 1430; Erwin G., HW 1644; Friedrich B., IIW 3143. BDC, files of Friedrich B., Hermann F., Erwin G. Ernst Hr., Erwin N., Ernst R., and Walter Z.

14. Heinrich H., HW 973; Bruno D., HW 1880.

15. Rudolf B., HW 409.

16. Himmler Aktenvermerk, October 2, 1942, Hoffmann/Wohlauf indictment, 320–22.

17. Trawniki indictment, 104–6.

18. For Erntefest, see Helge Grabitz and Wolfgang Scheffler, Letzte Spuren: Ghetto Warschau—SS-Arbeitslager Trawniki—Aktion Erntefest (Berlin, 1988), 262–72, 328–34; Jozef Marszalek, Majdanek: The Concentration Camp in Lublin (Warsaw, 1986), 130–34; ZStL, 208 AR-Z 268/59 (Staatsanwaltschaft Wiesbaden, 8 Js 1145/60, indictment of Lothar Hoffmann and Hermann Worthoff, KdS Lublin case):316–31, 617–35, 645–51; Trawniki indictment, 159–97; YVA, TR-10/1172 (Landgericht Düsseldorf, judgment against Hachmann et al.; hereafter Majdanek judgment):456–87.

19. Werner W. (KdO liaison to SSPF Lublin), HW 600–601.

20. Majdanek judgment, 459; Marszalek, 130; Grabitz and Scheffler, 328–29.

21. Majdanek judgment, 459; Werner W., HW 601–2.

22. Helmuth H., HW 2206.

23. Rudolf B., HW 409–10; Herbert F., HW 1392; Martin D., HW 1610.

24. For the number of Jews shot at Majdanek on November 3, 1943, see ZStL, II 208 AR-Z 74/60 (Staatsanwaltschaft Hamburg, 141 Js 573, indictment of August Birmes):126–29; Majdanek judgment, 456–57, 471.

25. Rudolf B., HW 410; Herbert F., HW 1392; Martin D., HW 1610; Paul H., HW 1655; Bruno R., HW 1856; Bruno P., HW 1928; Otto H., HW 2229; Wilhelm Kl., G 109.

26. Fritz B., HW 804–5; Otto H., HW 2228–29.
27. Heinrich Bl., HW 467–68.
28. ZStL, 208 AR-Z 268/59 (Staatsanwaltschaft Wiesbaden, 8 Js 1145/60, indictment of Lothar Hoffmann and Hermann Worthoff, KdS Lublin case):633–35.
29. Heinrich Bl., HW 468; Alfred L., HW 1354; Martin D., HW 1610; Bruno R., HW 1856; Wilhelm Kl., G 109.
30. Alfred L., HW 1354; Johannes L., HW 1444; Bruno R., HW 1856; Bruno P., HW 1928.
31. Martin D., HW 1611–13.
32. Wilhelm Gb., HW 2155.
33. Karl E., HW 900.
34. Johannes L., HW 1445; Eduard D., HW 433–34.
35. Wilhelm K., HW 1777–78.

16. AFTERMATH

1. Wolfgang Hoffmann, HW 768; Kurt D., HW 1224.
2. Heinrich Bl., HW 469.
3. Wolfgang Hoffmann, HW 790, 2922–24.
4. Heinz B., HW 649, 825; Arthur K., HW 61.

17. GERMANS, POLES, AND JEWS

1. Wolfgang Hoffmann, HW 780.
2. Heinz B., HW 826.
3. Bruno P., HW 1919.
4. Lucia B., G 597.
5. Wolfgang Hoffmann, HW 2299.
6. Walter H., G 602.
7. Bruno P., HW 1925–26.
8. Wolfgang Hoffmann, HW 2921.
9. Kurt D., HW 2886–87.
10. Alfred K., G 582; Ernst R., G 608, 612d; Georg S., G 635.
11. Hermann Bn., HW 3067, 3214–15, 3512, 3515; Rudolf B. and Alfred B., HW 3514.
12. Erwin G., HW 2503; Alfred B., HW 2520.
13. August Z., HW 3368.
14. Erwin G., HW 1640, 2504; Conrad M., HW 2682; Anton B., HW 2710; Kurt D., HW 4338; Hermann Bg., G 101.

15. Bruno D., HW 1876; Anton B., HW 4347; Kurt D., HW 4337; Wilhelm Gb., HW 2149.
16. Rudolf G., HW 2491.
17. Ernst Hd., HW 3088–89.
18. Georg W., HW 1733.
19. Gerhard K., HW 3083.
20. Friedrich Bm., HW 2097.
21. Karl G., HW 2200.
22. Erwin N., HW 1690.
23. Friedrich Bm., HW 2103; Hellmut S., G 652.
24. Hans K., HW 2265.
25. Friedrich P., G 247; Wilhelm K., G 517–18; Walter N., HW 3354.
26. Oskar P., HW 1742.
27. Wilhelm J., HW 1322; Friederick V., HW 1540; Emil S., HW 1737; Ernst Hr., HW 2717.
28. Wolfgang Hoffmann, HW 2294.
29. Rudolf B., HW 407; Friedrich B., HW 1592; Martin D., HW 1609; Heinrich E., HW 2171; Georg K., HW 2640; August Z., G 285; Karl S., G 663.
30. Gustav M., G 169.
31. Bruno P., HW 1924.
32. Bruno P., HW 1918–19.
33. Wilhelm J., HW 1324.
34. Friedrich Bm., HW 2104; Anton B., HW 2709–10; August Z., HW 3367, G 286.
35. Bruno G., HW 3301; Hans K., HW 2265.
36. August Z., HW 3365, 3367.
37. Anton B., HW 2710–11.

18.   ORDINARY MEN

1. John W. Dower, *War Without Mercy: Race and Power in the Pacific War* (New York, 1986), especially 3–15 ("Patterns of a Race War") and 33–73 ("War Hates and War Crimes").
2. The Polish name for the town is Bydgoszćz. Ethnic Germans living there were killed in the first days of the war, and in the following month the occupying Germans carried out particularly intensive executions and expulsions. See Krausnick and Wilhelm, 55–65; Tadeuz Esman and Wlodjimierz Jastrzebski, *Pierwsje Miesiac Okupacji Hitlerowkiej w Bydgoszćz* (Bydgoszćz, 1967).
3. As for overt encouragement, after machine-gunning Japanese soldiers

in the water for more than an hour, the commander of the submarine *Wahoo* was awarded both the Navy Cross and the Army Distinguished Service Cross. Dower, 330, n. 94.

4. Dower, 11.

5. Both Richard Rubenstein, *The Cunning of History* (New York, 1978), and Zygmunt Bauman, *Modernity and the Holocaust* (Ithaca, 1989), have elaborated on the implications of Hilberg's work in this regard. In *Eichmann in Jerusalem: A Report on the Banality of Evil* (New York, 1965), Hannah Arendt presented Eichmann as the "banal bureaucrat," a small cog in the bureaucratic machine. While Eichmann is not in fact the best example of the "banal bureaucrat," the concept is still valid for understanding many Holocaust perpetrators. Hilberg and others have certainly documented the extent to which ordinary bureaucrats, performing functions vital to the mass murder program in exactly the same routine way they performed the rest of their professional duties, made the Holocaust possible. The evil was not banal; the perpetrators most certainly were. It was precisely this gap "between the unspeakable horror of the deeds and the undeniable ludicrousness of the man who perpetrated them" (54) that Arendt tried to bridge with her notion of the "banality of evil."

6. Hans-Heinrich Wilhelm, unpublished manuscript.

7. Bettina Birn, *Die Höheren SS- und Polizeiführer* (Düsseldorf, 1986), 363–64; ZStL, II 208 AR-Z 74/60 (Staatsanwaltschaft Hamburg, 141 Js 573/60, indictment of Birmes):62–65.

8. Sereny, 83–88.

9. T.W. Adorno et al., *The Authoritarian Personality* (New York, 1950), 1–10.

10. Adorno et al., 222–279.

11. Bauman, 153.

12. John M. Steiner, "The SS Yesterday and Today: A Sociopsychological View," in *Survivors, Victims, and Perpetrators: Essays on the Nazi Holocaust,* ed. Joel E. Dimsdale (Washington, 1980), 431–34, 443.

13. Ervin Staub, *The Roots of Evil: The Origins of Genocide and Other Group Violence* (Cambridge, 1989), 18, 128–41.

14. Staub, 26, 126. Staub includes one Vietnam veteran's story that parallels the experience of the policemen of Reserve Battalion 101 who felt initial distress at Józefów but soon became accustomed to the killing: "Flying over a group of civilians in a helicopter, he was ordered to fire at them, an order he did not obey. The helicopter circled over the area and again he was ordered to fire, which again he did not do. The officer in charge then threatened him with court-martial, which led him to fire the next time around. He vomited, felt profoundly distressed. The veteran

reported that in a fairly short time firing at civilians became like an experience at a target-shooting gallery, and he began to enjoy it" (134).

15. Bauman, 166–68.

16. Craig Haney, Curtis Banks, and Philip Zimbardo, "Interpersonal Dynamics in a Simulated Prison," *International Journal of Criminology and Penology* 1 (1983):69–97.

17. Haney, Banks, and Zimbardo, "The Stanford Prison Experiment: Slide show and audio cassette."

18. Gustav M., 169–70; Heinz B., HW 2439–40.

19. Herbert Jäger, *Verbrechen unter totalitärer Herrschaft* (Frankfurt, 1982), 81–82, 95–122, 158–60.

20. Stanley Milgram, *Obedience to Authority: An Experimental View* (New York, 1974), 1. For reactions to Milgram's experiments, see Arthur G. Miller, *The Obedience Experiments: A Case Study of Controversy in the Social Sciences* (New York, 1986).

21. Milgram, 13–26.

22. Milgram, 32–43, 55–72, 93–97, 113–22.

23. Milgram, 135–47.

24. Milgram, 148–52.

25. Milgram, 7, 177.

26. Milgram, 9, 176–77.

27. Milgram, 113–15.

28. Stanley Milgram, "Group Pressure and Action Against a Person," *Journal of Abnormal and Social Psychology* 9 (1964):137–43.

29. Milgram, *Obedience to Authority*, 142.

30. Milgram, *Obedience to Authority*, 177.

31. Bernd Wegner, *Hitlers Politische Soldaten: Die Waffen-SS 1939–1945* (Paderborn, 1982); Krausnick and Wilhelm.

32. BA, R 19/467 (RFSS and chief of German police directives of October 27, 1942, and April 6, 1943, signed by Winkelmann).

33. BA, R 19/308 (guidelines for training of police battalions, January 23, 1940).

34. BA, R 19/308 (guidelines for training police reserves employed in the Schutzpolizei of the Reich and the communities, March 6, 1940).

35. BA, R 19/308 (training of Order Police formations and Reserve Police on precinct duty, December 20, 1940).

36. BA, R 19/308 (six-day officer education plan).

37. BA, R 19/308 (staff plan for National Socialist instruction, January 14, 1941).

38. BA, R 19/308 (guidelines for carrying out ideological training of the Order Police in wartime, June 2, 1940).

39. YVA, 0-53/121 W I (KdO, Police Regiment 25, December 17, 1942, Christmas/NewYear's greetings and recognitions, signed Peter).

40. BA, RD 18/15-1, Gruppe A and 2, Gruppe B: *Politscher Informationsdienst, Mitteilungsblätter für die weltanschauliche Schulung der Orpo.*

41. BA, RD 18/15-1, Gruppe A, Folge 16, June 10, 1941.

42. BA, RD 18/15-1, Gruppe A, Folge 27, December 1, 1941.

43. BA, RD 18/15-2, Gruppe B, Folge 22, September 20, 1942.

44. BA, RD 18/42, *Schriftenreihe für die weltanschauliche Schulung der Ordnungspolizei*, 1941, Heft 5, "Die Blutsgemeinschaft der germanischen Völker" and "Das grossgermanische Reich."

45. BA, RD 18/16, 1942, Heft 4, "Deutschland ordnet Europa neu!"; RD 18/19, 1942, Sonderheft, "SS-Mann und Blutsfrage."

46. BA, RD 19/41, 1943, Heft 4–6, "Rassenpolitik."

47. BA, R 19/305 (chief of Order Police guidelines for combatting partisans, November 17, 1941).

48. Bruno, D., HW 2992.

49. Gustav, M., G 169.

50. Primo Levi, *The Drowned and the Saved*, Vintage edition (New York, 1989), 36–69.

AFTERWORD

1. Daniel Jonah Goldhagen, "The Evil of Banality," *New Republic* (July 13 & 20, 1992), 49–52; Daniel Jonah Goldhagen, *Hitler's Willing Executioners: Ordinary Germans and the Holocaust* (New York, 1996), which contains more than thirty footnotes discussing my work; Daniel Jonah Goldhagen, "A Reply to My Critics: Motives, Causes, and Alibis," *New Republic* (Dec. 23, 1996), 37–45; "Letter to the Editor," *New Republic* (Feb. 10, 1997), 4–5.

Daniel Jonah Goldhagen began his research in the records of the *Staatsanwaltschaft* in Hamburg several months after I finished my work there in May 1989. He became aware of my work on the topic of Reserve Police Battalion 101 in the fall of 1989 at the latest.

I in turn have criticized Goldhagen's work: Christopher R. Browning, "Daniel Goldhagen's *Willing Executioners*," *History & Memory* 8/no. 1 (1996), 88–108; and "Human Nature, Culture, and the Holocaust," *Chronicle of Higher Education* (Oct. 18, 1996), A72. We also had an exchange of views at the opening academic symposium of the U.S. Holocaust Memorial Museum in December 1993, though these papers have not yet been published.

2. At least two anthologies of responses to *Hitler's Willing Executioners* have already appeared: Julius H. Schoeps, ed., *Ein Volk von Mördern?* (Hamburg, 1996), and Franklin H. Littel, ed., *Hyping the Holocaust: Scholars Answer the*

Holocaust (Merion Station, Pa., 1997). More are apparently on the way. The two most detailed and sustained critiques of *Hitler's Willing Executioners* are: Ruth Bettina Birn, "Revising the Holocaust," *Historical Journal* 40/no. 1 (1997), 195–215; and Norman Finkelstein, "Daniel Goldhagen's 'Crazy' Thesis: A Critique of *Hitler's Willing Executioners*," *New Left Review* 224 (1997): 39–87. Another very detailed assessment is: Dieter Pohl. "Die Holocaust—Forschung und Goldhagen's Thesen," *Vierteljahrshef Für Zeitgeschichte* 45/1 (1997), 1–48.

3. Raul Hilberg, *The Destruction of the European Jews*, cited from the revised and expanded edition (New York, 1985), 1011, 994.

4. Herbert Jäger, *Verbrechen unter totalitärer Herrschaft* (Frankfurt/M., 1982), 81–82, 95–122, 158–60.

5. Goldhagen, *Willing Executioners*, 106

6. Goldhagen, *Willing Executioners*, 85.

7. Goldhagen, *Willing Executioners*, 399, 443.

8. Goldhagen, *Willing Executioners*, 39, 43.

9. Goldhagen, *Willing Executioners*, 582, fn 38; 593–94, fn 53.

10. Goldhagen, *Willing Executioners*, 35–36.

11. Goldhagen, *Willing Executioners*, 444.

12. Hans-Ulrich Wehler, *The German Empire* (Leamington Spa, 1985). James Retallack, "Social History with a Vengeance? Some Reactions to H-U Wehler's 'Das Kaiserreich,'" *German Studies Review*, 7/no. 3 (1984), 423–50. Roger Fletcher, "Recent Developments in West German Historiography: The Bielefeld School and Its Critics," *German Studies Review* 7/no. 3 (1984), 451–80.

13. George Mosse, *The Crisis of German Ideology* (New York, 1964); Fritz Stern, *The Politics of Cultural Despair* (Berkeley, 1961); Jeffrey Herf, *Reactionary Modernism: Technology, Culture and Politics in Weimar and the Third Reich* (Cambridge, 1984), and "Reactionary Modernism Reconsidered: Modernity, the West and the Nazis," forthcoming.

14. John Weiss, *Ideology of Death: Why the Holocaust Happened in Germany* (Chicago, 1996).

15. Shulamit Volkov, "Anti-Semitism as a Cultural Code," *Leo Baeck Institute Yearbook*, 23 (1978), 25–46. See also: Peter Pulzer, *The Rise of Political Anti-Semitism in Germany and Austria* (London, 1964).

16. History of Anti-Semitism List, 5.15.96.

17. Gavin Langmuir, "Prolegomena to Any Present Analysis of Hostility Against the Jews," reprinted in *The Nazi Holocaust*, vol. 2, ed. by Michael Marrus (Westport, Conn., 1989), 133–171, esp. 150–154; and "From Anti-Judaism to Anti-Semitism," *History, Religion, and Antisemitism* (Berkeley, 1990), 275–305, esp. 289–97.

18. Saul Friedländer, *Nazi Germany and the Jews* (New York, 1997), 73–112.

19. Goldhagen, "Reply to My Critics," 41.

20. Goldhagen, *Willing Executioners*, 399, 85.

21. William Sheridan Allen, *The Nazi Seizure of Power* (Revised Edition: New York, 1984), 84.

22. Goldhagen, "Reply to My Critics," 41.

23. Ulrich Herbert, *Best: Biographische Studien über Radikalismus, Weltanschauung und Vernunft 1903–1989* (Bonn, 1996).

24. Ian Kershaw, "The Persecution of the Jews and German Public Opinion in the Third Reich," *Leo Baeck Institute Yearbook* 26 (1981), 261–89; *Popular Opinion and Political Dissent in the Third Reich: Bavaria 1933–1945* (Oxford, 1983); *The Hitler "Myth": Image and Reality in the Third Reich* (Oxford, 1987); "German Popular Opinion and the 'Jewish Question,' 1933–1943: Some Further Reflections," *Die Juden im Nationalsozialistischen Deutschland: 1933–1943* (Tübingen, 1986), 365–85. Otto Dov Kulka, "'Public Opinion' in Nazi Germany and the 'Jewish Question,'" *Jerusalem Quarterly* 25 (1982), 121–44 and 26 (Winter 1982), 34–45; and Otto Dov Kulka and Aaron Rodrigue, "The German Population and the Jews in the Third Reich: Recent Publications and Trends in Research on German Society and the 'Jewish Question,'" *Yad Vashem Studies* 16 (1984), 421–35. David Bankier, "The Germans and the Holocaust: What Did They Know," *Yad Vashem Studies* 20 (1990), 69–98; and *The Germans and the Final Solution: Public Opinion Under Nazism* (Oxford, 1992). See also: Marlis Steinert, *Hitler's War and the Germans* (Athens, Ohio, 1977); Walter Laqueur, "The German People and the Destruction of the European Jews," *Central European History* 6, no.2 (1973), 167–91; Sarah Gordon, *Hitler, Germans, and the "Jewish Question"* (Princeton, 1984); Robert Gellately, *The Gestapo and German Society: Enforcing Racial Policy, 1933–1945* (Oxford, 1990). In contrast, see: Michael Kater, "Everyday Anti-Semitism in Prewar Nazi Germany," *Yad Vashem Studies* (1984), 129–59.

25. Friedländer, *Nazi Germany and the Jews*, 298, 327–28.

26. Bankier, *Germans and the Final Solution*, 151–20.

27. Kulka and Rodrigue, "German Population and the Jews," 435.

28. Kershaw, "Persecution of the Jews," 288.

29. Kulka and Rodrigue, "German Population and the Jews," 430–435.

30. Goldhagen, *Willing Executioners*, 439–440, 592.

31. Goldhagen, *Willing Executioners*, 279, 185.

32. Goldhagen, "Reply to My Critics," 40.

33. Goldhagen, *Willing Executioners*, 279.

34. Goldhagen, *Willing Executioners*, 241, 231, 451.

35. Goldhagen, *Willing Executioners*, 386, 414.

36. Goldhagen, *Willing Executioners*, 416, 392.

37. In addition to his "Reply to My Critics" and "Letter to the Editors" in the

New Republic, see also his "Letter to the Editors," *New York Review of Books*, Feb. 6, 1997, 40.

38. As many critics have noted, one comparison Goldhagen does not make is between German and non-German anti-Semitism. This does not deter him from asserting, "No other country's antisemitism was at once so widespread as to have been a cultural axiom. . . . German antisemitism was *sui generis.*" *Willing Executioners*, 419.

39. Goldhagen, *Willing Executioners*, 348–351. In most of the narrative, Goldhagen speaks of the guards as a monolithic group without distinction, often referred to simply as "the Germans." Yet he himself provides telling details that point to important situational, institutional, and generational distinctions. In contrast to the eight to ten young ethnic German men, the eighteen to twenty older male guards (according to one survivor) "were for the most part good-natured and did not beat or otherwise torment us." Recruitment of ethnic Germans outside the Reich was, of course, in the hands of the SS. The young women guards—uniformly cruel (though six deserted quickly)—had all sought out their profession as guards. (*Willing Executioners*, 335, 360).

40. The statistics are taken from Danuta Czech, *Kalendarium der Ereignisse im Konzentrationslager Auschwitz-Birkenau 1939–1945* (Hamburg, 1989), especially 126–132, 179; Steven Paskuly, ed., *Death Dealer: The Memoirs of the SS Kommandant at Auschwitz Rudolph Höss* (New York, 1996), 132–34.

41. Michael Thad Allen, "Engineers and Modern Managers in the SS: The Business Administration Main Office (Wirtschaftsverwaltungshauptamt)," Ph.D. dissertation, University of Pennsylvania, 1995.

42. Yehoshua Büchler, "First in the Vale of Affliction: Slovakian Jewish Women in Auschwitz, 1942," *Holocaust and Genocide Studies* 10, no. 3 (1996), 309.

43. Goldhagen, *Willing Executioners*, 410–11.

44. Goldhagen, *Willing Executioners*, 398, 410.

45. Henry Friedlander, *The Origins of Nazi Genocide: From Euthanasia to the Final Solution* (Chapel Hill, 1995), 110, writes: "The staff at Hadamar arranged for a celebration when the number of patients killed there reached 10,000. On the orders of the physicians, the entire staff assembled at the basement crematorium to participate in the burning of the ten thousandth victim. A naked corpse lay on a stretcher, covered with flowers. The supervisor Bünger made a speech, and a staff member dressed up as a cleric performed a ceremony. Every staff member received a bottle of beer."

46. Friedlander, *Origins of Nazi Genocide*, 389.

47. Primo Levi, *The Drowned and the Saved*, (Vintage edition: New York, 1989), 125–26; Gita Sereny, *Into That Darkness* (London, 1974). 101.

48. Fred E. Katz, *Ordinary People and Extraordinary Evil: A Report on the Beguilings of Evil* (Albany, 1993), 29–31, 83–98.

49. Goldhagen, *Willing Executioners*, 408.

50. Goldhagen, *Willing Executioners*, 409.

51. Subsequently published as: Browning, "Daniel Goldhagen's *Willing Executioners*," esp. 94–96.

52. Goldhagen, *Willing Executioners*, 463.

53. Goldhagen, *Willing Executioners*, 467.

54. Goldhagen, *Willing Executioners*, 464.

55. Goldhagen, *Willing Executioners*, 601, fn.11.

56. Goldhagen, *Willing Executioners*, 467.

57. Goldhagen, *Willing Executioners*, 221.

58. On a footnote on p. 537 he notes the testimony of Ernst G., G 383. He does not note the testimony in this regard of: George A., HW 421; Alfred L., HW 1351; Bruno P., HW 1915; Heinz B., HW 4415; Henry L., G 225; August Z., G 275; and Hans K., G 363.

59. Georg A., HW 439; and Erwin N., HW 1685.

60. Friedrich B., HW 439; Bruno R., HW 1852; Bruno D., HW 1874; Bruno P., HW 1915; and Bruno G., HW 2019.

61. Oskar P., HW 1743.

62. Goldhagen, *Willing Executioners*, 240.

63. Goldhagen, *Willing Executioners*, 241.

64. Bruno P., HW 1925–26. It should also be noted that the witness to this incident freely offered a great deal of incriminating testimony and is often cited by Goldhagen on these other counts, so his general reliability is not in question.

65. Needless to say, Goldhagen has deemed my selection and use of evidence tendentious and misleading as well. His points often strike me as nitpicking, but on occasion they are well-taken. For instance, he correctly notes that I should have provided the full quotation and precise attribution of Trapp's admonition, after he observed "the maltreatment of the Jews," that the men "had the task to shoot the Jews, but not to beat and torture them." Goldhagen, "Evil of Banality," 52.

66. Heinz Buchmann, HW 2439–40.

67. Goldhagen, *Willing Executioners*, 249–50.

68. Heinz Buchmann, HW 2441.

69. Heinz Buchmann, HW 4416.

70. Goldhagen, *Willing Executioners*, 248.

71. Goldhagen, *Willing Executioners*, 235-36; Hermann B., HW 3066–67, 3214, 3515.

72. Bruno D., HW 1874.

73. Wilhelm E., HW 2239.

74. Goldhagen, "Reply to My Critics," 38.

75. Goldhagen, *Willing Executioners*, 381–82.

76. These are the factors Goldhagen credits with dismantling anti-Semitism in postwar German culture. Goldhagen, *Willing Executioners*, 582, 593–4.

77. Goldhagen, "Reply to My Critics," 40.

78. Herbert C. Kelman and V. Lee Hamilton, *Crimes of Obedience: Toward a Social Psychology of Authority and Responsibility* (New Haven, 1989).

79. The Nazis occasionally understood that preserving such a distinction was necessary for the mindset of the majority of the perpetrators. While there were no trials of men who refused to shoot Jews, there were investigations (and in one case a murder trial) for the "unauthorized" killing of Jews even in the bloodiest year of the Holocaust—1942. For example: Military Archiv Prague, Varia SS, 124: Feldurteil in der Strafsache geger Johann Meisslein, Gerricht der kdtr. des Bereiches Proskurow (FK183), March 12, 1943.

80. James Waller, "Perpetrators of the Holocaust: Divided and Unitary Self-Conceptions of Evildoing," *Holocaust and Genocide Studies* 10, no.1 (Spring 1996), 11–33.

81. Goldhagen, *Willing Executioners*, 13.

82. Goldhagen, *Willing Executioners*, 383.

83. Goldhagen's most recent technique of alleged refutation ("Letter to the Editor," 5) is quite original and unusual. He invents or fantasizes a hypothetical or counterfactual verbatim testimony concerning peer pressure, and announces that the absence of just this particular verbatim testimony proves the absence of peer pressure as a factor entirely.

84. Goldhagen, "A Reply to My Critics," 38–40. In his book, Goldhagen made the same claim: "The conventional explanations . . . deny the humanity of the perpetrators, namely that they were moral agents, moral beings capable of making moral choices." *Willing Executioners*, 389–92.

85. Stanley Milgrim tested rather than assumed that "deference to authority" was a cross-cultural phenomenon, and he explicitly acknowledged that prejudice toward and indoctrination against the victim would undoubtedly intensify a subject's willingness to inflict pain upon the victim. Zimbardo intentionally screened out prejudiced subjects precisely because their participation would obviously skew the results. Kelman and Hamilton affirm that cultural factors—such as a negative attitude toward the victims—will facilitate peoples' compliance to legitimate authority's policies of sanctioned mass murder.

86. Goldhagen, *Willing Executioners*, p. 389.

87. Goldhagen, *Willing Executioners*, 27, 269.

88. Goldhagen, *Willing Executioners*, 34.

89. Goldhagen, *Willing Executioners*, 106.

90. Goldhagen, *Willing Executioners*, 399, 85.

91. Goldhagen, *Willing Executioners*, 443.

TWENTY-FIVE YEARS LATER

1.Heiner Lichtenstein, *Himmlers grüne Helfer: Die Schutz- und Ordnungspolizei im "Dritten Reich"* (Köln: Bund-Verlag, 1990).

2.Konrad Kwiet, "From the Diary of a Killing Unit," *Why Germany?*, ed. by John Milfull (Oxford: Berg, 1991), pp. 92–110, and "Auftakt zum Holocaust. Ein Polizeibataillon im Osteinsatz," *Der Nationalsozialismus. Studien zur Ideologie und Herrschaft*, ed. by Wolfgang Benz, Hans Buchheim, and Hans Mommsen (Frankfurt am Main: Fischer, 1993), pp. 191–208. Andrej Angrick, Martina Voigt, Silke Ammerschubert, and Peter Klein, "Da hätte man schon ein Tagebuch führen müssen. Das Polizeibataillon 322 und die Judenmorde im Bereich der Heeresgruppe Mitte während des Sommers und Herbstes 1941," *Die Normalität des Verbrechens: Bilanz und Perspektiven der Forschung zu den nationalsozialistischen Gewaltverbrechen*, ed. by Helge Grabitz, Klaus Bästlein, and Johannes Tuchel (Berlin: Edition Hentrich, 1994), pp. 325–386.

3.Winfried Nachtwei, " 'Ganz normale Männer.' Die Verwicklung von Polizeibataillonen aus dem Rheinland und Westfalen in den nationalsozialistischen Vernichtungskrieg," *Ville Ten Hompel: Sitz der Ordnungspolizei im Dritten Reich*, ed. by Alfons Kenkmann (Münster: Agenda Verlag, 1996), pp. 54–77.

4.Richard Breitman, *Official Secrets: What the Nazis Planned, What the British and Americans Knew* (New York: Hill and Wang, 1998), pp. 45–53, 63–66, 79–80.

5.Edward B. Westermann, " 'Ordinary Men' or 'Ideological Soldiers'? Police Battalion 310 in Russia, 1942," *German Studies Review* 21, no. 1 (1998), pp. 41–68.

6.Klaus-Michael Mallmann, "Der Einstieg in den Genozid. Das Lübecker Polizeibataillon 307 und das Massaker in Brest-Litovsk Anfang July 1941," *Archiv für Polizeigeschichte 1999*, pp. 82–88.

7.*Wessen Freud und wessen Helfer? Die Kölner Polizei im Nationalsozialismus*, ed. by Harald Buhlan and Werner Jung (Köln: Emons Verlag, 2000). *Im Auftrag: Polizei, Verwaltung, und Vernichtung*, ed. by Alfons Kenkmann and Christoph Spieker (Essen: Klartext Verlag, 2001).

8.Stefan Klemp, " 'Ab nach Siberien?' Zur Sanktionierungspraxis gegenüber Polizeibeamten des Dritten Reiches: Der Fall des Polizeibataillons 9," *Im Auftrag*, pp. 278–300.

9.Stefan Klemp, "Ermittlungen gegen ehemalige Kölner Polizeibeamte in der Nachkriegszeit: Die Verfahren gegen Angehörige des Reservepolizeibataillons 69 und der Polizeireservekompanie Köln," *Wessen Freund und wessen Helfer?*, pp. 602–618.

10. Harald Welzer, *Täter: Wie aus ganz normalen Menschen Massenmörder werden* (Frankfurt am Main: Fischer, 2005).

11. Edward B. Westermann, *Hitler's Police Battalions: Enforcing Racial War in the East* (Lawrence: University of Kansas Press, 2005).

12. Karl Schneider, *Auswärts eingesetzt: Bremer Polizeibataillone und der Holocaust* (Essen: Klartext, 2011).

13. Wolfgang Curilla, *Die deutsche Ordnungspolizei und der Holocaust im Baltikum und in Weissrusssland 1941–1944* (Paderborn: Ferdinand Schöningh, 2006) and *Die Judenmord in Polen und die deutsche Ordnungspolizei 1939–1945* (Paderborn: Ferdinand Schöningh, 2011).

14. Schneider, *Auswärts eingesetzt*, pp. 118–177.

15. Ibid., pp. 413–417.

16. Ibid., p. 137.

17. Curilla, *Die deutsche Ordnungspolizei und der Holocaust im Baltikum und in Weissrussland*, pp. 828–833; Curilla, *Der Judenmord in Polen und die deutsche Ordnungspolizei*, pp. 838–845. I have rounded off Curilla's statistics to the nearest one hundred.

18. For a wider review of the literature on perpetrator studies in general: Thomas Kühne, "Der nationalsozialistische Vernichtungskrieg und die 'ganz normalen' Deutschen: Forschungsprobleme und Forschungstendenzen der Gesellschaftsgeschichte des Zweiten Weltkrieges," *Archiv für Socialgeschichte* 39 (1999), pp. 580–662; Gerhard Paul, "Von Psychopathen, Technokraten des Terrors und 'ganz gewöhnlichen' Deutschen: Die Täter der Shoah im Spiegel der Forschung," *Die Täter der Shoah: Fanatische Natoinalsozialistischen oder ganze normale Deutsche?*, ed. by Gerhard Paul (Göttingen: Wallstein Verlag, 2002), pp. 13–90; Donald Bloxham, "Perpetrators and Perpetration," *The Holocaust: Critical Historical Approaches*, ed. by Donald Bloxham and Tony Kusher (Manchester: Manchester University Press, 2005), pp. 61–175; Claus-Christian W. Szejnmann, "Perpetrators of the Holocaust: A Historiography," *Ordinary People as Mass Murderers: Perpetrators in Comparative Perspective*, ed. by Olaf Jensen and Claus-Christian W. Szejnmann (Blasingstoke: Palgrave Macmillan, 2008), pp. 25–47.

19. James Waller, *Becoming Evil: How Ordinary People Commit Genocide and Mass Killing* (Oxford: Oxford University Press, 2002), p. xiv. Waller presents a succinct summary of the model in: "Becoming Evil: A Model of How Ordinary People Commit Genocide and Mass Killing," *Lessons and Legacies*, vol. VII: *The Holocaust in International Perspective*, ed. by Dagmar Herzog (Evanston: Northwestern University Press, 2006), pp. 142–155.

20. Leonard S. Newman, "What Is a 'Social-Psychological' Account of Perpetrator Behavior? The Person versus the Situation in Goldhagen's *Hilter's Willing Executioners*," *Understanding Genocide: The Social Psychology of the Holocaust*, ed. by Leonard S. Newman and Ralph Erber (Oxford: Oxford University Press, 2002), pp. 43–67.

21. Edward B. Westermann, *Hitler's Police Battalions: Enforcing Racial War in the East* (Lawrence: University of Kansas Press, 2005), p. 7.

22. Ibid., pp. 237–239.

23.Jürgen Matthäus: "Ausbildung Judenmord? Zum Stellenwert der 'welt-anschaulichen Erziehung' um SS und Polizei im Rahmen der 'Endlösung,' " *Zeitschrift für Geschichtswissenschaft* 47, no. 8 (1999), pp. 673–699; "'Warum wird über das Judentum geschult?' Die ideologische Vorbereitung der detuschen Poli-zei auf den Holocaust," *Die Gestapo im Zweiten Weltkrieg: 'Heimat' und besetzten Europa* (Darmstadt: Primus Verlag, 2000), pp. 100–124; "An vorderster Front: Voraussetzungen für die Beteiligung der Ordnungspolizei an der Shoah," *Die Täter der Shoah: Fanatische Nationalsozialisten oder ganz normale Deutsche?*, ed. by Gerhard Paul (Göttingen: Wallstein Verlag, 2002), pp. 137–166; "Die 'Judenfrage' als Schulungsthema von SS und Polizei: 'Inneres Erlebnis' und Handlungslegitimation," *Ausbildungsziel Judenmord? "Weltanschauliche Erzie-hung" von SS, Polizei und Waffen-SS im Rahmen der 'Endlösung,'* ed. by Jürgen Matthäus, Konrad Kwiet, Jürgen Förster, and Richard Breitman (Frankfurt am Main: Fischer Taschenbuch Verlag, 2003), pp. 35–86.

24.Klaus-Michael Mallmann, "Vom Fussvolk der 'Endlösung.' Ordnungspolizei, Ostkrieg, und Judenmord," *Jahrbuch für deutsche Geschichte* 26 (1997), pp. 355–391.

25.Ibid., pp. 386–391.

26.Harald Welzer, *Täter: Wie aus ganz normalen Menschen Massenmörder werden* (Frankfurt am Main: S. Fischer Verlag, 2005). See also: Harald Welzer, "Wer waren Täter? Anmerkungen zur Täterforschung aus sozialpsychologischer Sicht," *Die Täter der Shoah*, pp. 237–253; and "On Murder and Morality: How Normal People Become Mass Murderers," *Ordinary People as Mass Murderers: Perpetrators in Comparative Perspectives*, ed. by Olaf Jensen and Claus-Christian W. Szejnmann (Basingstoke: Palgrave Macmillan, 2008), pp. 165–181.

27.Thomas Kühne: *Kameradschaft. Die Soldaten des nationalsozialistischen Krieges und das 20. Jahrhundert* (Göttingen: Vandenhoeck & Ruprecht, 2006); "Male Bonding and Shame Culture: Hitler's Soldiers and the Moral Basis of Geno-cidal Warfare," *Ordinary People as Mass Murderers: Perpetrators in Comparative Perspective*, ed. by Olaf Jensen and Claus-Christian W. Szejnman (Blasingstoke: Palgrave Macmillan, 2008), pp. 55–77; and *Belonging and Genocide: Hitler's Com-munity, 1918–1945* (New Haven: Yale University Press, 2010).

28.Kühne, *Belonging and Genocide*, p. 64.

29.Ibid., pp. 6–7, 73.

30.Ibid., p. 63.

31.Ibid., pp. 67 and 71.

32.Ibid, p. 171.

33.Ibid., p. 83.

34.Ibid., p. 87 (Künhe's translation, cited from *Deutscher Osten 1939–1945*, ed. by Klaus-Michael Mallmann, Volker Riess, and Wolfram Pyta (Darmstadt: Wissen-schaftliche Buchgesellschaft, 2003), p. 120.

35.Kühne, *Belonging and Genocide*, pp. 83–7, 112–117.

36. "The 'Willling Executioners'/'Ordinary Men' Debate," Occasional Paper of the United States Holocaust Research Institute, USHMM, 1996.

37. Testimony of Heinrich E. Landgericht Hamburg 141 Js 1957/62, pp. 2167, 2169, 2172, 3351.

38. Roger Vietor, "Ich hatte eine Beschützer," *Freiwellegekompanie 1940–1945*, ed. by L. Jacoby and R. Trauffler (Luxembourg: St. Paul, 1986), pp. 220–221.

39. Jean Heinen, "Das Schicksal einer Gruppe," *Freiwellegenkompanie 1940–1945*, pp. 207–219.

40. Christopher R. Browning, "Goldhagen's willige Vollstrecker," *Der Weg zur "Endlösung": Entscheidungen und Täter* (Bonn: Dietz, 1998), pp. 161–181, esp. 169–171.

41. Jean Heinen, "Die Luxemburger im Reserve-Polizeibataillon 101," *Luxemburger Wort*, August 3, 7, and 10, 1996.

42. Landgericht Hamburg 141 Js 1957/62, pp. 2245-67 (testimony of Hans K.)

43. Staatsarchiv Hamburg, Bestand 213-12, A 81/95D, Verfarhungssignatur 0022/003, pp. 1955–1956, 1970–1973 (signed statements of Johann Weber, Marcel Jean Speller, and Emil Konsbrueck, February 22–23, 1972).

44. Staatsarchiv Hamburg, Bestand 213-12, A 81/95D, Verfahrungssignatur 0022/003, pp. 1948–1954, 1956–1969 (interviews of Weber, Speller, and Konsbrueck, December 1973).

45. Staatsarchiv Hamburg, Bestand 213-12, A 81/95D, Verfahrungssignatur 0022/003, pp. 1986–2006, 2040–2044 (interrogations of Heinrich H., Heinrich F., Hans Karl P., Helmut S., and Friedrich B., January/February 1974).

46. Testimony of Frederick B., pp 2040–2044.

47. Testimony of Henrich H., pp. 1986–1989.

48. Testimony of Helmut S., pp. 2000–2006.

49. Paul Dostert, "Die Luxemburger im Reserve-Poloizei-Bataillon 101 und der Judenmord in Polen," *Hémecht: Zeitschrift für Luxemburger Geschichte* 52 (2000), pp. 81–99, esp. pp. 84–89.

50. Staatsachiv Hamburg: Bestand 331-8, Polizeiverwaltung—Personalakten, Nr. 792-802.

51. For the controversy over one of the most "iconic" of Holocaust photographs, see: Dan Porat, *The Boy. A Holocaust Story* (New York: Hill and Wang, 2010).

52. Emails from Daniel Uziel, Photo Archives, Yad Vashem, May 12 and 15, 2011, concerning the rival claims of Łuków and Tarnow. Yad Vashem is in possession of only the second and third photos but not the first.

53. Whatever the other controversies surrounding Daniel Goldhagen's *Hitler's Willing Executioners*, his book did have the merit of extensively analyzing photographs related to RPB 101. In this particular case, however, Goldhagen rather incautiously captioned the second and third pictures of this sequence: "Shortly before deporting the Jews of Łuków to their deaths in Treblinka, men of Police Battalion 101 take time out to force a group of Jews to pose for photographic momentos" (p. 260).

54.USHMM 49189/YIVO Łuków 1.

55.USHMM 49198A/Yad Vashem 117FO3a.

56.USHMM 18604/YIVO Łuków 2/Yad Vashem 117EO6, 74CO7, 4613/523, 2746/13, 68091/39, 8030/16.

57.Email from Daniel Uziel, May 15, 2011.

58.USHMM, Acc. 1999.99.1-3 O'Hara Collection. I am extremely grateful to Jürgen Matthäus for his research and analysis of these albums. Jürgen Matthäus and Christopher R. Browning, "Evidenz, Erinnerung, Trugbild. Fotoalben zum Polizeibatallion 101 im 'Osteinsatz,'" *Naziverbrechen: Täter, Taten, Bewältigungsversuch*, ed. by Martin Cüppers, Jürgen Matthäus, and Andrej Angrick (Darmstadt: Wissenschaftliche Buchgesellschaft, 2013), pp. 135–190, esp. 163–181.

59.USHMM 47432 and 47430.

60.USHMM 47441 and 47442.

61.USHMM 47438 and 47439.

62.USHMM 47453 and 47454.

63.USHMM 47447 and 47444.

64.USHMM 47436.

65.USHMM 57619/Lichtbildmappe 1;Lichtbildmappe 2; USHMM 57619/Lichtbildmappe 4.

66.Lichtbildmappe 18-22, 24-5; as examples here, 21 and 24.

67.Lichtbildmappe 15.

68.Lichtbildmappe 16

69.Christopher R. Browning, *Ordinary Men*, pp. 92–95.

70.Ibid., pp. 127, 149.

71.USHMM 57629-32/Lichtbildmappe 85-88

72.USHMM 57701/Lichtbildmappe 90.

73.Himmler Order, December 12, 1941, printed in: *Einsatz im "Reichskommissariat Ostland": Dokumente zum Völkermord im Baltikum und in Weissrussland 1941–1944*, ed. by Wolfgang Benz, Konrad Kweit, and Jürgen Matthäus (Berlin: Metropol, 1998), pp. 28–29.

74.Lichtbildmappe 17.

75.USHMM 57620-4/Lichtbildmappe 26-30). The photos were identified for the prosecution by a member of Gnade's Second Company, Herbert Kurt F., though apparently not at the time of his first interrogation in which he identified only later photos from Second Company's stay in Międzyrzec. LG Hamburg 141 Js 1957/62, pp. 1383-1393. (interrogation of Herbert Kurt F., July 1, 1963). This series of photos does not seem to have been used in the interrogations until mid-1965 (p. 2061, interrogation of Heinrich B., June 1, 1965).

76.Daniel Goldhagen, *Hitler's Willing Executioners*, pp. 224–225, suggests that because the distant German guard in the first photo is facing the camera with his back to the seated Jews, he is demonstrating that he is "proud of his actions, wanting not to conceal the image of him participating in a genocidal operation but to preserve it for posterity." I think this is stretching the photographic evidence considerably. At that distance it would be unlikely that he even knew his picture was being taken.

77.USHMM Photo Archive 89352/Landgericht Hamburg 141 Js 1957/62, Lichtbildmappe 39 and 69.

78.Browning, *Ordinary Men*, pp. 108–109.

79.Ibid., pp. 121–132.

80.USHMM 57627/Lichtbildmappe 91-92

81.Browning, *Ordinary Men*, p. 134.

82.USHMM 57625/Lichtbildmappe 33 and 59; USHMM 89237/Lichtbildmappe 58; USHMM 46321/Lichtbildmappe 36 and 60; USHMM 89328; Lichtbildmappe 37.

83.Lichtbildmappe 78.

84.USHMM 89329 and 8329A/Lichtbildmappe 62 and 63).

85.USHMM 89330

86.Lichtbildmappe 79

87.USHMM 89347/Lichtbildmappe 40 and 66; USHMM 61538 and 79067/Lichtbildmappe 41 and 64; USHMM 89349/Lichtbildmappe 38, 67, and 74; USHMM 89351/Lichtbildmappe 42; USHMM 89350/Lichtbildmappe 68 and 76.

88.USHMM 89346/Lichtbildmappe 32 and 70. One photo (Lichtbildmappe 75) of Lieutenant Dreyer in front of the barracks is not shown here.

89.USHMM 51233-5.

90.USHMM 57702-11; included here are 57704, 57708, 57709, and 57711.

91.Porat, *The Boy. A Holocaust Story*, p. 11.

92.Judith Levin and Daniel Uziel, "Ordinary Men, Extraordinary Photographs," *Yad Vashem Studies* XXVI (1998), pp. 267–268.

93.Ibid., pp. 266, 289–290.

94.Goldhagen, Hitler's Willing Executioners, p. 245, contains a photo of a classic beard-cutting ritual, credited to the *Zentrale Stelle*, in which his caption claims the chief perpetrator to be a member of Police Battalion 101. However, like the Łuków photos, this photo was not in the prosecutor's collection, and the perpetrator is not individually identified. Given what we now know about the Łuków photos, clearly caution would be advisable in this case as well.

INDEX

Note: An asterisk (*) designates a pseudonym, as explained on p. xx of the Preface.

Breitman, Richard, 227
Bremen, 42, 67, 229–230
Bremerhaven, 72–73
Breslau, 46
Brest-Litovsk, 202, 227–228
Bromberg, 160
Brünn, 28
Brunner, Aton, 28
Brustin-Berenstein, Tatiana, 105
Buchenwald, 248
Buchmann,* Heinz
  background, 47
  at Józefów (1942), 56, 60, 75–76,
    102, 242
  at Łuków, 111–113
  opposition to murder, 56, 75–76,
    101–103, 111–113, 151, 165,
    169, 171, 181, 188, 213–214
  trial and sentencing, 144, 153
Budzyn, 139
Bulgaria, 27
Bundesarchiv (German Federal
  Archives), 178
Bürger, Josef, 134

Cambodia, 207
Camps. *See also* Auschwitz
  (Birkenau); Bełżec; Deportation
  of Jews; Sobibór; Treblinka
  death or extermination, xvi, 27,
    49–54, 60, 77, 163–164, 176,
    206–207
  labor, xv, 2, 28, 55, 56, 60,
    116–117, 134–135, 136–138,
    161, 204, 209
  prisoner-of-war, 38, 52, 77
Carl, Heinrich, 23
Caucasus, xv–xvi
Central Agency for Jewish

Emigration, 26, 28
Central Agency for the
  State Administrations of
  Justice (Zentrale Stelle der
  Landesjustizverwaltungen), xvi–
  xviii, 144–145
Chelm, 28, 53
  county of, 105
Chełmno (Kulmnof), 50
"Chimeric" anti-Semitism, 197, 198,
  199
Christian values, 222, 237
Claasen, Kurt, 51
Cognitive dissonance theory, 234
Colberg, Bernhardt, 253–259, 289,
  291
Cologne, 248
Commissar order
  (Kommissarbefehl), 11, 13, 183
Communism (Bolshevism), 11, 13,
  48, 52, 75, 180, 183, 184, 202,
  235, 239
Competition for mercilessness, 241
Conformity, 71–72, 86–87,
  174–176, 232–241
Criminal Police (Kriminalpolizei or
  Kripo), 4, 9, 51
Croatia, 27, 207
Culture of brutality, 241
Curilla, Wolfgang, 229, 231
Czechoslovakia, 6, 27, 50, 53
Czemierniki, 91, 98, 105, 115, 267,
  294
Częstochowa, 28

Dachau, 248
Daluege, Kurt, 4–5, 7–8, 12–13, 15,
  24, 26–27, 184, 235
Danzig, 5

About the Author

CHRISTOPHER R. BROWNING taught history at Pacific Lutheran University and the University of North Carolina at Chapel Hill. He was a three-time winner of the National Jewish Book Award in the Holocaust category, including *Ordinary Men* in 1994. He was elected a Fellow of the American Academy of Arts and Sciences in 2006.